MICHAEL

THE

21 YEARS OF THE GLASGOW CITIZENS THEATRE

CITZ

N
H
B

NICK HERN BOOKS

A division of Walker Books Limited

For Susan and Thomas

1000647391 T

A Nick Hern Book

The Citz first published in 1990 by Nick Hern Books
a division of Walker Books Limited,
87 Vauxhall Walk, London SE11 5HJ

Cover photograph by John Vere Brown: mirror images in
The Balcony by Genet, 1982

British Library Cataloguing in Publication Data

Coveney, Michael
The Citz: 21 years of the Glasgow Citizens Theatre
  1. Scotland. Strathclyde Region. Glasgow. Theatres:
  Citizens Theatre (Glasgow, Scotland), 1969 – 1990
  I. Title
  792.0941443

ISBN 1 – 85459 – 033 – 2 Hardback
ISBN 1 – 85459 – 038 – 3 Paperback

Typeset by Action Typesetting Limited
Printed and bound by Biddles Limited, Guildford

CONTENTS

ILLUSTRATIONS

All photographs, unless otherwise credited, are by John Vere Brown

1   The Citizens Theatre, inside and out, old and new, between 1977 and 1990 (courtesy of the *Glasgow Herald*)
• The Citizens Theatre, exterior, in 1990 (John Barr)
• The three directors of the Citizens (John Barr)

2   Hamlet (Diane Tammes)
• Antony and Cleopatra (Diane Tammes)
• Tamburlaine (Diane Tammes)
• Troilus and Cressida (Diane Tammes)

3   Thyestes (Mike Henderson)
• De Sade Show (Mike Henderson)
• The Country Wife
• Figaro

4   Chinchilla
• Semi-Monde
• Summit Conference
• Painter's Palace of Pleasure

PREFACE

Giles Havergal and Philip Prowse, joined later by Robert David MacDonald, celebrate their 21st anniversary in charge of the Citizens Theatre, Glasgow, in September 1990, the year of Glasgow's nomination as Cultural Capital of Europe. It seemed the right time to attempt a critical and historical assessment of one of the most vivacious and idiosyncratic success stories in the arts of Great Britain.

The Citizens Theatre has been so called since 1945 when James Bridie changed the name of the Royal Princess's Theatre into which he had moved with the Citizens company. The Citizens, therefore, is both the name of the theatre in the Gorbals of Glasgow and of the company which lives there.

The name of the company, deriving from the 1909 manifesto of the Glasgow Rep, was first adopted in 1943 by James Bridie with a final possessive apostrophe. This apostrophe has since led a chequered existence, especially over the past two decades, and I have followed recent practice at the theatre in dropping it altogether, except, of course, when using the genitive case.

The title of the book was a problem. The Citizens

Theatre is widely referred to today as 'The Citz', but not by anyone who works in the building. The sobriquet sounds right in some respects, over-familiar and ingratiating in others. I avoid it throughout. But 'Citizens' might have been confused with either a BBC radio serial of that name or last year's magisterial documentation of the French Revolution by Simon Schama. And anything else might have sounded too much like the title of an official handbook, which this isn't, or a plodding treatise, which I hope it isn't.

The other word which I worry about is 'style'. It is one of my submissions that there is no single style of production at the Citizens, but in moments of weakness I have found no alternative to suggesting there might be.

I knew this book had to be written, and that I needed to write it. But I would never have started without the prompting of Nick Hern, and his encouragement and perceptive editing have been more than I expected and better than I deserved. Nor could I have accumulated any worthwhile experience of the Citizens without the support of the *Financial Times*, whose editors in my time there, Fredy Fisher and Sir Geoffrey Owen, thought it important we should review the productions. I am grateful to successive FT arts editors: B. A. Young, especially; Antony Thorncroft; and J.D.F. Jones. I also thank Gillian Widdicombe, my arts editor at *The Observer*.

In reconstructiong a history before and after 1969, which is only fleetingly recorded elsewhere, if at all, I am particularly grateful to everyone who spared the time to speak and to write to me. Their names are all in the text, and I apologise in advance for any errors of fact or misrepresentation. Thanks are due to three outstanding libraries in Glasgow: the Mitchell Library, Stirling's Library, and the Special Collections of the University Library. The Citizens' cuttings books were a major source of information to which I was allowed unconditional access. I have benefited incalculably from the friendship and opinions of many colleagues, especially my Scottish critical colleagues.

My torrential enquiries at the Citizens itself were answered with unfailing courtesy and efficiency by the staff, but Roberta Doyle, Morag Hendry and Paul Bassett bore the brunt of them with tact and good humour. Giles Havergal generously unpacked his great store of precise memories and vital knowledge without once insisting on how I should make use of it.

Michael Coveney
April 1990

GLASGOW, CITY OF CULTURE

In 1990, Glasgow is designated Cultural Capital of Europe, the sixth city to be so honoured in succession to Athens, Florence, Amsterdam, Berlin and Paris.

1990 also marks the 21st anniversary of the current artistic regime at the Glasgow Citizens Theatre in the Gorbals. The two events are, as they say, related. For one way of demonstrating the cultural Europeanism of Glasgow is to point to the track record and consistency of the Citizens Theatre since 1969. You might go further and say that the success story of the Citizens made possible the nomination in the first place.

But this is not a story of cultural status symbols and overnight recognition. It is a tale of a theatre company's struggle and survival in a desolate and changing landscape while creating an artistic reputation not without attendant controversy and in defiance of all local and national example.

In the most unlikely of physical circumstances, the Citizens has provided the most exciting European-based repertoire in the British theatre over the past twenty years; has produced more fine young actors than any comparable organisation; has saved and renovated a crumbling Victorian theatre; and has survived both politically and financially during a bleak and generally difficult time for the arts in Great Britain. In more ways than one, it has gone magnificently against the grain.

James Bridie's legacy and its renunciation

The Citizens Theatre, so named by James Bridie in 1945, is a classic Victorian jewel in the Gorbals on the south side of the Clyde river in Glasgow, a mere fifteen-minute walk from the city centre. It stands, much transformed in outward appearance, while all around has tumbled before the bulldozers in the name of clean-up and progress. Bridie's dream of a Scottish national theatre was launched when he formed the Citizens company in 1943, moving with them as chairman into the present building in 1945. Bridie died in 1951. His influence and renown lived on, but only fitfully.

Bridie had taken the makeshift name for his new company from a manifesto for the Glasgow Rep in 1909: 'The Repertory Theatre is Glasgow's own theatre. It is a citizens' theatre in the fullest sense of the term. Established to make Glasgow independent of London for its dramatic supplies, it produces plays which the Glasgow playgoers would otherwise not have an opportunity of seeing.'

Nationalist idealism vied with grass roots political and artistic aspiration throughout the twentieth century's Scottish theatre. The two camps rarely coincided on the same terrain. The Repertory Theatre survived for only four years. Then came the Scottish National Players, in the 1920s, to which Bridie's war-time initiative was in clear succession. It was also in stark contrast to the left-wing Glasgow Unity, which had been founded in 1941 after an inspirational visit to the city by Michael Redgrave and Sybil Thorndike. When Unity broke up at the end of the 1940s, many of its actors joined the Citizens, and the Gorbals theatre continued to present a mixed repertoire of new Scottish plays and standard classics during the 1950s.

In 1964, a publication to mark the twenty-one years since the Citizens' formation was dominated by memories of the Citizens' founding father. But Iain Cuthbertson, the general manager, and Andrew Leigh, the house manager, now boasted of running one of the best half-dozen reps in the land. They excoriated the locals for not believing that the Citizens on their own doorstep could be as good as the claims made for it; and they denied the implicit assumption that Sassenachs who worked there (such as Leigh and many of the actors) must be failures from down south.

Such wimpering defensiveness soon proved inappropriate. In 1970, amid puritan uproar and nationalist outrage, Giles Havergal changed the theatre's course entirely with his all-male production of *Hamlet*. He had been appointed the previous year at a time of acute crisis: audiences had slumped, there had been five artistic directors since 1962, and the building itself was under threat of demolition.

Bridie's bruited independence from London is more marked today than it was in the 1950s and 1960s. Glasgow playgoers, after two decades of solid rather than spectacular programming, suddenly feasted on a repertoire without comparison in Britain. At one stroke, Havergal impudently installed the most radically chic, and sexiest, young company in Britain, with a majority of English actors, in the quondam cradle of Scottish nationalist drama. His immediate predecessors had failed precisely because the Citizens had become just another ordinary British repertory company.

In the succeeding twenty-one years, Havergal and his fellow directors, Philip Prowse and Robert David MacDonald, have run a theatre of visual delight and European orientation which bears no relationship whatsoever to the great upheavals in British theatre since the mid-1950s: John Osborne's *Look Back In Anger*, Joan Littlewood's Theatre Workshop at Stratford East, and the formation, at the end of the decade, by Peter Hall of the Royal Shakespeare Company in London and Stratford-upon-Avon.

Today the Citizens has renounced Scottishness, but renounced Englishness, too. A swaggering cultural cruade was designed to knock an audience out of its sense of composure and into a forbidden garden of sensual, aesthetic, intellectual and moral riot. There have been nods in the direction of the mainstream humanist European post-war theatre of Bertolt Brecht, Giorgio Strehler, and Roger Planchon; eclectic flashbacks to the more Slavic extravagances of Meyerhold and Eisenstein; a succession of Goldoni discoveries, rare Coward revivals and Wilde melodramas; British premières of Lermontov, Hochhuth, Goethe and Karl Kraus; new adaptations of Proust, Tolstoy, de Sade, Offenbach and Balzac; and high-voltage, daring assaults on the darker recesses of the Jacobean and Restoration repertoire.

Unique and inimitable, the post-1969 Citizens has nonetheless proved profoundly and insidiously influential. Without question, the Havergal Citizens has been the most outstandingly interesting British theatre company of the past two decades. And the success is a political and artistic vindication of a city's intention to combat its popular image of violence, poverty and industrial decline through investment in cultural and architectural renewal.

The delightful irony, and one that no doubt accounts for the reluctance of Glaswegian tourism bureaucrats to mention the Citizens in the same breath as the Burrell Collection and Scottish Opera, is that the company is 'tasteless', anarchic, unpredictable, and gloriously inimical to the whole idea of prestige and sponsorship. The rumpuses, on the whole, have faded, as we shall see, but not always the rumps. There is always a fair chance that a bottom might be bared, at least metaphorically, to split the groundlings and fart in the face of Culture.

So while the cultural renaissance of Glasgow is in large measure due to the sustained reputation of the persistent Citizens, the theatre's achievement has also prompted a profound Glaswegian cultural cringe, an ambiguously appreciative scepticism developed in direct ratio to increasing national and international recognition. Parochial pride in the Citizens has been tempered, more often than not, with parochial disavowal.

Moreover, we shall see that survival has been linked to political cunning and an economic efficiency, on a shoestring budget, without parallel in the British arts of the period. In twenty years, the books have always been

5

balanced and the policy, seen at first in some quarters as the product of preening self-indulgence by a bunch of incompetent weirdos, vindicated as a success with the public.

Historical mixed fortunes and culture in the Gorbals

At the beginning of the nineteenth century, Glasgow was the second city of the British Empire. A majority of all the ships that sailed the seven seas were built in the Clyde shipyards. Maurice Lindsay, the Glaswegian poet and historian, has suggested that the city is now embarked on a second period of greatness; but, whereas the great days of the cotton industry, the steel works and the shipyards were instigated by native individual Glaswegians 'with business acumen and fierce Presbyterian energy', the present resurrection and regeneration is dependent on kick-starting the private sector with an initial investment of public funds.

The recovery, slow and painful, dates from the 1950s. Even in 1977, the novelist Allan Massie could write in a fiction review that 'there is no city in Western Europe so evidently decaying as Glasgow'. As the slums were cleared, a whole set of new problems arose in the new towns and in 'the schemes' – the high rise blocks and huge peripheral housing estates of Drumchapel and Easterhouse, Castlemilk and Pollok – which were mistakenly thought to hold solutions to social ills.

The Gorbals, once an agricultural village surrounded by crofts, on the south side of the Clyde, is a particular and tragic example of good city-scheming intentions gone badly awry. At the end of the eighteenth century, with the proceeds of wealth stemming from the cotton and tobacco industries (half of the latter commodity imported into Britain was coming through Glasgow), speculators bought up land to build for themselves superior residences. But these were soon crowded out by lesser dwellings and small businesses (Glasgow Corporation had no jurisdiction south of the river until the mid-nineteenth century). From 1830, the notorious tenements, sub-divided into many one- and two-room family homes, sprang up everywhere and were soon absorbing thousands of Irish immigrants fleeing the poverty and potato famines of the 1840s. By the 1880s, the Gorbals was one of the worst slums in Europe.

Theatre, and particularly music hall and pantomime, was proffered as an opium to the people. Alongside the Irish, who loved the 'crack' of theatre, was another key immigrant population – the Jews from Poland, Lithuania, Hungary and Bohemia, a community which was temperamentally inclined to make a contribution in the performing arts, to supply that 'crack'. Between 1862 and the outbreak of the Great War in 1914, no fewer than eighteen major theatres were built in Glasgow (in the same period, seven were built in Edinburgh, six in Dundee, four in Greenock, itself now an absorbed outpost of Glasgow, and three in Aberdeen). Only four of these Glasgow houses still stand – the Pavilion, the King's, the Theatre Royal (in its third incarnation and, since 1975, the home of Scottish Opera) and the Royal Princess's, renamed the Citizens in 1945.

In 1983, the Queen opened the imaginative new building erected to house the Burrell Collection, bequeathed to the city by a wealthy ship-owner, Sir William Burrell (1861 – 1958). She described it as 'proof, if it is needed, that Glasgow leads from the front in artistic matters'. Her Majesty's speechwriter was obviously mindful that Glasgow has (and also had; much has been tragically lost) some of the finest Victorian public architecture and statuary in Britain; that Charles Rennie Mackintosh (1868 – 1928), architect of the still astonishing Glasgow School of Art, was a leading light in the European modern movement; that the first British performances of Mozart's *Idomeneo* and of Berlioz' *The Trojans* were given in Glasgow in the mid-1930s; and that the Glaswegian music hall is one of the greatest undocumented cultural phenomena of these islands.

The new Burrell home cost £20m to build. A few years later, in 1988, Peter Brook would bring his *Mahabharata* not to London or even Edinburgh, but to the Old Transport Museum, now re-christened the Tramway, in the Pollokshields area of the city. In the same year, the third National Garden Festival, previously held in Liverpool and Stoke-on-Trent, was the fourth of Glasgow's Great Exhibitions since 1888, and attracted over four million visitors.

Now, in 1990, Pavarotti is giving a recital. The new concert hall is due to open at a cost of £23m, final and lone legacy of the arts complex that nearly absorbed the Citizens (with what would have been, I am sure, disastrous consequences) in the early 1970s. Between 1959 and 1984, Alexander Gibson transformed the Scottish National Orchestra into a band of international renown. He also launched Scottish Opera in 1962, and

£3m was raised by the administrator, Peter Hemmings, to convert the Theatre Royal from the headquarters of Scottish Television into the company's new home in 1975.

'Glasgow is one of the cleanest, most beautiful cities in the world', wrote Daniel Defoe when he returned as a tourist to the country he had spied on under the name of 'Alexander Goldsmith' with a view to precipitating the Union of 1707. Defoe's praise was invoked by the Lord Provost in 1973 in a message to those who were then planning the new Glasgow as 'a great Euro-City of the future'. The cultural renovation was all part of the 'new-look' campaign. The worst slums were cleared by the end of the 1960s and, in 1970, the Scottish Civic Trust and the Glasgow Corporation launched its 'Facelift Glasgow' programme. Housing renewal projects have faltered somewhat owing to cut-backs in public expenditure over the past ten years. But art, for all its seemingly cosmetic properties, could be a politically potent and useful public relations ploy.

In the case of Glasgow, the interaction of civic identity and cultural expression surely cuts more deeply than elsewhere in Britain. Coming up from London, you do feel you have crossed more than a national border. Like a character in the second of William McIlvanney's gripping Inspector Laidlaw novels, *The Papers of Tony Veitch*, you sense you have arrived in a city that is about proximity, not anonymity, a place that in spite of its wide vistas and south side areas of dereliction often seems 'as spacious as a rush-hour bus'. The social temperature is both warm and frightening, hugger-mugger, helter-skelter, inviting and dangerous. McIlvanney notes, or his character does, that Glasgow on a Friday night is 'the city of the stare'.

Mcllvanney is a notable post-Chandler crime story stylist, like his American counterparts Ross Macdonald and Ed McBain. His Glasgow, like that of another native novelist, James Kelman, is a city of the underprivileged and dispossessed. Their dour characters have nothing much to do with the punning 1983 promotional slogan 'Glasgow's Miles Better'; little has changed for the people these characters represent, except for the worse. The even grimmer 1990 slogan 'There's a lot Glasgowing on', dreamed up by the advertising men, must strike a good number of the city's population as either an insult or a sick joke.

Nonetheless, I have discovered that many Glaswegians think of the old slum tenements in the Gorbals as an invisible residue of 'lost happiness' and neighbourliness. As a native of London's once notorious, and in many ways comparable, East End, and of Irish antecedence like so many Gorbalites, I know the feeling. Ralph Glasser elaborates on this tenacious sentimentality in his pungent autobiography of escape, *Growing Up in the Gorbals*. A man may very easily and ruefully reflect upon the displacement of his past when wandering among modern Glasgow's great loops of motorway and slabs of high-rise brutalism.

During the slump of the 1930s, with the ship-building industry in decline, and Glasgow already a highly politicised left-wing city (the Scottish National Party had been launched in 1928), there was a marked rise in the city's gang warfare and street violence, elements that contributed to the mythology of hard-drinking macho men knocking hell out of each other on Friday nights. The Gorbals became synonymous with these exploits, and was rendered romantically notorious by several works of art: Alexander McArthur's 1935 novel *No Mean City*, and, in 1946, Arthur Bliss's ballet *Miracle in the Gorbals* and Robert McLeish's play *The Gorbals Story*. The latter was among the most important productions of the Glasgow Unity Theatre, a Chekhovian Expressionistic account of life among eight families in a Gorbals tenement. Russell Hunter and the late Roddy McMillan, each actor emblematic of so many later developments in Scottish theatre, were in the cast.

It is significant that Bridie was not all that keen on Unity, which was palpably committed to a 'people's drama' in a sense that he was not, and which presented a distinct threat to his pre-eminence as a creative Scottish figure. The company, founded in 1941, faded out within the decade, and many of its members joined the Citizens, but not before *The Gorbals Story* had transferred to the Garrick Theatre in London in 1948. *The Times* said the play struck a new and original note, while *The Observer*, having labelled it 'a minor Clydeside sequel to the major Liffey-side slum drama of O'Casey', drew some resonating conclusions:

The moral of it all is that no sort of reform is any good until we get houses, houses, houses. Why spend millions on education and drive the products back into this hell of verminous, overcrowded, insanitary human stabling, where any kind of peace and privacy is unthinkable? The search for a roof, even a bug-infested

11

roof, goes pathetically on: boy meets girl and neither meets a home. The play has no direct preaching: it drives at heart and mind by a dispersed picture of the Gorbalins, especially of its women-folk, who put up, in astonishing patience, with men who are soaks or bullies. English ears – indeed any ears unused to the ghastly havoc that Glasgow makes of decent Scottish speech – will find some of it difficult, but none of it is dull.

Pace the quaint notion of goblin 'Gorbalins' and the blank refusal to submit to the rhythms and vivacity of the dialect – London critics are still prone to turn a deaf ear to the vigorous musicality of Glaswegian – the response is fascinating. In the 1980s, the Scottish touring company, 7:84, has returned to the Glasgow Unity repertoire in order to build on the popular response to its political cabarets in the mid-1970s. Giles Havergal himself guest-directed Ena Lamont Stewart's *Men Should Weep* (1947) to great acclaim, inflecting the social realism of the piece with a stylish Citizens guile; when the production came to Stratford East in London in 1983, Irving Wardle in *The Times* welcomed 'a triumphant marriage between the allegedly decadent style of the Citizens Theatre and the wholesome virtues of the Labour stage'.

However, this attempt to revitalise the contemporary Scottish theatre by invoking a vanished heyday of popular drama has not been entirely successful. Another 1947 Unity piece, *Gold in his Boots*, by George Munro, proved a jejune embarrassment when revived by 7:84 in 1982. The football hero's rising career is undermined by both

Calvinism at home and managerial exploitation at work. Imitative of *Golden Boy* (1937), Clifford Odets' morality set among the boxing fraternity, it revealed neither individual merit nor political significance. Similarly, in 1988, when 7:84, now run by David Hayman, one of the original members of the Havergal Citizens and a leading light of the first decade, dramatised *No Mean City*, Joseph Farrell, a critic and lecturer at Strathclyde University, said 'the novel belongs to another age and is an embarrassment now'. He noted an attempt to stand the values of violence and hard drinking on their heads, but this only revealed a yawning gap at the play's centre. The Glasgow public flocked, however, packing out 7:84's visit to the King's and, just two months later, filling the Citizens for the same production during the first Strathclyde Summer Season.

Other ventures in establishing an ethnic, indigenous theatre culture will be discussed later. Suffice it to say that they all flared for a while and then failed. Another academic, Jan McDonald, Professor of Drama at Glasgow University, declared in 1984 that 'the haggis hunt for the great Scottish play has been the bugbear of the development of the theatre in Scotland', quoting Hazlitt's ingenious explanation for the Irish theatrical supremacy over the Scots: the cheerful, celebrating Irish character, he averred, was more suited for the stage than was the Scotsman's dour, secretive mien and gloomy outlook.

Patriotic scepticism, patronage and the soul of a city

In spite of all the surface friendliness and the legendary hospitality, Glasgow remains strikingly intense. Intense about football, boxing, politics and drinking. Intense, above all, on the subject of its own political identity. There is nowhere in Britain quite like it, not even Liverpool. But, like Merseyside, Glasgow has also been shown, courtesy of a report prepared in 1988 by John Myerscough for the Policy Studies Institute, to be intense about art. The link between the arts and business in the city was found to be particularly strong, and by no means a recent phenomenon.

The link is most visible in the stone legacies of the great industrialists. Some of these have an interesting and complex history in the city's life. For example, the house of William Cunninghame, a prominent tobacco lord, was built in 1788 in what is now Royal Exchange Square, and became the Royal Exchange in 1832. It was enlarged, and the Corinthian columns added at the front. Today the house serves as Stirling's Library, itself so named after the merchant and magistrate William Stirling, who bequeathed his books to the city in 1791.

Modern commercial patronage is less haphazard. Over half a million pounds a year was raised in arts sponsorship in Glasgow well before 1990; the annual turnover was £25m and the number of jobs in the arts over 1,800 (the comparable figures on Merseyside were £183,000 in business sponsorship, £14m turnover and 1,300 jobs).

Along with this high artistic profile goes a well-thumbed sceptical nose. Marcella Evaristi, the Glaswegian-Italian writer and actress, expressed the mood beautifully in a 1988 Garden Festival Mayfest sketch referring to the Transport Museum facelift for *The Mahabharata*: 'Glasgow has thrown away its flat cap and sand-blasted itself in the face . . . for every wino spewing up his Special Brew and sausage supper, there's a wine bar opening now!'

But the transformation at the heart of Glasgow is more spectacular than in any other British city. New shopping centres have sprung up with brash, chrome-plated confidence as the Strathclyde Regional Council, responsible to 1.7 million poll tax payers in the west of Scotland, has attracted £300m of investment in retail floor space. The latest monument to Mammon is the St Enoch Centre, containing 270,000 square feet of shopping space beneath the world's 'largest glass envelope', a glittering pyramidic roof structure which sits disappointingly squat and inert when viewed from across the river but which is exhilarating, and fun, to walk through. There is a wide selection of shops and food counters, a skating rink, artifical greenery, fountains and a curious array of glass monuments poking upwards towards a high-tech celestial jungle of tubular support structures, reflective glass walls, and a transparent ceiling. Outside, the patio-scape between the centre and the ever more incongruous whimsical little Jacobean-style St Enoch subway station is invariably populated by a few of Miss Evaristi's winos.

Such evidence of a divided city — ostentatious symbols of prosperity crowding out the misfits and drunks — is symptomatic of all urban improvement. But the more politically intense Glaswegian artistic community is serious in its contempt for City of Culture fever. Liz Lochhead, the poet and dramatist, pooh-poohs 'art as a function of property development'.

John McGrath, the founding director of 7:84, and a formidable Marxist polemicist, regards 1990 as another dastardly way of reinforcing the Act of Union of 1707, under which Scotland was incorporated into the re-named United Kingdom. In the *Weekend Guardian* of 1 April 1989, an issue devoted to Scotland, McGrath commented on the fact that every large Scottish cultural organisation – the Scottish Arts Council, Scottish Opera, the National Gallery of Scotland, the Edinburgh Festival, and Scottish Ballet – is now in the hands of English administrators and managers (significantly, and with some reason, he excludes the Citizens from his strictures; Giles Havergal can claim to be at least half Scottish, Robert David MacDonald wholly so): 'This is not a problem about any individual's place of birth. But it is worrying when so many and such powerful people take decisions based on assumptions that are not those of their audience, and create policies that do not grow from the specific potential of Scottish artists but from the need to compete in a cosmopolitan bazaar.'

The Glasgow District Council employed the advertising agency Saatchi and Saatchi, image-moulding advisers to Mrs Thatcher and the Conservative Party, to handle the 1990 account. In the build-up to the festivities, Glasgow arts bodies were advised by a man from the agency that 1990 was nothing to do with culture, but all to do with business re-location, and the target audience was the 18- to 35- year-old professional market in the South East of England.

Thus would the fears of McGrath seem to be confirmed. But I shall try to show later on that the strategic, political and economic aims of 1990 are both less despicable and more complex than McGrath claims. The Citizens under Havergal has increasingly become part of those aims over the years, and willingly so. It is my contention, too, that the success of the theatre is very much due to the fact that it 'belongs' to Glasgow.

In spite of both the 1984 'Glory of the Garden' Arts Council Report, which advocated decentralisation of resources, and the subsequent 1986 Cork Report, which proposed a network of six or seven equally funded and regarded national theatres, Britain's theatre culture remains prey to the damaging hegemony of metropolitan values and snobbery. The Citizens alone among our regional theatres pursues an artistic policy unrelated to the capital. It has lost interest in London, just as London has shown only a flickering interest in the Citizens' work. This spiritual and physical remoteness from London has been a crucially creative aspect of the Citizens' work since 1969.

As Ian McDiarmid, one of the early members of the company, and one of its few Scots, said to me, 'It is rather like the attitude now of the Glasgow artists; at the Citizens, they had, and have, a healthy contempt for London, and never felt, as many other regional British companies feel, including the Royal Exchange in Manchester where I worked for a time as an associate, that to get to London with a production was any big deal, any sort of aim or apotheosis'.

In that first year, 1909, of the Glasgow Rep, Bridie's

predecessors presented the British première of Chekhov's *The Seagull*, but their programme was mainly drawn from Ibsen and the Court Theatre's seasons in Sloane Square, London. There was a fair proportion of now forgotten Scottish plays by the likes of R.H. Powell and Neil Munro; but the staple diet for the four years of the Rep's existence under the pioneer directorship of Alfred Wareing was Shaw and Granville Barker, St John Hankin, John Masefield and Pinero. Later on, Bridie would produce his own Scottish plays at the Citizens, but there are those who suggest that he gave all his best ones to West End managements. London, in fact, was not as theatrically remote from Glasgow as it is today. On the whole, the Havergal regime has remained aloof and apart from London for twenty-one years, adhering more closely to that original manifesto than did ever its perpetrators.

The Citizens, in short, is both a feather in the cap of Glasgow 1990, and a stern reminder that, in matters of reputation and success, there is no time or excuse for window-dressing or hollow fanfare. I once asked Giles Havergal, what happens after 1990? '1991', he tartly replied. Like most sensible arts institutions in Glasgow, his theatre is using 1990 to hike up its grants and solidify a platform for the future. In 1988–89, Strathclyde Regional Council gave the theatre £150,000, Glasgow District Council £175,000, and the Scottish Arts Council £410,000. Between 30 and 37 per cent of all earned income is taken at the box office (attendances in the 641- seater theatre average over 80 per cent), making the whole annual turnover slightly in excess of £1m.

Many myths surround the Citizens, not least the one of

spendthrift luxuriance and aesthetic dilettantism. In fact, the organisation is penny-pinching and pragmatic to a degree. In this it is unique, and quite different from most deficit-happy British subsidised theatres or their more lavishly funded European counterparts. It is poised with perfect ambiguity between the show-off razzmatazz of Glasgow 1990 and the social and cultural aspirations of the folk on its doorstep. The Myerscough report summed up with just impartiality:

The Citizens Theatre remained the sole public building in a large part of the Gorbals which had been subject to clearance. Theatrical life was maintained as the sole vestige of city life in an urban wilderness, and the theatre audience continued to attend. The Citizens Theatre became both the symbol of continuity with the Gorbals past and the social node around which its future prospects could cohere. The quarter is now being successfully resettled and its soul has endured in the theatre and its audience.

2

THE CITIZENS THEATRE: 'NEW LAMPS FOR OLD'

You have to look for the Citizens Theatre these days. It is obscured, from the Gorbals Cross side to the north, behind a new Legal Services Centre and now shares with this latest architectural monstrosity, as part of its renovation deal with the Scottish Development Agency, a yellow brick exterior of the sort usually associated with Sainsbury's or Marks & Spencer. Hurry round to the new glass-fronted entrance, though, and the fun begins. A first sight of an airy, spacious white foyer will not even then prepare you for the splendours of the auditorium.

When I first visited the theatre, as a 24-year-old tyro critic, in February 1973, the place stuck out like a sore thumb, a good but dilapidated deed in a dirty night. Along with the swimming pool and baths opposite, and the immediately adjacent Palace of Varieties (a bingo hall since 1962), the theatre was the last public building left standing in the Gorbals. An incongruous façade of Corinthian pillars supporting six battered Victorian statues – four muses, flanked on the left (as you faced the frontage) by Shakespeare and on the right by Robert Burns, all the work of James Mossman – stared across what was once a bustling High Street at a dismal wasteland soon to be invaded by a grey group of 24-storey residential high-rise blocks. And then the final vulgarian touch: plastered by the front entrance, alongside what passed for a portico, was a notice declaring in huge block-black letters on a white background, ALL SEATS 50p.

Inside, a palace of delights; outside, a wilderness, a bleak terrain of broken up concrete, scrubland, the crumbling remains of a redbrick railway arch, no pubs, few people. When Lord Taylor of Gryfe resigned from the board in 1969, he had arrived at the painful conclusion that people would not go to a theatre in the Gorbals. But they would, and they did. After the first phase of renovation was completed in 1978, the American critic David Zane Mairowitz, writing in *Plays and Players*, welcomed a gorgeous *Threepenny Opera*, set in a pink and powder-blue salon, in the wider context of a devastated neighbourhood:

This brash interpretation, with a punk Polly Peachum, Mrs Peachum pushing a black pram with only a gin bottle inside, Macheath's gang of crooks doubling as his whores in drag, has certainly liberated the poet from the clutches of the Brecht Mafia. But it is no more unlikely a scenario than Britain's most exciting theatre company being housed in the middle of Scotland's (and perhaps Britain's) toughest square mile of bleak drudge. This curious dialectic between the Glasgow streets and the Citizens' stage is surely mirrored in this unique *Threepenny Opera*. This is theatre with a sense of itself and its rather singular geographical fix; this is a theatre of imagery which, in spite of its grim girdle of Gorbals, bears constant witness to the pleasure principle.

The theatre thrives nowadays precisely because it does contradict its surroundings. Local kids would congregate at the stage door not because they wanted to know about the theatre or to collect autographs, but because they knew something delicious and probably forbidden was going on inside. When Noël Coward's *Semi-Monde* was given its world première in 1977 (the play attracted the London critics in force for the first time; even Bernard Levin, then serving a stint on *The Sunday Times*, came up), the local urchins marked the event by setting fire to a vehicle in the car-park. Such bravura clashes of style and extremities of statement lie at the heart of the whole operation.

Journey to the centre of the Citizens

I remember the first time I made my way to the Gorbals across the Clyde from the city centre, having stopped off to check in at the now demolished St Enoch Hotel, the nearest I've ever come in the flesh to Mervyn Peake's Gormenghast. I like to cross the river on foot, and a route can be taken via one of three bridges: the sturdy Victoria and Jamaica Bridges, uncompromising totems of the iron and steel ages; and the one on which I invariably settle, the elegant 1853 suspension bridge for pedestrians only that divides the other two.

The suspension bridge was purpose-built to service the newly resident merchant class on the south side, with a halfpenny toll for the privilege of using it. This forms a direct approach to the neo-classical pink stone terrace of Carlton Place, the first attempt in Glasgow at organising a whole street into a symmetrical composition. The terrace was designed by Peter Nicholson in 1802 and admirably restored after the last war; it cheats you into thinking it's all like that over there. And indeed it once was. Ida Schuster, a Glasgow Unity actress and a regular in many Citizens companies since, including Havergal's, rhapsodised to me about the district's lovely Victorian tenements and big, wide, beautiful streets, all now bulldozed; her brother-in-law, Avron Greenbaum, had founded the Jewish Institute Players, one of the arterial forebears of Unity, in South Portland Street, just behind the terrace.

Turning left off the bridge and holding the river for 150 yards, one used to arrive at a higgledy-piggledy area just before Gorbals Cross by the busy road coming in from Paisley. This patch is now occupied by the Sheriff's Court, as hideous an abomination of modern architecture as you could not wish to see, the sort of thing that convinces you after all that Hitler won the war. Inching precariously towards the Cross, now the crossroads, the Legal Centre and the Citizens are suddenly visible, and to the south of them, on Ballater Street, is a brash new mosque.

Looking back over the bridge, you can see lights twinkling on the nautical marquee of a trendy new establishment called Pier 39 — 'lounge bar, deli, ice-cream parlour' — on the Custom House Quay. With a shiver, I recall that the disappointed Lord Taylor thought the Citizens would stand a better chance of survival if they took up an available site on the Clyde riverside between the suspension and Jamaica bridges; instead we have Pier 39, and coffee and spirits priced for yuppies. The wind blows viciously across the scene of desolation, bleak even when the sun shines. Random piles of rubbish are accumulating along the outside perimeter of the mosque and the traffic hurtles past at more than a fair lick. We are at Gorbals Cross, once the centre of an impoverished community. As he drank from the fountain at the Cross, Ralph Glasser remembers reading an inscription printed in gold letters beneath the coat of arms: 'Let Glasgow flourish' was the shortened but now generally quoted version of a city motto which once carried the full moral credo of business ethics fuelled by religion, 'Lord let Glasgow flourish through the preaching of thy Word and praising thy name'. The Cross was removed by the City Fathers in 1932, as if to serve notice of future intentions; when Glasser returned to the Gorbals in later life, he had no idea where the Cross might have stood. His disorientation was complete.

The geographical location, or indeed dislocation, of the Citizens is important and has a direct bearing on the choice of play and indeed method of production. In a lecture to the Tenth World Congress of the International Federation for Theatre Research in 1985, Havergal told delegates that discussion on play choice often prompts one of the three directors to ask: 'Honestly, they are not going to schlep all the way down here to see that: would you?'

Stand opposite the new glass foyer. It used to be so

different. You had to squeeze through a stiff door into a box office area painted and carpeted in red (in the 1960s the public areas were predominantly off-white) and decorated with huge blow-up photographs of past productions. Here was Jonathan Kent as Cleopatra in a sarong and beaded hair-do, torso darkened and athletically strained against a background matted of rushes and bamboo (when this production went on tour, Kent was the first Cleopatra in Rome since Eleonora Duse). Here, too, was a languid collection of beach boys in white dungarees lolling around on the Venice Lido during *Chinchilla*, the 1977 Diaghilev play and company manifesto. Turning off the foyer into the tea room, more huge pictures: in Edward Bond's *Early Morning*, David Hayman chewed ecstatically on the sodden tendons of a severed arm (the property limb was generously stuffed with Mars bars).

As magic time approaches, the warm welcoming foyer bustles with a band of pleasant usherettes, girls and ladies in black skirts and white blouses (the troops are led, as they have been for twenty-eight years, by Mary Sweeney), one of whom conducts you to your seat within, past the bronze plaque that honours the Citizens' founding father, Dr O.H. Mavor, 'physician and dramatist', alias James Bridie (alias, too, 'Mary Henderson' in his early writing days). Then, as now, a duty roster operated so that each night's audience is personally greeted, and I *mean* greeted, at the front door by Havergal, or the house manager, or the general manager (there have been just two general managers since 1973, Clare Blenkinsop and Paul Bassett).

As you settle, you glance at the free programme which contains only the barest information about the play and details of the cast. The Citizens Company – comprising ushers, directors, cleaners, the wages clerk, publicists, wardrobe and canteen assistants, actors and carpenters – is listed by name in alphabetical order. About 120 of them, including all the part-time staff. Robert David MacDonald reports that one critic complained in print that the programme told him no more about Balzac's *Vautrin* than who was in it and who swept up afterwards, to which MacDonald replied: 'I think that's quite sufficient information to have at your fingertips if you are that type of lazy, uneducated critic. The audience don't care. Most of them don't know Balzac from a bull's foot, actually, and that's fine. You get what you get from our productions. We're not a branch of the Open University.' Other theatres in Britain have imitated this programme style, and have appeared hypocritical and pretentious; what for them is a gimmick is, for the Citizens, a truthful reflection of how the whole place works.

The interior in the early 1970s was painted red, gold, green and black. It was warm, cosy, the perfect setting for classical plays, with no confusion over the audience's physical relationship to the stage. The plaster-cast naked goddesses around the proscenium were sprayed in gold paint. For the Genet trilogy of 1982, Philip Prowse designed the auditorium into the set, reproducing the Victorian boxes in triplicate in their exact proportions, moulding and paintwork. In this voluptuous essay in Genetesque illusion, the biggest mirage of all turned out to be the revolution.

Illusion and deception are endemic to the Citizens. This was so even in the old days, as Ida Schuster will testify. She has no regrets about the nearby slums disappearing ('They had to go, there was terrible filth in those backyards along Thistle Street just behind the theatre, a high density of pubs and drunks spewing in the closes') and remembers queues trailing along the pavement outside the Palace next door. 'I'd come down to the theatre and think, ooh, we've got a good house tonight. But the queue was to get in to the Palace for the bingo!'

The renovation work, begun in 1978, was completed last year in time for the 1989 Mayfest production of *A Tale of Two Cities*. A new set of traffic lights seems to proclaim civic care and approval: don't get knocked down in the street before you get knocked out in the theatre. At dusk, the place is lit up from within like a great ocean-going liner. The four muses are restored on high, this time in a hi-tech glass pediment. You can see straight through them to a coloured window of the Royal Princess's Theatre, formerly hung on the old stair to the dress circle ('A sign of blessed continuity' said Stanley Baxter, a Citizens actor of the 1950s and one of the greatest of many great Scottish pantomime dames), now elevated like a monstrance on a glass altar.

The new foyer is a very public arena, its white stairs, hand-rails and curious portholes in the front wall reinforcing the nautical atmosphere, a setting, perhaps, for a jolly 1930s musical such as Cole Porter's *Anything Goes*. It is a place of air and sky and holiday spirits, where once it was an appealingly louche, red rabbit warren of corridors and corners. In daylight, the transparent enclosure is meteorologically vulnerable, altered in tone by scudding clouds or shafts of sunlight, while the auditorium beyond preserves its great dark secrets. Guarding the back wall of the stalls, four decorative plaster elephant heads, rescued from the Palace next door before it was razed to the ground, stand wisely in a row with the Bridie plaque. The four matching topless nautch girls who sat on top of the elephants around the Palace stage boxes, rather Amazonian in their armoured belts, stand sentinel in the two new bars, one on the upper deck, one below. The final bold stroke in this post-Modern Victorian culture clash is the restoration of the Shakespeare and Burns statues to their rightful, imposing position, left and right again, on the main raised level of the foyer.

Opinions differ on the overall effect. I like it more each time I go, though I miss the big dramatic photographs, and the snug little bar off the dress circle. The interior restoration is just as drastic. Gone the red and the green and the black; the entire place, including the elephants and nautch girls, has been painstakingly sponge-stippled in strawberry and gold leaf paint. The foyer is blindingly bright. And so, to start with, is the auditorium; the circle has been given a high-wattage nether belt of naked bulbs. The famous 'woods' in the surprisingly large gallery have long gone; there is comfortable seating up there now for over 200, the distinction between upper circle and gallery obliterated. Seats throughout are in red; two new raised rows at the back of the stalls often afford the best vantage points, though the circle overhang can fuzz up the acoustics.

Typically, the Citizens has made something bold and decisive of alterations partly enforced by political will and commercial development. The amazing thing, given the history of the building, is that it still stands in any shape at all.

'Don't clap too hard, lady, it's a very old building'

The beginnings of the first theatre on the south side were not auspicious. It closed almost as soon as it opened as Her Majesty's Theatre and Royal Opera House in 1878, ten years before Bridie was born, in what was then called Main Street, Gorbals. The *Glasgow Herald* found it hard to be encouraging. *Ali Baba and the Forty Thieves* had not gone well, and not least because the Philip Prowse of the day had been over-ambitious:

> As regards the scenery, all of which is fresh from the hand of the painter, and much of it highly artistic in character, it was in a state of mechanical rebellion, and the hard-working staff whose duty it is to reduce it to subjection found their efforts more than once unavailing on Saturday evening . . . the audience manifested a good deal of impatience, although Mrs McFadyen craved their indulgence in a sensible, business-like speech which might have had a kindlier response.

In other words, it was a riot. Little wonder that Prowse, whose philosophy of theatre design extends only to the belief that there is not a play in the world that cannot be done on one set, will have nothing to do with trucks, painted cloths, mobile flats and furniture removals between scenes.

The minute Her Majesty's closed, it was re-opened by Harcourt Beryl as the Royal Princess's Theatre. The Palace next door had been going as a concert hall since the 1880s, but was re-designed as a theatre in 1907 and decorated in the baroque Anglo-Indian style popularised by Walter Emden's Tivoli music hall in the Strand, London. Decorating the eight stage boxes were six elephants and six goddesses (the nautch girls); the two of each which eluded the Citizens' grasp are preserved in a striking reconstruction of a Palace box in the lobby of the Theatre Museum in Covent Garden, London.

The Royal Princess's was designed by Campbell Douglas, a friend and contemporary of Alexander 'Greek' Thompson, the genius most responsible for Glasgow's architectural pre-eminence as a Victorian city. The theatre seated 1,200 people, the Palace 2,000. On a good night, therefore, there were at least 500 more theatre-goers milling around in the vicinity than you could pack today into the three auditoria of the National Theatre. The façade was equidistant between the two theatres, and stuck on as an afterthought. The columns came from David Hamilton's Union Bank in Ingram Street, and James Mossman popped the statues on top. The feature is preserved today on some of the theatre's posters and publicity material.

Harcourt Beryl had promoted a successful mixed diet of melodrama, variety and pantomime, a policy continued by his assistant Richard Waldon, an Englishman. Waldon is almost as prominently commemorated as Bridie by a wooden relief plaque, also guarded by the elephants. Waldon, 'into whose possession this theatre came in

31

1886', was director and manager until he died in 1922. The theatre was then inherited by Harry McKelvie, 'the Pantomime King', who had worked his way up from programme-seller to manager. He wrote and produced the pantomimes that made him a fortune, although he was superstitious enough to insist always on a thirteen-letter title, a tradition that persisted into the post-Bridie era. He probably felt you could insure against disasters of *Ali Baba* proportions with shows called *Gaggiegalorum* or *Bletherskeite*.

McKelvie soldiered on while the Palace next door became a cinema in the 1930s (It closed altogether in 1947, re-opening for bingo in 1962). In 1945, McKelvie, now dogged by ill health, made a generous offer of tenancy to Bridie, who believed he could succeed with the Citizens in an unfashionable area, just as Lilian Baylis had succeeded with the Old Vic on the wrong side of the Thames. With the expiry of the ten-year lease imminent, the Corporation of Glasgow bought the Citizens for £17,000 and rented it back to the administration. This arrangement persists today, Glasgow District Council leasing the theatre to the Citizens Theatre Company Limited.

Plans for a cultural centre in Glasgow first surfaced in 1965. The threat to the Citizens, meanwhile, came not just from the rapidly declining state of the building. William Taylor, the lawyer and Citizens board member who served on the city's Labour council from 1952 to 1969 (retiring, undefeated, to become the theatre's chairman), was heavily involved in the major road planning now underway. One problem was the eastern flank of the inner ring road, which would necessitate the demolition of the theatre. Taylor was saved from embarrassment by the lack of capacity in the Corporation (which became the District Council in 1975) to sustain the amount of property acquisition necessary to execute this plan.

However, much time in the early years of Havergal's regime was consumed with discussing and approving plans for a new 650-seater Citizens, and 200-seater studio, within the proposed cultural civic centre on Buchanan Street, on the block between Sauchiehall Street and Bath Street. The models were publicised in 1973 and very hideous they looked, too. In addition to the theatres, wedged in a corner, was a concert hall seating 2,500, a smaller concert hall for the Royal Scottish Academy of Music and Drama seating 500 (the RSAMD now has its own splendid new honey-brick home with concert hall and horseshoe theatre on Renfrew Street, next to the Theatre Royal), a banqueting chamber and other amenities. A veritable little Barbican of the North. The theatres were expected to be ready in 1978.

By then, the economic squeeze had put paid to the eastern flank inner motorway and, in June 1976, the Secretary of State for Scotland instructed Glasgow District Council not to go ahead with the cultural centre, whose estimated costs had risen from £20m to £30m. (The concert-hall part of the plan was salvaged and it is this remnant that is due to open in late 1990.) To the Citizens' considerable relief, their own building received an official reprieve in December 1976, at which point Havergal started agitating for substantial renovations.

The pillars were removed in July 1977, and the four

muses and two poets put into storage (Burns appeared for a time in the bar of the Tron Theatre Club which opened in 1980). The Citizens, the Palace, and what remained of the adjoining tenements, were to be roofed over anew. Almost immediately, and without so much as a by-your-leave or a notice pinned on a lamp-post, the District Council decided to demolish the Palace. The Citizens' Manager, Clare Blenkinsop, achieved a brief stay of execution in order to salvage the elephants and goddesses; the exceedingly pretty jade box office was taken by the People's Palace on Glasgow Green, where it may be seen to this day.

The bulldozers moved in during November 1977, and Havergal recalls the destruction as an act of haphazardly perpetrated urban vandalism of the worst kind. 'It was outrageous enough that they weren't going to tell anybody; the place closed on a Saturday night, the last little old lady in a headscarf went home, and they were sending in the bulldozers on Monday morning. But they did it so *badly*.' The Scottish Development Agency 'landscaped' the surrounding area.

Thus another Glasgow theatre bit the dust. The Queens had disappeared in 1952, the Royalty in 1953, the old Metropole (managed in its latter years by Jimmy Logan) in 1961, and the Alhambra in 1971, in spite of a petition of 500,000 signatories. The most famous variety hall outside of London was the Glasgow Empire in Sauchiehall Street, the toughest house in the kingdom. The audience had perfected the art of expressing disapproval; they would yell, whistle and even throw things at unwelcome, usually English, comedians. The story goes that when

Morecambe and Wise played there for about the third time, they walked off to dead silence. 'They're beginning to like you,' said the stage doorman. The Empire closed in 1962, even though, in only the previous year, over 500,000 people had paid to see Andy Stewart during a twenty-week season; the site, opposite what is now the Electricity Board's headquarters, was sold for commercial development. In the same year, the last trams ran in Glasgow, and people wept openly in the streets. Popular culture and habitual ways of life were increasingly put at risk by city planners and the interests of big business.

Dawn of a new day

Art, however, was going up market. 1962 also saw the first stirrings of Scottish Opera: *Madame Butterfly*, sung in Italian, opened at the King's on 5 June. As Cordelia Oliver has noted, the company's connection with the Citizens in the early years was mainly forged through collaborations with two of Philip Prowse's designer protégées, Sue Blane and Maria Bjornson. Scottish Opera's staff producer, and subsequent director of productions, was David Pountney, who had been a contemporary at Cambridge University of Keith Hack, a member of the new Citizens company; Bjornson was to become Pountney's chief design colleague in Glasgow and subsequently at the English National Opera in London. Hack himself had come to Glasgow in 1970 as a trainee director.

When Keith Hack removed the Citizens' stalls for his boxing ring production of Brecht's *In the Jungle of the Cities*, he invited Pountney to provide the music. But the two enterprises have drifted apart since the early days;

35

Havergal occasionally directs opera, but not for Scottish Opera. Prowse and MacDonald later worked just once for the company: Prowse's great grey library for the Citizens' *Don Juan* was interestingly developed into Tamino's 'Age of Reason' book-lined study in Jonathan Miller's production of *The Magic Flute*; and MacDonald has elaborated ingeniously on Beaumarchais's *Barber of Seville* on both Citizens and Theatre Royal stages.

Havergal and Prowse came up to Glasgow from the Watford Palace in 1969, to take over a theatre that was proving almost as much of a graveyard for artistic directors as the Empire had once been for music-hall comics. The building was dishevelled, morale low, the board in disarray and the audience missing. At first, Havergal and Prowse carried on in much the same way as at Watford, where Harold Pinter had been persuaded to appear in his own play, *The Homecoming*, and Pinter's first wife, Vivien Merchant, enticed into playing the lead in the British première of Tennessee Williams's *Sweet Bird of Youth*.

Now in Glasgow, Constance Cummings appeared in Williams's *The Milk Train Doesn't Stop Here Anymore*, James Fox in *Heartbreak House*, and Miriam Karlin in a Christmas version of *Nicholas Nickleby* by Ned Sherrin and Caryl Brahms. Havergal had been particularly pleased with an *Importance*, designed by Prowse with a set of just three great art nouveau pillars, and Cecily got up like Mae West in a pink shiny dress. The cast also included Ambrosine Phillpotts 'in full flight' as Lady Bracknell; Anna Wing as Miss Prism; Robert Swann as Jack; and Ellen Sheean 'brilliant as Gwendolyn, the best

Opposite: the Citizens in 1977, shortly before the razing of the Palace next door, and the removal of the statues and façade. Overleaf: top, the redecorated auditorium of the Citizens in 1989; below, a view of the exterior in the Gorbals in 1982.

you've ever seen'. The key point about the predominantly unconventional presentation was that the audience loved it; Havergal and Prowse noted that the customers did not much care about what had been done with the play because they had heard of the title.

Attendance figures began to pick up a little, but not enough. A continued respectable repertory policy was not going to detain Havergal in Glasgow for long. It is interesting that the thunderbolt change of policy, the overnight aesthetic upheaval, was nothing much to do with artistic soul-searching, but rather with a simple desire to survive. Prowse decided, for the new season in September 1970, that they should employ a gang of kids and do all the plays the audience had heard of, but in a manner different from all expectations, including their own. 'If nobody likes what we do, we can do what we like' became the catchphrase. The first play was *Hamlet*. It opened on Friday, 4 September, and all hell broke loose.

Overleaf:
the new foyer in
May 1989, the
statues restored to
the frontage, but
under glass, the
high-rise flats
beyond.
Opposite: top,
the exterior by night
in April 1990;
below,
Philip Prowse,
Giles Havergal and
Robert David
MacDonald,
in April 1990.

HAMLET, AND THE STORY SO FAR

The first sniff of a scandal came the next morning, in the first review. 'Hamlet proves a tragedy for Citizens' seemed an innocuously disappointed headline in the Scottish Daily Express, but Mamie Crichton immediately went for the jugular, setting the predominant tone of gloomy Press reaction in an address now widely considered beyond redemption:

> The death-wish must indeed be upon Glasgow's ailing Citizens Theatre. At a time when the board and artistic director have acknowledged its struggle for survival, the Citizens' autumn season started off last night with a Hamlet of unbelievable ineptitude. So many were the gimmicks, so clumsy the cuts, so jerky and double fortissimo the lines and so insensitive most of the action, it was hard to remember this is a great play.

Even bigger guns were rolled up on Monday morning. With a weekend to think about it, The Scotsman, for the first and last time in its history, decided to print a review by Allen Wright in full on the front page under the headline 'Hamlet depicted as a gibbering oaf'. The production was crude, a travesty, a hideous spectacle, an unjustified indulgence of a director's pet theory. Wright 'wished that someone would have [had] the decency to bring down the curtain before any more wounds were inflicted on a work of art ... it is shameful that this should be the play's first production in Glasgow for ten years, giving many young people a warped impression of it'.

Christopher Small was equally certain in the *Glasgow Herald* that the new policy was doomed, sneaking in a learned pun on another director famed for an anti-*Hamlet*: 'Mr Havergal, determined only to do something new, at whatever cost, with the best known of all plays, is so to speak at his Marowitz end even before he is fairly started.' The refrain generally adopted was that the experiment was doubly misguided at this low point in the theatre's fortunes. 'It is no good and no service to the Citizens to keep up a pretence. The present direction of the theatre has been and continues to be disastrous.'

What had Havergal and Prowse done? The cast was all-male and unidentified in the programme, the grave-diggers dressed only in loincloths, the other costumes all black (Small invoked both Aubrey Beardsley and Charles Addams), the action preceded by a mimed scene of copulation between incestuous sheets. The text was ruthlessly cut (and minced and shredded), the company on the brink of a corporate nervous, hysterical breakdown with the exception, according to Small, of the venal and villainous — Polonius, Osric and Claudius. Most critics knew that local lad David Hayman was the prince, but this was no time for expressions of pride.

What was obviously cataclysmic in terms of Glasgow theatre was perhaps not so wildly aberrant by general theatre standards of the time. Looking back, Havergal only regrets that the production was not half as flamboyantly outrageous as the reviews suggested. This was, however, the first sign that mainstream Scottish theatre acknowledged a world elsewhere in the performing arts, although the Traverse in Edinburgh, the first British fringe venue, had been stirring things up for a coterie audience since 1963, and the homoerotic scenarios of Lindsay Kemp were attracting a cult underground following throughout Britain and in mainland Europe.

Kemp, who was based for a time in Edinburgh, was, and is, an outrageously maverick performer. Claiming descent from the Shakespearean clown, Will Kempe, he formed his own company in the mid-1960s to present works by Genet, Lorca and Shakespeare, among others, in a hothouse environment of nudity, emphatic make-up of white face and carmine lips, explicit mime, lush and loud recorded music, overt sensuality and audience-manipulating lighting effects. He both anticipated and influenced the Havergal Citizens in that he brought elements of the new fashionable androgyny, and the rock concert, into the theatre. He was a close adviser to David Bowie in the early part of Bowie's career as a rock star, and he directed an all-male version of Genet's *The Maids* in the Close Theatre, the Citizens' studio space, soon after Havergal arrived.

Theatrical censorship had been abolished in Britain by the Theatres Act of 1968, but the National Theatre in London at the Old Vic had already staged an all-male

41

production of *As You Like It* in 1967. The gimmick of stage nudity had been purged of any shock resonance or value by *Hair* in 1968, and *Oh! Calcutta!* in 1970.

The difference was that, unlike any of those shows, but like Lindsay Kemp, this *Hamlet* obviously did radiate a sense of sexual and political danger. Within two days, the *Glasgow Herald* was reporting the cancellation of school bookings and the convention of an emergency board meeting at the theatre. Bailie Derek Wood, who attended the first night, regretted that, only two days before the opening, a Corporation sub-committee had voted £200,000 of taxpayers' money towards the new theatre in the proposed cultural complex. He said the show deserved an X-certificate but conceded that his 21-year-old daughter had not felt as affronted as he had; perhaps he, aged forty-seven, was just 'an old fogey'. Having announced a season of classic plays to restore the artistic operation on an even keel, the theatre was alleged to have misled the funding bodies as to its intentions. The city treasurer, William Samuels, muttered darkly about what the consequences might be.

The immediate consequence, as always in these cases, was packed houses. The furore bubbled away in the newspapers and, as people came to see for themselves, opinions widened. Cordelia Oliver of *The Guardian*, who was to become the new regime's most powerfully loyal advocate, had not enjoyed *Hamlet* much but reported the first-night cheers of the younger people in the audience, concluding that if Havergal had indeed set his sights on a new constituency, this 'visually rewarding production' may not be so wide of the mark. A critic in the *Scots*

Independent concurred: 'There were boos, cheers, hisses at the end — but no one went to sleep . . . it was very exciting . . . a damned good try to get back a lost audience.' The chairman, William Taylor, staunchly defended the professional integrity of his director before he had even seen the production. He knew that the trend had been reversed and that, in spite of the cancellations by certain schools, 'the production had done what it had set out to do'. It put the Citizens firmly back on the map. People now knew something positive and very probably offensive was going on. Taylor went with his wife, Gladys, and son, Graham. 'Graham, a young man at the time, was wildly enthusiastic. I liked it very much. Gladys was, well, not very keen. This three-way split within one family reflected how other families and friends were divided, and it was important for me to know of these other opinions, some of them ahead of my own, some of them not.'

Three board members had resigned in the first year of Havergal's appointment. Within a few days of *Hamlet* opening, the administrator, J. Arnot Ferguson, and the literary manager, Anthony Paterson, a former schoolmaster who had been associated with the Citizens since 1952, also resigned. The controversy reverberated forty miles across country to Edinburgh, where it upstaged the last week of that year's Festival. Harold Hobson of *The Sunday Times* sprang inimitably into action without even seeing the production. He had, he said, much admired Havergal's work at the Watford Palace:

I know the fineness of its taste, its intelligence, its sympathy with everything good and commendable in

43

the modern theatre. Mr Havergal made Watford one of the most impressive repertory theatres in England. Yet in the storm of obloquy that has broken over Mr Havergal this week, in Edinburgh no less than in Glasgow, with threats that his theatre may lose its subsidy unless it loses him, one is asked to believe that the air of Scotland is so corrupting that a man whose work in England has never been subject to the least reproach has immediately after crossing the border produced something which is a public disgrace.

Paola Dionisotti had joined the new company to play in Pinter at the smaller Close Theatre. She had spent two years at the Liverpool Everyman and remembers going to see *Hamlet* in the pouring rain:

Even after Liverpool, there was a level of depression about [Glasgow] that I had never experienced before, hordes of small men standing on street corners waiting for the pubs to open. In the foyer were all these boards, as if it was a civic exhibition, full of outraged and furious reviews, and the city treasurer calling for emergency meetings to cut the grant. Of course the place was packed and I was absolutely fascinated. At that time, I had seen nothing that bold; you were thrown into the action from the word go, with this great copulating couple who turned out to be men, and yards and yards of black satin; the famous black parachute silk had hit the Citizens stage for the first of many times. It was *very* effective.

David Hayman had left drama school also to join the smaller Close Theatre company. The boy from the tenements in Bridgeton just along the river from the Citizens was suddenly thrust into the limelight as a classical actor, and remained a leading player there for ten years. The rehearsals for *Hamlet*, he says, were a series of explorations in different voices and at different speeds. He found nothing outrageous in it, because he had nothing to compare it with.

Also, I was a born radical. And I love getting up people's noses. Brecht said that theatre should create moral scandal, and Giles and Philip understood that very well. It was a heady time, and the life-style we were involved in was almost as exciting as the work itself. We were playing with our sexuality on stage and off. This was 1969, remember; [off-stage] I was wearing eye make-up, an ear-ring, a woman's fur coat, a great sombrero hat and my hair down to my shoulders. I was even ahead of Mick Jagger. I remember aunts and uncles of mine running from me in the street as this vision bore down on them. And here were a bunch of young actors straight from drama school doing the greatest ever European classic. Suddenly a city was saying here is a theatre in the front line of society; it was an extraordinary thing to be part of, very exciting. The schoolkids whose masters had cancelled their bookings took to the buses and came on their own.

Deep down, the *Hamlet* represented a calculated assault on Scottish Calvinism and the spirit of John Knox whose

45

statue glares down on the city from the highest point in the Necropolis, that great complex of tombs and memorials to the Glaswegian Victorian great and good, hard by the cathedral. But it also declared war on the narrow nationalist aspirations of the Scottish theatre, which had often been confused in the past with the broader struggles to establish a serious national forum for drama.

The Birth of the Citizens, Alfred Wareing and Bridie

The theatre in Scotland declined after the court of James VI removed to London in 1603, where the great years of patronage by Elizabeth I and her nobility had protected the English theatre companies from the Puritan civic authorities. In Scotland, the theatre did not find comparable or effective patrons until the prosperous new middle classes began to take an interest in the middle and late eighteenth century. The climate was tested by John Home's *Douglas* in 1756, which fell foul of the Kirk but inspired one enthusiastic Edinburgh first-nighter to utter the imperishable battle-cry 'Whaur's yer Wullie Shakespeare noo?' As Professor J.F. Arnott once ruefully remarked, the play was anyway performed by an English cast and written with a view to a production by Garrick at Drury Lane. English companies led by Mrs Siddons, Edmund Kean and Henry Irving toured to Scotland throughout the nineteenth century, and many leading English actors appeared as star guests with local stock companies. The real Scottish national theatre, as Lewis Casson pointed out, was in pantomime and variety.

But, as the twentieth century dawned, the rumblings in

the repertory movement gathered around the initiative of one of those extraordinary, dedicated characters whose do-gooding led to the 'art theatre', or 'theatre of ideas', the formation of the Arts Council and the network of subsidised houses that still sustain the dramatic tradition.

Alfred Wareing (1876–1942) was a stage-struck, virtually stone-deaf Englishman who had worked with Frank Benson's company and as a touring manager for Beerbohm Tree. While engaged with the latter in Dublin in 1906, he had seen the new Abbey Theatre and its Irish Players in the new work of Yeats and Lady Gregory. Infected by the repertory ideals, he returned to England and arranged, with Annie Horniman (the heiress of a tea merchant who financed the Abbey until she started her own, and England's first, repertory company in Manchester in 1907), a tour of the Abbey company. This took him to Glasgow, where the company made a handsome profit and he spotted a market, an opportunity to spread the gospel.

His proposal was a citizens' company funded by public subscription, rather than by the benefactions of a Horniman. The Glasgow Repertory Theatre opened at the Royalty, opposite the Empire in Sauchiehall Street, on 5 April 1909, with a production of Shaw's *You Never Can Tell*. I have already quoted from the manifesto Bridie latched on to; Wareing hoped to raise £2,000 in single pound shares, but in the event managed only half the amount. The theatre was rented to the company by Howard and Wyndham for £80 in the first season. The Rep ran at a loss for four seasons, and the outbreak of the

Great War closed it just as Lewis Casson, who had become director of the Royalty at the start of 1914, had cleared a profit of £700.

That money was placed in trust and eventually went to fund the Rep's successor, the Scottish National Players, in 1921. During the inter-war period, the Players produced over 100 new Scottish plays, including Bridie's first piece, *The Sunlight Sonata*, a farcical morality in which picnickers at Loch Lomond were besieged by visitors from heaven and imps from hell, directed at the Lyric (the new name for the Royalty) by Tyrone Guthrie in 1928. The Guthrie contact led Bridie into London theatrical circles; although he continued to give his work to the Players, as well as to other Scottish theatres, and eventually the Citizens, his plays were in demand in London from as early as 1932. Laurence Olivier appeared in *The King of Nowhere* in 1938 and a crucial association with Alastair Sim was forged during the 1940s, with the London premières of *Holy Isle* and *Mr Bolfry*.

It was against this background, and in large part due to the now distant inspiration of Alfred Wareing, that the Citizens came into being in 1943. The Scottish National Players had become increasingly amateurish as far as Bridie was concerned, and he was fed up with having his plays put on in a variety of unsatisfactory locations. According to Winifred Bannister, Bridie's biographer and a busy activist in the Glasgow arts scene of the day, it was she herself who was responsible for bringing together the three men capable of exerting sufficient influence to launch a new company.

The triumvirate comprised Bridie, Dr T.J. Honeyman,

who had been an innovative director of Glasgow Art Galleries since 1939, and George Singleton, who had opened, in the same year, the Cosmo cinema on the corner of Rose and Renfrew Streets. Honeyman was a showman determined to make his galleries attractive and lively, while Singleton had initiated a policy at the Cosmo of showing the best of contemporary European films. Bridie had already joined the Council for the Encouragement of Music and the Arts, CEMA, formed in 1940 and a model for the Arts Council which followed in 1946. He was thus in a good strategic position to make some structured contribution to Scottish drama beyond his own plays; he campaigned incessantly for the foundation, not realised until 1950, of the Scottish School of Drama, now the RSAMD. But Mrs Bannister claims it was she who first mooted the possibility of establishing a new Scottish company in the Athenaeum, the theatre owned by the Royal Academy of Music and frequently hired for performances by Glasgow Unity, the left-wing amateur company that was to prove such a thorn in Bridie's flesh.

In discussions with CEMA, Bridie had advanced his ideas of a Scottish national theatre based in Glasgow, and although CEMA considered Edinburgh to have an equal right to house the project, the vote swung in favour of settling on the Athenaeum in the centre of Glasgow.

Early in 1943, Bridie gave a dinner in the Glasgow Art Club and selected a six-man directorate, including Honeyman and Singleton, who in turn elected him chairman. His first deed in launching the Glasgow Citizens was to pass the hat round the dinner table and collect

£1,500. The first production in the Athenaeum, in October 1943, was a revival of *Holy Isle*, directed by an English woman, Jennifer Sounes, whom Bridie had engaged as resident producer (she only stayed for the first three productions). Although the critics were generous, Mrs Bannister records an inauspicious baptism: 'At the first night it was obvious at the first interval that everyone was delighted; at the second interval irritation had set in; there was a falling away from dramatic splendour and brilliant philosophy to an undramatic finale.'

(A poor production of *Holy Isle* at the Edinburgh Festival in Bridie's centenary year, 1988, confirmed this impression of galloping decline across the play's duration, though I am unable to vouch, even in its earlier stages, for much in the way of 'dramatic splendour' or 'brilliant philosophy'; the piece is an arch and static Utopian exercise of intolerable whimsicality set on the mythical island of Ultima Thule.)

The first Citizens company, which also presented Goldsmith's *The Good Natured Man*, a new adaptation by Bridie of Molnar's *Liliom*, and the première of J.B. Priestley's *Bull Market*, included Denis Carey, Yvonne Coulette, Duncan Macrae, Molly Urquhart and James Gibson, the latter two already well established as leading Scottish actors. Bridie was pleased with progress and the season broke even at the box-office. By the end of the second year, the Citizens was in profit. Increasing popularity necessitated the move to a larger arena.

It was at this point that Harry McKelvie's Royal Princess's Theatre in the Gorbals became available. With the help of a gift to the Citizens of £10,000, and buoyed up by promises of support from the Arts Council, Bridie crossed the river. The renovated Princess's opened as the Glasgow Citizens Theatre on 11 September 1945 with J.B. Priestley's *Johnson Over Jordan*. The production attracted wide attention, favourable comment and a fair sprinkling of top brass. Mrs Bannister, who had relinquished her post as 'theatre organiser', was installed in the gods as a fan:

I had elected to sit in the gallery. Harry McKelvie seemed to think some of his old regulars would turn up — if only out of curiosity — and I was interested in their reaction to a modern experimental play. My seat cost me the modest sum of one and sixpence (the front stalls were only six shillings). I was lucky. I sat beside a cheerful Gorbals man and wife who had come to see justice done to their theatre . . . They had never seen a play before — variety and pantomime were their theatre fare. The woman said she had imagined that plays were "more respectable"; the man said he found it "very interesting" but he hoped the next play would have "some go in it".

Over the next decade the Citizens became recognised as one of the leading theatres in Britain, with successful performances in Dublin and at the Edinburgh Festival, tours throughout Scotland and a growing reputation for mixing classical revivals with new native drama. Bridie was chairman until his death in 1951, and was succeeded by Norman Duthie (1951–55), who had been the company's accountant since its inception, and Dr Honeyman

51

(1955 – 58). George Singleton stayed on the board right the way through, only severing his active participation with the Citizens when he handed over the chairmanship to William Taylor in 1970.

Scottish authors remained a priority of the Citizens throughout the 1950s. Tyrone Guthrie and Denis Carey were among the directors, and the cast lists reveal a plethora of native acting talent. Stanley Baxter (who had sprung to national fame in the 1949 Citizens pantomime, *The Tintock Cup*), Molly Urquhart and James Cairncross appeared regularly, and Duncan Macrae built up an impregnable reputation in comedy and pantomime, in the wake of what Tony Paterson called his 'supreme claim to greatness' in Robert McLellan's *Jamie the Saxt* (1947).

Such was the fruit of the seeds Alfred Wareing had sown. After he left Glasgow, Wareing ran a theatre in Huddersfield and fetched up in Stratford-upon-Avon in 1931, where he initially worked as a librarian in the Memorial Theatre. His big undertaking, however, was the foundation in 1934 of the League of Audiences, through which he agitated 'to obtain Government recognition of drama and music and to promote personal interpretation'. He toured the country, canvassed opinions, enlisted the Vice-Chancellor of Oxford as his President and various church notables and aristocrats as his Vice-Presidents. He spent days upon end in the lobbies of the House of Commons peddling what many thought to be utopian, unpractical schemes.

When CEMA was transformed into the Arts Council in 1946, Bridie noted that the new body had been created 'on almost precisely the lines he [Wareing] had worked out. It administers a subsidy of ten times the amount suggested by him and the Treasury pays up with a smile. In none of the literature of the CEMA or the Arts Council has his name been so much as mentioned. But there is no doubt that he is its "onlie begetter". The Arts Council rests on his dream, on his hard work and on his martyrdom.'

The frontispiece of Wareing's biography by Winifred Isaacs is a photograph of a portrait painted in 1928 by William Oliphant Hutchison, and subsequently presented by Wareing's estate to the Princess's Theatre. It shows a rubicund, sociable fellow with a head of thinning, severely parted hair, dressed in a heavy worsted three-piece suit and holding an open newspaper from which he has been momentarily, but not annoyingly, distracted. The portrait was first hung in the Society Club Room. It was later screwed to the wall of the Green Room (now a store-room) by the stage, where it was paired with a full-length portrait of Duncan Macrae as Jamie the Saxt. Shortly after Giles Havergal arrived, a bad leak from the roof rotted the picture clean away, though its frame is still preserved. The Macrae picture is on permanent loan to the People's Palace on Glasgow Green.

Wareing's legacy was Bridie's career, the Citizens Theatre, and the recognition in subsidy of the dignity of dramatic art. But parallel to such publicly authorised endeavour ran the emergence of the political, popular Glaswegian theatre focussed by Unity and the Jewish Institute Players. There was a division, and not much love lost, between Bridie's sort of theatre and the grass roots. These conflicts would flare up again in the 1970s, with the emergence of John McGrath's 7:84 and other left-wing companies.

Ida Schuster is adamant that Bridie did not establish a Scottish theatre: 'Bridie wrote for the West End'. But the best Scottish actors did gravitate towards Bridie's Citizens, even though he started off by importing English actors. Bridie disliked both the amateur status and the politics of Unity, and his influence (he had been chairman of the Scottish committee of CEMA) was thought to be partly responsible for the withdrawal of Unity's Arts Council guarantee and its subsequent demise. In a lecture to the Royal Philosophical Society in 1949, Bridie praised Unity's record while seeming to justify the Arts Council's action. He said the company had as many Achilles' heels as a centipede:

> It is difficult to find high artistic ambition and sound judgement in the same place ... I got the impression that the audiences were more of a brake club than a collection of lovers of the drama ... And they had a deadly love of the cheap laugh. I thought, in short, that they might not be reliable, and that they might have a dangerous influence on the actors.

Like J.M. Barrie, a more magically poetic dramatist, Bridie was by temperament an Anglo-Scot and throughout his career sustained a double life either side of the border, entering into many interesting and enduring correspondences with actors and directors such as Alastair Sim and Tyrone Guthrie. A recent study by his son, Ronald Mavor, attempts to establish for Bridie a divided personality as reflected in much Scottish writing, from Hogg's *Confessions of a Justified Sinner* and Stevenson's *Dr Jekyll and Mr Hyde* to R. D. Laing's study of schizophrenia in *The Divided Self*. There is certainly a tension in Bridie between the private professional family man and doctor, and the public dramatist on easy terms with James Agate and St John Ervine. Puffing up with Glaswegian pride, Bridie once reminded the latter that his unfairly maligned home city had given the world the internal combustion engine, political economy, antiseptic, aseptic and cerebral surgery, the balloon, the mariner's compass, the theory of Latent Heat, Tobias Smollett — and James Bridie. Mavor fails to see that Bridie's view of what the theatre could be was itself handicapped by his ambivalent, London-oriented nationalism. Touchingly ambitious and over-anxious to please, Bridie's talent is hedged around with the considerations of respectability. The demands he makes of theatre are not, finally, very great:

A stage play is a method of passing an interval of time by putting an actor or actors on a platform, and causing them to say or do certain things. If it is amusing, that is to say if it succeeds in making the spectators unconscious of the passing of time, it fulfils its function and has merit. Other qualities of a play — its educative, its thought-provoking, its exciting, its poetic qualities, are not basic.

Convulsions and controversy in the 1960s

The Havergal Citizens could not embody a philosophy more diametrically opposed to Bridie's decent gentility. The idea of theatre as an amusing diversion between lots of other amusing diversions, an after-dinner digestive, an intellectual bromide, is precisely what the Citizens reject in their heritage. At the end of the 1960s, they needed to, in order to keep Bridie's theatre open, let alone alive.

For while the Citizens maintained its reputation through the late 1950s, and was indeed often cited as a model of what a repertory theatre should be, the 1960s proved far more convulsive. Michael Goldberg, scion of a wealthy warehouse-owning family in the city, succeeded Dr Honeyman as chairman in 1958. Goldberg was a civilised man with an interest in European modernism, and the theatre began to reflect a wider spectrum of dramatic literature. Scottish plays became fewer.

In the 1964 anniversary pamphlet, Christopher Small advocated a permanent stock of Citizens plays based on Bridie, but also envisaged the theatre as part of an international community whose other members included the Berliner Ensemble, the Théâtre National Populaíre, the Royal Court and Theatre Workshop. He questioned the value of the Scottish national theatre grail, with all its implications of 'tourist attractiveness and tartan wrappings . . . the Citizens are citizens of Glasgow, yes, Scotland, yes, but also of the world'.

This prophetic rallying cry did not find a fully sustained echo for a few years, but the ambition seemed at least plausible under Iain Cuthbertson's artistic stewardship (1962 – 65). In 1963, Albert Finney played in Pirandello's

Henry IV (the play with which the Citizens kicked off the 1990 season). And in 1964, Cuthbertson himself, a commanding actor who spoke Lallans, created a sensation in the leading role of John Arden's *Armstrong's Last Goodnight*, a sinewy and Shakespearean political parable about a sixteenth-century feudal chief on the Scottish borders, probably the best 'Scottish play' ever written. Cuthbertson was subsequently invited to join the Royal Court in London (but he soon returned to Scotland). At his own suggestion, his job was split between a general manager, Andrew Leigh, who had been at the Citizens since 1963, and a new artistic director, David William.

The next three or four years, though not without significant work, were chaotic. Andrew Leigh says that most problems arose from the board's interference in artistic matters. William was carpeted after directing John Arden's violently funny *Live Like Pigs*, a 1958 piece about the settling of a family of gypsies on a housing estate; it caused a furore. After just one year, William, too, was enticed away for what may have appeared to be a better job, at Stratford, Ontario (in a subsequently peripatetic career, it is an odd coincidence that William has returned to the Stratford theatre in 1990). As William departed, he suggested to the confused board that they should appoint two actors in the company, Michael Meacham and Michael Blakemore, one English, the other Australian, as co-directors.

This they did, but relations, always strained, were pushed to breaking point when the board thwarted Blakemore's plans to present the British première of

Tennessee Williams's *Sweet Bird of Youth* starring Vivien Leigh. The coup meant nothing; the play was deemed unsuitable for Glasgow. The board was happier with Meacham's invitation to Tyrone Guthrie to return and direct Bridie's *The Anatomist* with Tom Fleming in the lead.

In spite of the rockiness, Blakemore did pull off two famous productions in his brief two-year sojourn. The first was the world première of Peter Nichols's *A Day in the Death of Joe Egg*, a black comedy about the domestic tensions arising from the care of a severely handicapped child. Every London management, including Michael Codron, Kenneth Tynan at the National Theatre, and Tony Garnett at the BBC, had turned the play down. Nichols remembered his Citizens triumph when he wrote his autobiography nearly twenty years later: 'On the first night in Glasgow a microscopic moment of history passed, a taboo was broken. We knew by the final applause that we'd won . . . I would always be grateful to Glasgow for giving me one of the happiest and most decisive weeks of my life.'

In the next season, Blakemore directed Leonard Rossiter in Brecht's *The Resistible Rise of Arturo Ui*. When the board refused to allow the production to transfer to the Edinburgh Festival, Andrew Leigh resigned his post and, with the board's blessing, took the production there himself. The performance in Edinburgh made Rossiter's name overnight, Laurence Olivier invited Blakemore to join him at the National Theatre, and *Arturo Ui* caused a further sensation when it came south to London and played a short season at the Saville

Theatre in 1969 (the Saville became a cinema in 1970). Although the two Michaels left quietly enough, and much of their work was generally considered admirable, the succession of brief regimes was taking its toll. Attendances were in decline, and they plummeted still further in the following year under the artistic directorship of Robert Cartland, yet another recruit from the acting company. The festering grievances of both board and artistic management erupted nastily with the sacking of Cartland in the early summer of 1969. Cartland promptly took his complaints to the Press. A ding-dong correspondence ensued in the *Herald*, and the board appeared more foolish by the day.

Resignations followed as yet another quest for an artistic director began. George Singleton, reluctantly installed in the chair, interviewed Havergal and appointed him in July 1969. As Havergal and Prowse swung into action, Singleton anxiously sought his own successor as chairman. One year later, he finally turned to William Taylor, who had been on the board for a few years and had just resigned from his duties on the Corporation. Taylor took on the chairmanship he has steadfastly held ever since.

George Singleton had succeeded Michael Goldberg as chairman. Goldberg's chief initiative, and one he more or less financed himself, was the Close Theatre Club, which opened with seating for 150 people in 1965. This informal arena was situated within the Citizens above the box office to the right, exactly where the new circle bar is today. The space it occupied was once a dance hall and, before that, a place for cock-fighting. The Close became an opposite number to the Traverse in Edinburgh, staging the première of Simon Gray's *Spoiled*, and the first performances in Scotland of John Osborne's *Hotel in Amsterdam* and of plays by Stanley Eveling, Genet and Sam Shepard.

Within a few months of the Close opening, Charles Marowitz produced a *Dr Faustus* that led to a public uproar. Ida Schuster recalls that Goldberg wanted Marowitz to cut a scene in which the Queen was clearly ridiculed as the figure of Sloth. Andrew Leigh says that various members of the board stood up before the performance began in order to disassociate themselves from what was to follow; at this point, Marowitz stuck his head through the window of the lighting box at the back of the room and yelled vituperatively at the patriotic dissenters. The performance was adjourned, everyone went to the bar, and there followed a great meeting of the Close membership during which Goldberg was firmly advised by a majority not to interfere in matters of artistic licence.

Clearly shaken by this, Goldberg struggled on before resigning, deeply hurt, at the end of the decade. Havergal testifies that Goldberg was a truly elegant and refined man whose idea of theatre culture was eclipsed in the artistic and social climate of the late 1960s. He was tough, sophisticated and generous, and he wanted the Close to be a genuinely intellectual forum of debate and discussion, with drinks, dinner and a spot of Ionesco. What he was perhaps unprepared for was David Hayman sitting on a bed in a pair of Y-fronts declaiming a Sam Shepard monologue about riotously unrestrained orgasms. Although Goldberg cut himself off from the theatre when he resigned, his contribution to its evolution under Havergal was obviously immense; like the new regime, he was European both in instinct and outlook, and he could not resist returning many years later, in 1980, to see the Proust adaptation. He was one of those rare benefactors of the arts without whom progress, at whatever the cost, would be impossible.

The Close continued to make waves until it was destroyed in May 1973 by a fire which threatened, briefly, the stability of the whole building. Shortly before the fire, I had seen Steven Dartnell's all-white, neurasthenically intense production of Strindberg's *The Father*, and its extraordinary quality was something the Citizens managed to incorporate over the years into the main stage work. Havergal thinks the loss of the Close was a blessing in disguise, in that he was forced to concentrate on the main house: 'In the old days, the Close was a leech, using a lot of manpower and resources, and it drove us mad. But once we were up and running we felt differently about its loss — to the extent that, today, we feel we could once again do with another space, and there are indeed plans to inaugurate one, very close to the theatre, I hope.'

David Hayman had been a member of the Close company, in the first 1969–70 season, which had been put through its paces by two talented young associates of Havergal and Prowse, Robert Walker and Keith Hack. Robert Walker ruffled a few feathers by instructing his actors to strip naked for a Press photo-call. The play, in March 1970, was Artaud's adaptation of Shelley's *The*

Cenci. 'Sex play is one big yawn' moaned the *Evening Times*, and Christopher Small in the *Herald* obviously considered the piece less *Cenci* than kinky, defining Artaud as a theatre-hater and a man of 'unhappily deranged talents', which he undoubtedly was; but Small was here flying under a moralising banner and, indeed, a headline of 'Unhealthy masochism'.

Hack, who later caused a rift in the company, had first worked at the Citizens as Michael Blakemore's assistant director on *Arturo Ui*. He had met Blakemore when the latter visited the Berliner Ensemble, where Hack was on student attachment, to see the Arturo Ui of Ekkehard Schall. Hack returned to Glasgow in 1970 as a beneficiary of the Thames Television Trainee Director scheme; he was assistant director on the *Hamlet*, and directed five productions of his own before leaving in 1973. Robert Walker, whose main contribution was in the Close, left in 1971 to pursue his career first at the Lincoln Rep and later in London, where he took over, and ran with notable success and a Citizens-style panache, the Half Moon Theatre in the East End, before embarking on a still flourishing career in television. Both Walker and Hack are part German in antecedence, and they brought a Continental outlook and youthful bravado to the Citizens that is still acknowledged by the directorate.

All the controversies and disasters were building to a head. The *Hamlet* was both the last straw and the first major new fling. Havergal and Prowse were set on a course that had attracted attention to the theatre, had put it once more on the local map, and had even seen that a daringly outrageous policy might well pay off at the box-office.

The idea of adventures in the world classical repertoire had been broached, and the cultivation of natively parochial Scottish drama placed on the back burner, where it was to remain. The stock explanation for this, when requested, was that if any outstanding new Scottish plays were to come their way, then Havergal and Prowse would indeed consider them. This was a polite way of saying that the Scottish national theatre of Bridie's heyday was not a priority. As a result, new Scottish plays went elsewhere, and if something like John Byrne's slice of Paisley cartoon realism, *The Slab Boys*, did come Havergal's way – as indeed it did – he would acknowledge receipt of the script and pass it on without too much dithering. *The Slab Boys* was sent to the Traverse in Edinburgh.

One Scottish dramatist had, however, crept in the back door and been encouraged to stay. Elgin-born Robert David MacDonald, who had given Havergal his first job in rep, at Carlisle in 1961, had adapted Robert Louis Stevenson's novel *Ebb Tide* for the first Citizens season under Havergal in the spring of 1970. There was to be rather more flow than ebb about MacDonald's contribution at the Citizens in the years to come.

4

THE 1970s: DIVINE DISTRACTIONS OF DECADENCE

The early years of the new era were marked by a rapid assimilation of styles and influences as Philip Prowse, ensconced from the start as Havergal's resident designer, worked towards the distinctive, divinely decadent stage compositions that characterise the middle period of the 1970s. Glasgow had nearly a century of modern European theatre to catch up with, and the process was to be violent and sudden.

At the same time, Robert David MacDonald, whose first main stage production was Otway's *Venice Preserv'd* in 1972, embarked on his dramaturgical voyage of discovery among the world's lost masterpieces. And Havergal held it all together, producing the money-spinning pantomime each year – both preserving the old Gorbals tradition and introducing his own special brand of charm and expertise; the Citizens' pantomimes assumed a new creative status within the overall artistic policy.

As the decade passed, Havergal emerged as a considerable director in his own right, while Prowse, who directed rarely to start with, became increasingly determined to assume total control of the productions he designed. This fluctuation of responsibility within the directorate undoubtedly contributed to the astonishing variety and range of project in the first decade. MacDonald was a languidly corrosive intellectual with a dizzying command of at least half a dozen languages and a wide cultural horizon; Prowse, who had rapidly made his mark at the Opera House, Covent Garden, after working there with artists like Franco Zeffirelli and Leslie Hurry, was a man of strong will and strong vision, and soon recognisable as the outstanding costumier bar none in the British theatre − his pragmatic genius lies at the root of the entire Havergal undertaking; and Havergal himself maintained his abiding interest in the mainstream British repertory while running an exceedingly tight ship. It was, and is, a formidable combination of talents, thrown together more by luck than design and destined to survive intact the stormiest of personal rows and artistic scandals.

The three directors each had different interests, and rarely clashed in wanting to do the same play. The point was that they sparked each other off and remained constructively critical of any productions in which they were not directly involved. There tended to be an agreement about what type of actor would be employed, and all three would hold auditions in London to which drama school graduates were very soon flocking.

Ian McDiarmid remembers auditioning in Glasgow for Havergal, but auditioning again in London with 'the mob' for Prowse's benefit. 'I did something of *Dingo* by Charles Wood, then some *Richard II*, then I offered a piece by Stewart Conn, a Scottish writer, but they wouldn't hear of it and waved it away.'

Sian Thomas, who joined the company much later, in 1977, also remembers her audition:

I did a bit of Tennessee Williams in which I prided myself on being rather moving. But the three directors just sat there laughing their heads off; I responded to this extraordinary reaction by changing what I was doing as I went along. We sat down to talk, and I remember being struck by their presence. We immediately had an argument. I said I did not like theatre where the actors were just puppets and Philip said, "Oh, really?" And I thought I had blown the job. And they said, well, it is all like a dark wood and you have to fight your way through and meet up with us on the other side, but if you'd like to come and work with us, enter the wood. And when I got there, it was like falling in love. It was the most exciting thing that had ever happened to me.

This seeming stand-offishness from the process of acting is a complex issue to be discussed in a later chapter. It is fundamental to the history of the company and, paradoxically, the reason why so many outstanding performers, from McDiarmid to Sian Thomas, matured in their time there. The young actors, many of them thrown into demanding classical roles way beyond their experience and, often, technical resources, were encouraged to preen and strut, to lay down their presence like a gift and dare the audience to reject it. I do not think the company was ever interested in avant-garde methods of alienation or audience-baiting along the lines of the Living Theatre's theatrical terrorism; but they were, and are, interested in extending an audience's notion of pleasure in theatre and in challenging its aesthetic values by offering a series of uncompromisingly stated values of their own.

Patrick Hannaway, who has appeared in over seventy productions, and worked with all three directors, says, 'There is really no such thing as the so-called house style; the house style is the buzz you get when you go into the theatre, and it's nothing to do with whether there's a glamorous set on the stage, or just a load of old boxes'. There have indeed been glamorous sets on the stage, and loads of old boxes; and Hannaway's remark is, I believe, profoundly correct. More than in any other theatre in Britain, the experience of crossing the threshold remains one of welcome, expectancy and the sense of an integrated effort to seduce and entertain the customer. As John Mullin, the financial controller of Strathclyde Regional Council, expressed it, this is not a sensation you acquire after a few visits; you smell it the instant you enter the place.

A policy of 'artistic sensationalism'

It is one of the extraordinary tricks, or illusions, that while a very great number of people soon developed an idea of what a Citizens production was like, there was in fact no single prototype. The theatre managed to project an image and an identity while never settling for an official version of either. But the timing was important. The cult of the personality was all the rage; Andy Warhol had said that soon everyone would be famous for fifteen minutes. And, certainly in the early years, the appearance of an

Opposite:
The first *Hamlet*, with Mike Gwilym and David Hayman (centre), Jeremy Nicholas and Luke Hardy (above).
Overleaf:
Jonathan Kent in *Antony and Cleopatra*.

actor, his or her physical demeanour, was of paramount importance. Havergal told *Plays and Players* in 1974 that an ensemble 'should be eighteen or so stars – a lot of glitterers glittering away'. The directors knew full well that in the age of the rock concert, and in the city of Rod Stewart, the theatre had to speak the language of the young in order to attract the new audience. Sexual ambiguity, the appeal of the androgyne, an essential element in what Susan Sontag calls the Camp Sensibility, was not a closet phenomenon in the early 1970s; it was out on the streets and climbing the charts, as David Bowie's alter ego, Ziggy Stardust, soon proved.

What Allen Wright was to call, disapprovingly, a policy of 'artistic sensationalism' was exactly that. But the policy was firmly based in a seriously iconoclastic and intellectually provocative approach to classic drama and new adaptations. There was undoubtedly, in the first productions, a sense of shocking for shock's sake. But it soon became clear that there was a serious undertow and a consistent artistic credo in the mayhem.

We must here nail certain colours to the mast. Journalistic theatre criticism, no less in England than in Scotland, has become not less, but more reactionary over the past fifteen years. Every week you can read a critic who believes that inventiveness or elaboration on the part of a director 'at the expense of the play' is a cardinal sin. Give us the Bard straight, they cry, don't mess around with sub-plots, stay in the period of the play's composition, all hail Kenneth Branagh and the Renaissance Theatre Company, do not interpose any experience or clutter between the literary artefact and the spectator.

Overleaf:
James Aubrey and
Jeffrey Kissoon in
Tamburlaine.
Opposite:
Jeremy Blake,
Di Trevis (top),
Angela Chadfield,
David Yelland,
David Hayman,
Patrick Hannaway,
Mike Gwilym (top)
and Rayner Bourton
in *Troilus and
Cressida.*

I think these critics are wrong. A lot of their complaints are based on the supposition that theatre is an art form subsidiary and inferior to literature, and one best put firmly in its place whenever a name like Shakespeare, Marlowe, Webster or even Oscar Wilde crops up. Such attitudes do not get you all that far with the Citizens, nor with an understanding of their appeal to audiences. Interpretation, indeed criticism at the highest level, is an art form in itself, and the governing vision Philip Prowse can impose (that's another dirty word in contemporary critical parlance) on a play like *The Duchess of Malfi* or *'Tis Pity She's a Whore* is worth, as theatre, any number of more literal, earth-bound and 'faithful' renditions. Libraries are where you imagine your perfect, complete, uncut and civilised versions of the classics; the theatre is where you see them anatomised, dismembered, reconstituted and discussed, through the necessarily distorting and subjective process of theatrical production.

These arguments have been taken for granted in Europe for years. But the British theatre culture is heavily steeped in its dramatic literary heritage, chiefly because we have so much more of it to be steeped in than any other European country. We are enslaved by it. Which is why it is the theatre's business to liberate us from those shackles and give us another vantage point. Sporadic interventions have been made in this field over the years by fringe artists like Pip Simmons (whose rampantly crude and pungent *The Tempest* was years ahead of its time) and Charles Marowitz (in his Shakespeare collages), and also by Jonathan Miller, adopting more conventional modes of intellectual deconstruction. The Royal

Shakespeare Company, constrained by its charter, dares not mess around with the Bard at all, except at the most superficial of levels, so the really adventurous rule-breaking productions are the rarities rather than the norm. The RSC, because of its size, and now its ever-increasing deficit, its reliance on tourism and desperate search for another blockbuster commercial hit like *Les Misérables* (a show which in fact *did* have an organic relationship to the company's work) is fundamentally inimical to inquisitive risk-taking.

The ironic paradox in all this is that the Citizens, engaging responsibly with all manner of texts over the years, has consistently been our most interesting centre of dramaturgical endeavour; the work of MacDonald alone is without rival over the same period at either the National or the RSC. And these experiments have prospered in the lively, informal atmosphere of the Gorbals theatre, unhampered by sponsors' evenings, remote from metropolitan expectations, rehearsed quickly and lightly for a few weeks by people who know and, on the whole, like each other, and all at a cost ranging from a literally zero budget on costumes or sets to a very occasional top whack of £17,000 for both.

MacDonald had acquired in the 1960s a national reputation as a translator of Rolf Hochhuth's contentious history plays, *The Representative* and *Soldiers*, but his career as a director and actor in rep, before joining Havergal, had been uncontroversial, indeed virtually unremarked. B.A. Young, I recall, had once complimented him in the *Financial Times* on a conventional production of *The Tempest* at the Thorndike in Leatherhead, a pleasantly sedate theatre in the Home Counties. But the new mood in Glasgow was obviously contagious. His production of *The Government Inspector* was the first show I saw at the Citizens. The actors fell over and broke wind with appalling regularity. Gogol's commissioner for schools, much to the delight of all schoolchildren present, was a pigeon-toed, knock-kneed pansy. Khlestakov and Osip were satirical analogues of Little Lord Fauntleroy and Tommy Steele, their divisions of age and class not so much annihilated as proposed in a new way. Small-town seediness became a self-satisfied, habitual posturing.

This sort of thorough reinterpretation was, and remains, unusual on British stages, to say the least. In a couple of years, emboldened and encouraged by success at the box office, the Citizens had consolidated their *Hamlet* breakthrough and were soon to confound the head-shaking of the drama lecturer in Aberdeen, who had angrily told the *Herald* that 'Since Mr Havergal's arrival, we have watched the Citizens being killed off'. Allen Wright on *The Scotsman* has never been able to disguise his revulsion for long, but he did admit a few months after *Hamlet* (he had much preferred the productions which followed) that 'Mr Havergal is a living reproof to those who would chop and change artistic directors'. At the same time, January 1971, the city treasurer, William Samuels, started muttering again when news reached him of a pantomime genie clad in little more than a jockstrap. The application for more grant aid might meet resistance 'in view of their past record'.

This record was now extended to include the first major

foreign tours. In May 1971, Keith Hack's Close Theatre version of *Titus Andronicus* visited the Wiesbaden Opera House and caused a mild stir when the cast, as was then company policy, did not take a bow, in spite of receiving tumultuous applause. In 1972, *Antony and Cleopatra* and *Saved* visited Rome, *Antony* going on to Antwerp and Hanover. In the same year, Hack's *Tamburlaine* and Havergal's *Twelfth Night* were invited to the Edinburgh Festival. The first had its title role famously divided between Rupert Frazer, Jeffrey Kissoon and Mike Gwilym. The company had an average age of twenty-four, and the weekly wage was £29. (The weekly wage is the same for all actors in the company to this day, and has usually been fixed in excess of the Equity minimum; it stands currently at £220 a week.)

The joint was jumping and confidence was high. Ian McDiarmid told *The Stage*, *à propos* of certain critics' lack of broad criteria by which to judge the company's work, that he looked back on Barrie and Bridie 'more with a sense of shame than of reverence'. Havergal told Michael Billington in *The Guardian*: 'I'm like the Madame of a brothel. I have my girls on one hand and my clients on the other and the delicate art is to bring them together.' The provocation to politicians could not gainsay the sudden acquisition of an international reputation. Glasgow Corporation increased the annual grant for 1972–73 by 65 per cent, from £15,000 to £25,000. And the Lord Provost, William Gray, awarded the company the city's Loving Cup for 1972 in recognition of its achievements.

73

First and last exit to London

Too much, perhaps, had happened too soon. 1973 was the year of the palace revolution when, according to Patrick Hannaway, 'half the company upped sticks and went to London with Keith Hack'. It was a classic case, on Hack's part, of misunderstanding the nature of the enterprise. Havergal and Prowse had long-term objectives; Hack was in a hurry. He thought the time was right to strike in the capital, after directing highly acclaimed productions of Brecht's *In the Jungle of the Cities*, Büchner's *Danton's Death*, and *Timon of Athens*.

Hack, with the confidence of gifted youth, had won the trust first of Michael Blakemore and then of Havergal. But he was not a chap to sit still, and he had no strong feelings about staying in Glasgow. In London, he rapidly inveigled himself into the friendship of Tony Richardson, with whom he had co-directed an appalling production in the West End of *The Threepenny Opera* (starring Vanessa Redgrave and Barbara Windsor). The producer of that show was Michael White and, 'out of chats', according to Hack, came the idea of a three-play season at The Place, near Euston Station, featuring many of the actors who had helped to make Hack's name at the Citizens.

The splinter company included Cheryl Campbell, Patti Love, Jonathan Kent and Ian McDiarmid. The latter two deny that they walked out on Glasgow; Kent says all the actors had been there for eighteen months and had already left before the season at The Place was proposed. McDiarmid felt persuaded that there would be another eighteen months of comparable excitement, but wrenched himself away nonetheless ('I've been wrenching myself away ever since, really'). Even today Hack claims that the Havergal Citizens could have come to London and been as influential in the 1970s as Joan Littlewood had been two decades earlier.

But Hack, for all his undoubted talent and palpable ambition, was doomed to fail. He was trying to promote in London an operation cut off from its roots. And any likelihood of a splinter Citizens movement in London was soon dealt with: The Place season was a fiasco. It ran out of money and lost its nerve. The second and third productions were cancelled. Hack says that the first production, *In the Jungle of the Cities*, played to packed previews and ran into bad notices merely because he and White made the mistake of asking the critics to pay for their seats. That was indeed a terrible error! But the crisis went deeper than that. Hack and White were asking for trouble by arrogantly trying to cash in on a theatre enterprise that was geared to a particualr urban environment, and which had hardly had a chance to take proper root.

Feelings ran deep back on the farm, but William Taylor diplomatically glosses over the episode, saying it did not harm the Glasgow operation, which was his only concern. It affected the Citizens only to the extent that a company identifiable as ex-Citizens was a commercial failure in London. The episode had a profound influence on the way the Citizens now viewed itself, and was probably instrumental in confirming a resolution to stay put and have nothing to do with London managements.

The splinter operation had come about partly because, in the early, heady days of the new Glasgow company, meetings and open discussions were encouraged. There was a dangerous outbreak of democracy. Angela Chadfield recalls a tempestuous company meeting when Prowse was announced as the director of *The Relapse*; the actors were unhappy, mainly because they did not feel they knew him very well, and certainly not as a director. Patrick Hannaway says that the meetings started to go out of control and.things were said that people did not want to hear. 'That was the point when the [Keith Hack] revolution happened.'

Angela Chadfield admits that the actors were really too young at that stage to know what they were talking about and failed to see the larger context. For instance, Prowse the designer used to sidle into the first rehearsals, go away, and when the director returned the next day, everything was changed. None of the actors had the faintest idea what was going on; but Prowse was subtly, and effectively, directing by proxy, even when working – and working to magnificent effect – with Keith Hack. Company meetings have long since been abolished. But not the memory of the Hack/Prowse collaborations. Hack says of Prowse that he was more properly challenged by his demands than at any time in his working life. The creative relationship was very special indeed, and crucial to the evolution of the company.

A new Jacobean theatre of blood, guts and sexuality

MacDonald's place in the hierarchy was fully established by 1973, possibly as a compensation for Hack's defection. He pressed home his authority with three outstanding productions, to designs by Prowse, that, in successive seasons, bristled with brainy passions. The first was Brecht's *St Joan of the Stockyards*, a play about industrial lock-outs that reflected the political turmoil of 1974 and the unrest that had precipitated the demise of Edward Heath's Conservative Government. When Di Trevis as Joan informed the assembled Chicago meat-packers that 'In this town, the people with jobs are starting to help the jobless', the audience sent a ripple back to the stage. The pious Salvationist became a furious activist, locked in combat with Patrick Hannaway's mustachioed, Hitlerite Pierpont Mauler. Prowse's design was an arrangement of blood-stained planks in zigzag formation, fitted out with banners, a huge organ and falling snow. When Trevis got to the great speech about political systems, applause broke out on the line about a see-saw needing many more at the bottom to maintain a few at the top. Brecht always went down big in Glasgow.

For Cordelia Oliver, though, the highlight of that season was MacDonald's *Camille* in which the fictional tragic romance of Marguerite Gautier was counter-pointed with the more sordid reality of Dumas' own affair with Marie Duplessis. The production was obviously a trailer for the great *fin de siècle* salon extravaganzas of the mid-1970s, and it also emphasised the full emergence of MacDonald the dramatist. In *De Sade Show* (1976), which MacDonald compiled and wrote using the source material of the mammoth *120 Days of Sodom* and the novels *Justine* and *Juliette* (with a bit of Marivaux thrown in), MacDonald and Prowse launched a gorgeous attempt to illustrate the basics of Sadean philosophy. It was, inevitably, too basic for Allen Wright who was apparently craving more space on the front page: 'By presenting a hideous exhibition of profanity and obscenity, the Citizens Theatre in Glasgow is defiling the name of drama . . . we are debased by this production.'

Some people are more easily debased than others, of course, but the theatre is not a church and blasphemy not a civil crime. Indeed, far from being the sort of gratuitous spectacle of sodomy and corruption feverishly imagined by *The Scotsman's* critic, the show was a cunningly arranged distillation of de Sade's intellectual themes, presented with Genetesque bravura and a high count of witty aphorisms and Wildean quips which were to become a hallmark of a MacDonald text. All good theatre makes voyeurs of its audience; but it is a commonplace in recent French literary criticism that de Sade's pornography is not really pornography at all, but a symptom of his revolutionary, inflamed and systematic writing. The ferociously penned arguments of de Sade's brilliant libertines proved as thrilling in the theatre as they are on the page; their substance is summarised by Mme Duclos's protestation that 'all life is an offensive against the repetitive mechanism of the universe'.

The setting was one of de Sade's castles of torture where two sisters were subjected to the educational process of a trial. Prowse's blood-stained floor was decorated with head-high pillars, clusters of candles and interrogation lights. Four languid valets in pink loincloths and jewelled dog collars glided subserviently among four representatives of the Three Estates assembled for the orgy. Johanna Kirby as Justine, the figure of Virtue Defiant, put horror in her aspect, radiance in her voice, thus enriching de Sade's ironic adjectives of disparagement when describing her tormentors' conduct. The Marquis himself supervised the proceedings and a vile bishop led a litany in praise of orgasm in the course of a Black (and blue) Mass, complete with steaming thuribles and a life-size Madonna. A transvestite Madame tore off her clothes and persuaded Justine to dance with the corpse of a lacerated valet. A duke, threatening to drown the world in his demonic sperm, went berserk in a torrent of Nietzschean fury.

The electrifying ambience of punk Jacobean excess and high-voltage, anarchic debate was like nothing I ever imagined seeing in a theatre. It presaged, too, Prowse's great string of Elizabethan and Jacobean productions in its X-certificate carnality and instant contemporary appeal. No argument or pose seemed risible because the actors were emblazoned, recognisable totems of style and swagger, not remote thespians in ruffs, furbelows and general period clobber spouting prim doggerel or historic irrelevancies. The stage sang – and spat.

Havergal was given a new four-year contract in 1975, and it was understood between him and the board that the continued participation of Prowse and MacDonald was guaranteed. The company was invited to take Prowse's production of *The Duchess of Malfi* to the Theatre of Nations Festival in Warsaw, and on to Belgrade, Frankfurt and Brussels. The visit to the Belgrade International Theatre Festival, BITEF, was significant because, run by Jovan Ćirilov and the late Mira Trailović, BITEF has consistently been a focus for major developments in world theatre, East and West. I was in

Belgrade, not with the Citizens, but as a regular guest of the festival, which was required viewing for anyone wishing to 'keep up' during the 1970s. The Citizens appeared, by no means to any disadvantage, alongside Roger Planchon's *Tartuffe* for the Théâtre National Populaire, La Mama's *Trojan Women* directed by Andrei Serban, Karolos Koun's *The Birds* and Peter Stein's unforgettable *Summerfolk*. I recall a blessedly unstuffy British Council reception at which the Citizens disported themselves colourfully in bandannas, make-up and exotic jewellery (the girls looked pretty smart, too) while Gladys Taylor, the chairman's wife, provided a useful contrast in her elegant cocktail dress and best pearls.

Prowse's design for *Duchess* was a baroque black and gold tabernacle adorned with images of death, in which was enshrined, and entombed, Suzanne Bertish's morosely severe Malfi. The company was gathering some outstanding performers at this time. Bertish was one; Jonathan Hyde, who was a lasciviously wicked Cardinal, another. Rupert Frazer had been away but returned as a rampageously petulant and lycanthropic Ferdinand. The madhouse sequence was particularly stunning, edited into a nightmarish tableau, while a cowled figure of Death opened a morbid tome for the recitation of the epiphanous couplets. Although Prowse did a very good *Malfi* for the Ian McKellen and Edward Petherbridge National Theatre group several years later, he never recaptured the gothic consistency of vision in this production.

Even more extreme was Prowse's 1976 treatment of *The Changeling*, which dispensed with the sub-plot, the madhouse and the title character, Antonio, and came across as an exquisite piece of spaghetti-Western kitsch about love and intrigue, performed in a cinematic fastness by a troupe of Spanish dancers. When Richard Eyre did the full text twelve years later at the National Theatre, the occasion was weighed down with painterly references to Goya and transformed into expensive High Art; as a result, it was dead theatre. Prowse, on the other hand, went gallivanting after the central images of blood, lust and betrayal: Gerard Murphy as Piraquo was gorily and horribly despatched; Johanna Kirby as Beatrice was gruesomely deflowered downstage as the corps de ballet tangoed sensuously in the background to the soundtrack of *Sunset Boulevard* and her breasts popped tantalisingly from a fragile black corset. David Hayman was slithering through the action as a beggar moaning 'Flores para los muertos', echoing the blind Mexican woman in *A Streetcar Named Desire;* he disappeared into the noonday sun as a harmonica emitted the haunting theme of *Once Upon A Time in the West*. It was as camp as a row of pink tents, and lusciously disrespectful to Thomas Middleton. I was rather put out by it at the time, but remember thinking that if you lived round the corner and were not dead set on becoming a drama critic, then you would probably have considered your 50p very well spent.

This issue of butchering classic texts has never been resolved between the Citizens and its critics, though when *The Spanish Tragedy* was severely tampered with in 1978, the company did announce the event as 'a production from the play'. Even that did not deter Allan Massie from taking up cudgels in *The Scotsman*: 'What is intolerable – and this is surely the indictment of all that is currently done at the Citizens – is the contempt that is shown for the work being interpreted . . . the work is their toy.' So indeed it was, and continued to be.

Contempt is a very strong word. Lack of respect is surely a positive theatrical virtue. And it would be wrong to underestimate the seriousness with which the theatre went about its hacking and patching. When Prowse amalgamated three Jacobean tragedies – *Malfi, 'Tis Pity She's a Whore* and *The White Devil* – into one four-hour evening called *Painter's Palace of Pleasure* (1978), after William Painter's compendium of tragic fable, he took three heroines, and their three brothers, and translated each trio into one consistent character to run right through his own artefact. The Duchess, for instance, was thus supplied with a background she lacks in the play as it stands. Cordelia Oliver described in *Plays and Players* the extraordinary white brick setting that both trapped and dwarfed the mad rush of killers and victims swathed in sinister cloaks and black velvet:

It's a forbiddingly bleak enclosure, as though part of some gaunt, Romanesque palazzo; a space which you see as blind and sealed-off until several entrances reveal themselves – immensely tall slits silently opening and closing . . . this white space contracts and darkens at will, carrying the smell of intrigue, eavesdropping and malice in the oppressive black walls and heavy furniture that slide in and out as scene follows scene.

The nationalist alternatives

While the new Citizens had dropped anchor in the Gorbals, the Scottish theatre around them was not exactly quiescent. John McGrath had founded in 1971 the 7:84 Theatre Company, and a visit to the Edinburgh Festival of 1972 with John Arden and Margaretta D'Arcy's brilliant and hard-hitting *The Ballygombeen Bequest*, about exploitative, absentee landlordism in Ireland ('a kind of political pantomime', Peter Ansorge called it) had given the new company a sharp national profile. In the following year, McGrath founded a Scottish 7:84. There was also renewed nationalist talk in Edinburgh at the Royal Lyceum, where the artistic director was Clive Perry and his energetic associate, in succession to Richard Eyre, was Bill Bryden.

McGrath's 7:84 was to become a regular visitor to the Citizens' summer seasons, invariably packing the theatre, as indeed did the Edinburgh Lyceum when they came west in 1972 with Bryden's own play about his Clydeside grandfather, *Willie Rough*, and, in 1973, with Roddy McMillan's first play for fifteen years, *The Bevellers*, about the author's early life in a small glass-bevelling business. Both 7:84 and Bryden's distinguished troupe — the latter included Rikki Fulton, James Grant, Joseph Brady, John Grieve, James Cairncross and Fulton Mackay ('the Lyceum's band of ethnic lovelies', Havergal good-naturedly dubbed them at the time) — were using history to address a contemporary audience. And both had their roots in the old days of Unity and the Scottish National Players. In their different ways, they were nostalgic throwbacks, appealing to a sense of community and conviction about a world that had entirely vanished or been suppressed.

While *Willie Rough* packed the Citizens, Havergal suffered the humiliation of emptying the Lyceum on an exchange visit to Edinburgh with MacDonald's production of *Venice Preserv'd*. The play had attracted only modest business in Glasgow; in Edinburgh, the Citizens died a death. One great idea of MacDonald's, an economic one, too, was to have the senators doubled with the conspirators so that they destroyed themselves, as it were, from within. Havergal considered the production 'very lovely, with a most fabulous set by Philip, and Douglas Heard as Death, so beautiful you could die'. The company did much better on this Edinburgh trip with the second production they took, *Tartuffe*, which had done less well in Glasgow. They always cherished, apparently, a remark at a little 'do' in Edinburgh after the first night of the Molière – there are always little 'do's' in Edinburgh – when one of the hosts said 'You can say anything you like In Edinburgh, as long as you say it with wit; not humour, mind you, but wit'.

There was a distinct definition at this point to the fortunes of the Edinburgh Lyceum. Under Clive Perry and Bill Bryden, there was a push towards a renewal of the Scottish National Theatre ideal. And the Citizens, it was intended, were to perish by comparison. The plot was never fulfilled. The Lyceum plays were photographic essays in grainy naturalism, lovingly designed by Geoffrey Scott with accurate period costumes by Deirdre Clancy. Their energy was atmospheric, not kinetic. Of his play about the south side boxing hero and tragic alcoholic, Benny Lynch, Bryden said he imagined it as a terrific movie of 1938, made by Warner Brothers, with James Cagney as Benny Lynch and Pat O'Brien as the priest. One or two of Bryden's actors voiced contempt for what was happening at the Citizens as 'funny clothes and make-up ... just amateur stuff', but the quality of the Lyceum commitment was unsound. Bryden never got the much larger investment from the Scottish Arts Council that he deemed necessary to compete with London attractions, and he was soon lured away down south (he had already established a reputation at the Royal Court) to join Peter Hall's National, where he did some of the best work of that period: the O'Neill productions, *Larkrise to Candleford, The Mysteries*. The company disbanded and the idea of a Scottish National Theatre was forgotten again for a few years.

There was more rough vitality, and more future, in the quite different nationalist aspirations of 7:84 (Scotland). The first show was *The Cheviot, the Stag, and the Black, Black Oil*, a cabaret play about the changing face of Scotland across two hundred years performed by a brilliant company at the heart of which were Bill Paterson, Alex Norton and John Bett, the trio who later performed John Byrne's *Writer's Cramp*, the hit of the 1977 Edinburgh Festival fringe. The avowedly left wing of Scottish theatre was facing the future by confronting the past. *Cheviot* stormed round the countryside reminding audiences of the rape of their country during the Highland clearances and the alleged parallel dispossession during the oil boom. After a long tour, the two weeks at the Citizens meant a great deal to McGrath, and, he reckoned, to

Glasgow, 'whose people were nearly all driven off their land, Scottish or Irish, and who are now demonstrably at the mercy of the whims of capitalism'.

McGrath's 7:84 spawned other exceptional touring companies – Borderline, Wildcat, Communicado – which refined and developed the political cartoon cabaret to a point where its limitations, by the end of the 1980s, had become dangerously exposed. But the audience was, and remains, ecstatically loyal to the companies, and nowhere more so than in Glasgow itself. McGrath wrote a production diary and manifesto in the February 1974 issue of *Plays and Players*, usefully summarising his beliefs:

> The theatre can never *cause* a social change. It can articulate the pressures towards one, help people to celebrate their strengths and maybe build their self-confidence. It can be a public emblem of inner, and outer, events, and occasionally a reminder, an elbow-jogger, a perspective-bringer. Above all, it can be the way people find their voice, their solidarity and their collective determination.

Windows on the world, mirrors in the salons

The theatre of direct political exhortation was not the Citizens' style, but it suited their backbone audience who made little qualitative distinction between the work of good visitors and of their own gifted residents. They could laugh with equal relish at either McGrath's aristocratic lampoons or a brutish neo-Wildean line of MacDonald's such as 'You must expect the cream of society to be both rich and thick'.

The line comes from MacDonald's version of Lermontov's *Maskerade*, the first ever in English of a play staged by Meyerhold in 1917, according to Alexander Matsin, as 'a tragedy within the framework of a carnival'. Like Prowse in his Genet season, Meyerhold and his designer, Golovin, often matched the stage decor with the gilded interior of the Alexandrinsky Theatre, and did so this time in a production widely perceived as a sombre requiem for the dethroned Romanov dynasty, a burial service for the old days. There were five curtains, their movements 'giving mood to each episode', and tall frosted mirrors which faced the illuminated auditorium and reflected a sea of lights. One critic described it as 'an opera without music'; Meyerhold devised a sort of acting score with punctuated movement that presaged his concept of biomechanics. Prowse, like Meyerhold, has made inventive use over the years of mirrors, traverse curtains, heavy swagging, reflected images and a liberating choreography of actors often achieved simply through what they wear. Meyerhold rehearsed for five years and built his production, according to one critic, like a pharaoh building his pyramid. He had 200 actors in the cast (MacDonald, directing his own text, had fourteen), and the play remained in the repertory until 1941 when a German bomb put paid to the store which housed the sets and costumes. The Citizens' version, given in repertory for a few weeks with Brecht's and Weill's *Seven Deadly Sins*, made use, as usual, of any materials to hand and recycled all the costumes in the company wardrobe.

MacDonald's slight twist in Lermontov's title, a 'k'

replacing the 'qu' of a regular translation, served notice of jaunty intentions. He also loosely updated the action to the 1890s, in order to convey at a sarcastic remove, almost, the absurdity of these hordes of foppish gamblers and lovelorn aristocracy gossiping around card tables. The central character, Arbenin, rejects this shallow scene and commits himself to marriage. But the denizens plan to recapture him because his flair, and his money, are missed on the green baize. Arbenin sees his own past in the antics of a pathetic prince who, at a beautifully staged masked ball, declares undying love to a baroness. She is sincere in returning his devotion, and he is a fraud. Arbenin detects a paradigm of his own situation, and the two stories mingle over a bracelet, worn by the prince, which he identifies (wrongly) as the one he gave his wife. He poisons her ice-cream at a grand ball, and she dies very slowly while he ruminates on the awfulness of Life. The melodrama was underpinned by surging quotations from Rachmaninov's First and Second Symphonies.

The confidence of this production may have emanated from the installation of a company which was one of the strongest assembled in the entire twenty-one years: Julia Blalock, David Hayman, Jonathan Hyde, Mark Lewis and Gerard Murphy were augmented by flying visits from past regulars such as Paola Dionisotti, Di Trevis and Douglas Heard. There followed a glorious run of work culminating in spring 1977 with the production of *Chinchilla*. The laconic, luxuriant salon style, with characters in impeccable evening dress lighting cigarettes from candles around the nearest catafalque while some cynical know-all cracks smart, and smart-ass, remarks on the sidelines, was defined by *Maskerade*, and later perfected in rare Coward and Wildean high melodrama. As the downfall of Arbenin, the Byronic man, was complete, Jonathan Hyde declared drily, 'Someone has clearly had a hand in all this; I should like to shake him by it'. When the disgraced prince returned to Arbenin's house with the mysterious avenging figure of death who stalked the lower depths from the upper level, he entered through a mirror which swung open to duplicate the theatre and its dumbstruck audience in swift and brilliant reflection. Meyerhold had been vindicated and restored to new life.

This season was full of scenic and literary invention. MacDonald's conflation of Beaumarchais's two Figaro plays was an extended revelation of the complex comic character of the servant, an essay in romantic love turned sour, with Hyde as Dr Bartolo once again latching on to MacDonald's quirky turns of phrase with unseemly relish; 'they have thrown a young man on my cucumber frames' may not look a funny line, but it brought the house down. The design was a spectacular one of movable white towers against a huge curtain whose colours were graduated through the costumes. The towers were similar to those seen just two months before in Prowse's own production of *The Country Wife*, inhabited by two dandyish stagehands who pulled back and forth three dazzling white drops in a stage picture entirely composed in blacks and whites. Although Prowse cut the Alithea/ Harcourt sub-plot, he did the hard part, the sexuality, better than any other production of this play I have seen. Heard's Horner was a diffident beauty who revelled in his false reputation as an eunuch; the trio of London ladies well-versed in sexual deceits were played, outrageously, by men in drag, including Giles Havergal as Old Lady Squeamish tearing her fan to tatters; and Julia Blalock's Margery appeared in a flimsily diaphanous blouse before the Playhouse, thus giving a double resonance to the attentions lavished upon her. The sexual itch, urge and ambiguity of the play were new-minted by young, attractive performers to whom the most untutored audience could respond with pleasure. During the run of *The Country Wife*, BBC TV transmitted an 'official' version that was anaemic, genteel and sexless, the epitome of an English classical tradition to which the Citizens stands in sworn opposition.

Lodged between *Maskerade* and these two productions came an event of at least equal significance: the first official production, in 1977, of the four-act version of *The Importance of Being Earnest*, prepared by Vivyan Holland from a German translation first published in 1903. Havergal and Prowse had done the play in their first season, but this was a quite different project. Havergal retained all the improvements in the 1894 three-act version which we know best today and which Wilde had prepared in haste at George Alexander's insistence for the first production. But Wilde had lost many fine lines from the full version, such as Lady Bracknell's comment, with thunderous caveat, on a salon rival of disguised age: 'Lady Dumbleton is very much admired . . . in the evening.' Even more baby had gone out with the bath water with the loss of the 'Gribsby scene', in which a solicitor arrives to escort 'Ernest Worthing' to Holloway prison. There is a small matter of a large bill, unpaid, at the Savoy Hotel. Algernon's incensed riposte – 'I really am not going to be imprisoned in the suburbs for having dined in the West End' – is one of his funniest, and the whole interlude was seen to reinforce the social quality of the play to marvellous effect. Also restored were the delightful proposal of Canon Chasuble to Miss Prism (played most touchingly by Gerard Murphy) in the last scene, and the skulking gardener, Moulton. Wilde's last two acts are set in the drawing room, but Havergal dallied *en plein air* in Prowse's wonderful creation of tall birches, four mounted flower pots full of pink roses, and a Victorian red brick archway. Jonathan Hyde's Lady Bracknell, complete with black bustle, parasol and galleon hat, was not a drag act, but a fully fledged, brilliant piece of feminine characterisation, sounding like Edith Evans but looking like Martita Hunt. Jill Spurrier's original Gwendolyn – large, snobbish and frightfully Belgravian – was going to become just like her mother in a good deal less than Ernest's 'about a hundred and fifty years'.

Diaghilev, Noël Coward, and more notes on Camp

Philip Prowse's affection for Venice was to prove a creatively significant obsession in the coming years. When Robert David MacDonald embarked on his Goldoni excavations, Prowse immediately responded in 1976 by relocating one of the more famous comedies, *La Locandiera*, in Venice, as opposed to its original Florentine setting. Suzanne Bertish was tremendous as the newly eponymous Mirandolina, seeing off her soppy suitors, including Hayman's Benedick-style 'cavaliere' and Hyde's seethingly demure marquis, with battling brusqueness before marrying the servant, just as her father wished.

To see this play reduced and transformed, over ten years later, into a little England vehicle for Penelope Keith's Thatcherite suburban bossiness (at the Chichester Festival Theatre, July 1987) was to see very clearly why the Citizens' internationalism is of paramount creative significance; it is nothing to do with a perverse desire to appropriate classic drama to a particular British culture, but an ambition to understand the great theatre of the world through the application of an intense and liberating vision.

MacDonald restored some deleted scenes with two spurious lady gentry and Prowse covered the grey exterior walls of the inn with countless sheets of newspaper, a veritable sea of graffiti, of speculation and gossip; the designer then filled the stage with happy hues, with graduated costume colours of powdered greys, soft pinks and browns, and the determined deep blue of Mirandolina's gown. With housework to be done in the third act, the stage was awash in a tumultuous, un-ironed plethora of sheets of another kind.

Prowse provided a severely contrasted, abstract view of Venice in his own landmark production of *Chinchilla* (1977). Everything about *Chinchilla* stemmed from Prowse – the idea, the setting, the events – and his conception resulted in MacDonald avowedly writing for the company, almost to order. The script struck analogous sparks off the backstage squabbles of the Ballet Russes at that point in its fortunes when the impresario Diaghilev (nicknamed 'Chinchilla' because of a prominent white quiff in his shiny black hair) had replaced one leading dancer, Nijinsky, with another, Massine, in the forefront of his professional and personal affections. The encounters on the beach at the Venice Lido were highlights of Chinchilla's career flashing before him as a prelude to death. Echoes abounded of Thomas Mann's von Aschenbach in *Death in Venice*, but MacDonald and Prowse also created a physical, gymnastic context appropriate to the Diaghilev ballet to Debussy's *Jeux*. 'A ball bouncing on a brightly lit stage' was the opening image, though Maxim is none too happy about always having to do that ballet 'about three boys having each other at a croquet match'. Richard Buckle's Nijinsky biography can be heard behind such lines, with its anecdote of Sarah Bernhardt confusing the English pastimes of cricket and football.

The play was sub-titled 'Figures in a Classical Landscape with Ruins' and contained many speeches in which Chinchilla and his associates define their impulse for artistic endeavour in an almost valedictory tone. The designer declares that when Maxim dances, 'it will be us out there on the stage'. Although MacDonald himself did not appear on stage in the production, Havergal did, as the loyally affable regisseur Grigoriev; over the years, MacDonald and Havergal were to make increasingly regular incursions onto the stage as performers while Prowse lurked manipulatively in the wings.

The opening was unforgettable. On a bare white stage, we heard the sound of waves lapping quietly behind the exquisite, ethereal music of Stravinsky's *Apollon*

Musagète. The lights rose and fell five times, revealing in snapshot style five increasingly populated beach tableaux: two boys in white towels arranged among a group of swish bohemians. Then, from the far depths of the stage, a hunched, drained man in a black coat with an astrakhan collar, climbed into the centre of everyone's attention. A sulky, heavily tanned boy in an Edwardian bathing suit was defined as the man's 'new great love', and also the new choreographer. Chinchilla had turned from Vatza to Maxim.

Other recognisably iconic but unspecified characters inhabiting the sculpted terrain of mirrors, raffia chairs, and a strategically placed look-out platform, included the designer Leon Bakst; Misia Sert, Diaghilev's closest woman friend; another lady admirer incorporating elements of the dancers Pavlova and Rambert; and the impresario Gabriel Astruc, the Ballet Russes' initial French connection. A cinematic jump-cut returned us, in the end, to the present and its fraught inquests into past artistic and emotional muddles. Chinchilla defends the apparent masturbation at the end of *L'Après-midi d'un faune* with the explanation to a fuming Astruc that it's a hot afternoon, Vatza's been chasing nymphs around for eleven minutes, what do you expect, etc., while David Hayman's muscular star limbers exotically in front of a large mirror that does a new version of the 'Meyerhold effect' on actor, theatre and audience.

This extraordinary comedy, written in a bright, hard, epigrammatical vernacular of jealousy, recrimination and stinging aspiration, was the climactic statement of the work in this decade, and the most eloquently honest appraisal of how the Havergal Citizens had chosen to collaborate fiercely on what they believed to be good theatre in the teeth of ridicule, misunderstanding and critical contempt. Some commentators diagnosed hubristic self-advertising in the creation of a metaphor of the Citizens in the figures of Diaghilev and his entourage. But the point was that the Citizens *did* dare to see themselves in the full European context of the great twentieth-century revolutions in art, and that the painful emergence of integrated, self-obsessed ensemble enterprises, full of spite, envy and creative pride, *was* seen, quite correctly, as endemic to those advances.

By now the idea of a Noël Coward world première in the Gorbals might not have seemed all that far-fetched. And that is precisely what happened at the start of the 1977 – 78 season, to which *Chinchilla* had posed a 'follow that' threat of alarming menace. *Semi-Monde* was written in 1926 while Coward was on tour with *The Vortex* in America. Originally titled 'Ritz Bar', it resembled an upmarket, more louche, version of *Cavalcade* set in the public rooms of that grand hotel. Basil Dean, apparently, had some good ideas on how it should be produced, and Max Reinhardt was keen to direct it in Germany (where a translation was prepared). But the play had slipped quietly into oblivion, unperformed. In 1957 Coward wrote to Beverley Nichols: '*Ritz Bar* was as jagged with sophistication as all get out; the characters were either demi-mondaine or just plain mondaine, shared their apartments and their lives with members of the opposite, or the same, sex and no wife dreamed for one instant of doing anything so banal as living with her husband.'

95

The world of gossip and intrigue was like that of *Maskerade* without the melodrama, though Prowse stretched Coward's skim across three years between the Wars into a parable of 'doomy' foreboding across twenty, from 1919 to 1939. They were, it seemed, taking the last orders on the Titanic. At the piano, a cadaverous MacDonald modulated from Charleston to wistful romance; a page boy previously in search of Mrs Simpson called finally for 'Madame la Duchesse de Windsor'; sirens mingled with Debussy and the hotel vacuum cleaner; beige flower bowls of pink and blue lilacs were re-stocked with tiger lilies; and in one moment of vintage Coward, an ageing novelist took his farewell of a beautifully attired socialite while fighting back tears with banal comments about the latest hit revue.

Rival schools of butch lesbians and screaming, highly strung young men hit each other with handbags and jumped on tables; two married couples exchanged partners; a Russian was shot dead by an irate rival; a sad loner pursued one of the married ladies. The sexual permissiveness of Coward's world was unstuffily related to a contemporary idea of its suffocating insouciance. Sandy Wilson, author of *The Boy Friend*, travelled north to see the show for *Plays and Players*. While he half-regretted the portentous over-loading of Coward's 'little charade', he was anxious to record his general enthusiasm:

The large cast were, almost without exception, splendid. I particularly enjoyed Katherine Kitovitz's Dorothy, gold lamé and chinchilla slithering off her shoulders as she agonises into her Bronx over her

Russian gigolo, and Sian Thomas, as her acidulated side-kick, Suzanne, all hard black hats and eye-veils, was equally good. Ann Mitchell, Angela Chadfield and Alison Mullin make a dashing trio of battling dykes, and Robin Pappas skilfully portrays the progress of Beryl, the American ingénue, from naive innocence to grasping duplicity. The men's roles have less meat to them and one or two of the actors had understandable difficulty in coping with the dated romantic lines; but Paul Bentall conveyed just the right air of bewildered outrage as the wronged English husband, and Pierce Brosnan came on as a dead-ringer for Clark Gable, dimple on the chin, ears and all.

Even if it had all been much less good than it was, *Semi-Monde* would have been well worth seeing for the clothes alone. Evening gown after evening gown, cocktail frock after cocktail frock, the parade passed by, including a couple of stunning lace numbers worn by Pauline Moran in that intrinsically Thirties shade known, I believe, as saxe blue, until by the end of the evening I felt I had seen, in a couple of hours, a decade of George White's Scandals. A special salute to Philip Prowse, designer, and to the astonishingly resourceful wardrobe of the Glasgow Citizens Theatre. Now, when are they going to do *The Women*?

Oscar Wilde said that one should either be a work of art, or wear a work of art, and this moral and habitual narcissism was what some critics found difficult to stomach at the Citizens. Undoubtedly some of these productions were informed by the sort of camp vision in art that has only ever been seriously discussed by Susan Sontag in her *Notes on Camp*. Admitting a sharp conflict in her own sensibility – as strongly drawn to Camp as offended by it – Sontag brilliantly analyses the phenomenon in terms of the canon of Camp (random examples include *Zuleika Dobson*, Aubrey Beardsley's drawings, Bellini's operas, Visconti's direction of *Salomé* and *'Tis Pity She's a Whore*, women's clothes of the 1920s, the novels of Ronald Firbank and Ivy Compton-Burnett), and points out the overlap with homosexuality by which moral seriousness is asserted, and its formulating metaphor of theatre as life. Taking her yardsticks, much of the Citizens' work may be defined as Camp, and this explains the reluctance of perfectly intelligent but disapprovingly strait-laced critics to discuss it. But theatre audiences, of most sexual and political persuasions, adore Camp, whether it is feathers and glitter at the Folies Bergères, the ball scene in *Cinderella* or *Swan Lake*, Oscar Wilde's epigrams, *Der Rosenkavalier*, or Barry Humphries as Dame Edna Everage. It is clear, therefore, that Camp is not anathema to good art.

If the Citizens' work of this decade was indeed Camp, its most distinctive product, *Chinchilla*, was far too austere and sinuous to be included under that heading. And the theatre itself has never struck me as a seedbed of the sort of indiscriminate promiscuity characterised in *Semi-Monde* and which outsiders might take for granted as part and parcel of working in such a company. David Hayman claims it was rather communal and orgiastic in the first two or three years, but Fidelis Morgan, who first joined the company in 1978, says it is now the one theatre

in Britain where you can work most often without meeting
a homosexual actor:

A lot of theatres have everyone sleeping with each
other; well, it's not one of those. There's a terrific
bonhomie, and a great feeling of friendship. You enter
friendships you then revive once a year for ten years, as
opposed to those awful claustrophobic physical ones
you can have for three weeks. And I think that's all very
healthy. It's not at all "actorish". On the whole, you get
rather sensible people up there; people with personality, obviously, but real people as opposed to
theatrical queens and screamers.

Semi-Monde had been comparatively expensive, so it had
always been planned to balance it against a cheaper play,
and 'cheap' in theatrical budget parlance means 'hardly
any actors' or a one-man show. The standing joke is that
they can always send on Giles Havergal (whose salary
covers his acting contributions) reciting St Mark's Gospel
in his own polo-neck, the ultimate cheap show to pack
them in. The company has never had to resort to this,
though they came perilously close ten years later. What
was needed was a three-hander to pay for the Coward,
and MacDonald volunteered to write one.

The idea for the resultant *Summit Conference* was
Prowse's, and incontestably camp; a fictional encounter
between the mistresses of Hitler and Mussolini, Eva
Braun and Clara Petacci, on the eve of the invasion of
Russia in 1941. These 'two people who are not asked to
functions' were walled up inside a cavernous smoky-grey

upper room in the Berlin Chancellory discussing, under the surveillance of a young soldier, Hollywood movies, fashion, sex and persecution. Critics complained that nothing much happened; but nothing much happens in Coward's *Fallen Angels*, a conversation piece to which this play bore more than a passing resemblance in both structure and tone. Four white architectural models on Prowse's set – of a pyramid, a mosque, a fortress and a triumphal arch – conveyed exactly that arid Nazi sense of power lust, while an Olympic flame tower burst to life as Eva and Clara sealed their conspiratorial relationship with a loving kiss. One remembers, too, the remarkable inset cocktail cabinet, briefly glimpsed to make the surprise point that while the Führer disapproved of alcohol for the masses, he did not deny it in his private hospitality. The girls gang up on the guard who, once humiliated, outlines his antecedence as a German Jew of Polish origin and strikes to the heart of Nazi ideology: 'In every country, someone within its frontiers is defining a group of fellow-citizens whose actions, while in no way considered criminal at present, are to be in some way restricted: and there, assured by bureaucratic continuity, are the seeds of an efficient killing operation.'

Four years later, the play was re-mounted in London with the same set but a different cast: Glenda Jackson and Georgina Hale replaced Ann Mitchell and Julia Blalock; Gary Oldman, Garry Cooper. The campiness became campier and too much to bear for many critics. Irving Wardle said the play never got going and suggested something Giraudoux might have written on a bad day, while Jack Tinker in the *Daily Mail* could not recall a

Opposite:
Mark Lewis,
Rupert Frazer,
Paul Bentall and
Philip Bloomfield in
Thyestes.
Overleaf:
Suzanne Bertish
and Oengus
McNamara in
De Sade Show.

toshier play 'that aspired so high and sank so low'. Robert Cushman in *The Observer* commented adversely on the general camp effect: 'You might respect a dramatist who tried to put Hitler and Mussolini directly on stage, however painfully he failed; to do it at this remove is merely to add a layer of titillation . . . Mr MacDonald says nothing new and says it aridly.'

Pride against parochial prejudice

The Citizens never had to go to London for their brickbats. There were still plenty flying around on the doorstep. And they could attract them even by being merely hospitable. In the 1977 summer season, Havergal gave Pip Simmons his first main house date after ten years on the fringe. Years later Simmons recalled the week with affection: 'The first time we played to a *real* audience in Britain was at the Glasgow Citizens, when Giles Havergal (typically, I'd say) invited us up there with *The Dream of a Ridiculous Man* and *Dracula*. We had all sorts of people, old ladies and young kids who laughed and screamed and found it shocking and went away saying they'd had a bloody good 50p's worth.' Not the Lord Provost, Peter McCann, though, who got wind of nude actors crawling through the front stalls in *Dracula* and called for the sacking of the Citizens management. He alleged that the show was 'kinky claptrap' appealing only to 'mentally ill weirdos' and summoned the four councillors who sat on the Citizens' board. One of them, Mrs Jean McFadden, now the deputy leader and treasurer of the District Council, had boldly declared that she did not find nudity offensive. Today, she recalls that McCann tried to persuade them to

Overleaf:
Barry Philips,
David Hayman,
Garry Cooper,
Gerard Murphy,
Julia Blalock,
Giles Havergal,
Ciaran Hinds,
Jill Spurrier and
Mark Lewis in
The Country Wife.
Opposite:
Mark Lewis and
Julia Blalock in
Figaro.

take action, but they were all supporters of the Citizens, and its policy, and he had to retreat in disarray.

None of this had any effect on the programme. Having started the decade with plays everyone had heard of, the repertoire was widening at an alarming rate to accommodate the enthusiasms and whims of its directors. At no point was a policy change declared to contradict the opening gambit of subjecting well-known titles to interpretative overhaul, but the company felt sufficiently safe in its residency to widen the dramaturgical scope. The process was gradual, unannounced and clearly essential to the creative well-being of the operation. The odd, the unexpected and the downright adventurous were now coming thick and fast. MacDonald did two ingenious, outrageous adaptations, of the James Hadley Chase thriller *No Orchids for Miss Blandish*, and of the 1950 Cocteau film, *Orphée*. The first, in a blood-smeared white box, all car chases deleted, was a gruesomely unsettling study in menace and sexuality, while the Cocteau, directed by Geoffrey Cauley, using the Gluck music, was an entirely bizarre, faintly anachronistic experience which replaced Cocteau's agent of mortality, the talking horse, with a magnificent 1926 gleaming white Rolls-Royce open tourer (the first ever seen in the Gorbals, it was said) and made much of the key line, retained from the play, 'If you look in a mirror, you will see Death at work like bees in a glass hive'.

Even on the grounds of a play's curiosity value, it was becoming difficult for a London-based critic to avoid the journey up to Glasgow at least six or seven times a year, a situation that would only intensify in the 1980s as the other regional theatres battened down the hatches and heeded the Arts Council's injunctions to give the people what they thought they wanted. I was fortunate to be working during this period for a newspaper thoroughly committed to covering the arts in the regions and in mainland Europe, so I had no trouble in convincing anyone that the Glasgow Citizens had become an immovable fixture among our priorities.

When Richard Eyre left the Nottingham Playhouse in 1978 he did his best to tempt the Citizens directorate to succeed him. Havergal took the invitation very seriously indeed, but had certain conditions to put to the Nottingham board, one of the most notoriously conservative of all regional theatre boards, at least in those days. It was taken as read that he would come with Prowse and MacDonald, but he also insisted on bringing his own general manager. The Nottingham chairman said that he and his colleagues could not countenance a night of the long knives among the administration, so Havergal said fair enough, and that was that. But for a time the move did seem a distinct possibility. Havergal now says that the degree of flexibility achieved in Glasgow happened because he took over a theatre on its beam end; the process of running the place works well chiefly because it is mercifully unhampered by continual referral of every tiny bit of business to the board. And anyway, he adds, 'taking over from a success, like Richard Eyre, would have been very hard'.

The decision not to move at that stage reduced the likelihood of them moving thereafter. The theatre renovations were well in hand, and the 1980s would see a return on Havergal's successful stewardship in the form of renewed contracts and increased funding from both the regional and district councils. But could the pattern be sustained?

All three directors had now emerged in full spate, and MacDonald had been a remarkably prolific writer throughout. When I saw the 1979 *Macbeth*, I declared that the house style had been temporarily discarded. In fact, Havergal was here launching a new, stripped down approach that was to become a feature of his work at the Citizens, and as a guest director with Shared Experience, in the next decade. The production remains the piece of work of which David Hayman, who was about to leave, is most proud. There were no crowns, no robes, no apparitions, no blood, and one sound effect (the porter's knocking). The fight with Macduff was done not with swords but with stage braces. There was no budget for scenery or costumes. The actors wore what they turned up in that day and waited for their cues on the periphery of an area lit by working lights and furnished with classroom desks and benches. Like the *Hamlet* at the top of the decade, the cast was all-male. But the text was not mangled; it was spoken with utter clarity, and Hayman as Lady Macbeth was as muscularly taut and dynamically watchable as he had ever been as Bosola in *Malfi* or Sparkish in *The Country Wife*. Gerard Murphy was equally memorable as Macbeth, and the production did as much as any, I suppose, to scotch the idea that the Citizens was an exclusively epicene or, indeed, camp entertainment factory. A few titters greeted Hayman on his first foray in white T-shirt and rehearsal dress, but they lasted barely five seconds. The play and performance gripped like a vice and I have never flinched from placing this version in a personal pantheon that includes the much derided William Gaskill Royal Court production (with Alec Guinness and Simone Signoret) and the Trevor Nunn RSC chamber production (with Ian McKellen and Judi Dench).

As if to prove that he could switch styles with the best of them, Havergal ended his tumultuous decade with a superb *Pygmalion*, incorporating the ballroom scene and Higgins's farcically Hungarian pupil Neppomuck from the film version, as well as bits of Shaw's first draft (performed in Vienna in 1913) and a string of aphorisms trawled from the play's preface. Havergal often resorts to the 'theatre-ness' of theatre as a framing device, but always with a high degree of freshness and bite. The idea here was that Higgins was not just a suave impresario but also a pathetic mother's boy who fights any onrush of sexual passion as fiercely as he upholds the phonetician's conviction that purity of speech is nothing to do with class. Giving the play an interesting tilt, this slightly deranged Svengali (played by MacDonald) manipulated his doll-like Trilby into a position of social and domestic acquiescence. Johanna Kirby thus related the guinea-pig element of Eliza to her submissive Sadean portrayal. The effect, however, was not reactionary, but radical in the sense that Higgins — and this was a valid, if ironic, Shavian point — knew perfectly well how to stage-manage people, but not how to live with them.

In spite of all the recognition, and the invitation by John Drummond to take part in his first Edinburgh Festival as director in succession to Peter Diamand, the Citizens continued to strike on raw nerves. The reactions of Allen Wright continued to be those of the gut, which is what made them interesting, and not of the brain, which is why they are of limited value. Reviewing the *Orpheus*, Wright clearly objected to people outside Scotland finding the company worthwhile, thus demonstrating the classic parochial cringe of denigrating something as of right because it belongs to you: 'Sometimes, when I read eulogies to the effect that Glasgow has one of the most brilliant theatre companies in Britain, I wonder if I have been taking the wrong turning at Gorbals Cross. Perhaps there is some other theatre on the south bank of the Clyde where one can see some excellent acting . . .'

It depends what you mean by 'excellent acting', and more of that later. Wright, through no fault of his own, had been completely outflanked by the Citizens' success. He no doubt felt that the clock could and should be turned back. In 1973, for instance, when a production of Bridie's *Daphne Laureola*, with Lennox Milne, Leonard Maguire and Ron Bain in the cast, had visited the Gorbals as part of the summer Clyde Fair, a predecessor of the Mayfest, he breathed a short sigh of relief: 'Civilised wit returns at the Citizens' ran the headline.

The uncivilised wit of MacDonald was simply not what Wright and many commentators, and indeed playwrights, wanted to hear. In this same article, Wright quoted with approval the opinion of the playwright Donald Campbell, who had written that 'in the context of Scottish Theatre, the Citizens is a monumental irrelevance. It does absolutely nothing to examine or reflect the concerns and mores of contemporary Scotland.'

Feelings ran high on the subject. In the mid-1970s, Chris Parr had initiated another new Scottish writing policy at the Traverse in Edinburgh. There was some good, slight stuff by Liz Lochhead and other writers, but nothing very much came out of it. The Traverse never really found a considerable new Scottish writer until the Jenny Killick era, when John Clifford emerged writing plays that were, significantly, as little to do with 'the concerns and mores of contemporary Scotland' as anything by MacDonald. Hector MacMillan faded after early success; one of the more pathetic Traverse offerings was his *The Gay Gorbals* in which he charted the attempt of gay social workers to take over a church hall in the Gorbals for the sole convenience of their own social group. The Provost of Glasgow was finally unmasked as a rampant pooftah and the city regeneration policy defined as something to do with a newly discovered link between permissiveness and productivity. As satire, this was wretched, but as aesthetic commentary, it was certainly indicative of a homophobic resentment towards the Citizens that had taken hold in some theatrical quarters.

One even encountered this in London, where ill-informed prejudice against the Citizens was to be found in the most unexpected places, among actors, directors and designers. Lord Provost McCann had said, at the time of the Pip Simmons row, that he did not have to go down a sewer to know that it stank. What was the cause of this rabid dislike of the Citizens? It was something to do with the fact that they flew in the face of everyone. They ignored London. They despised the National and the RSC. They were camp, and they were successful. They did everything people in the British theatre were supposed not to do. They were invited abroad and admired when they got there. And all of this was exacerbated because puritanism is very much more ingrained in the Scottish character than it is in the English. The playwright Tom McGrath declared on a Radio 3 programme about the Citizens in 1979 that they murdered Shakespeare and Brecht, and revived uninteresting Coward; that they also did abstruse classics, not very well, which was OK if you had seen them done before; that, although he liked and admired them all, the acting that went on there was of the type that made his flesh creep.

McGrath had written a play about Jimmy Boyle, the Glaswegian hard man who was the most celebrated inmate of the Barlinnie Special Unit and who had found redemption partly through art. Once he had left the Citizens, David Hayman was to play this character in a film. Hayman, who underwent something of a Pauline conversion, also came to view the Citizens as perpetrating an irrelevant view of the world, and none at all of that section of it on its own doorstep. The fundamental debate here is whether art has a function in society by virtue of what it discusses, or by virtue of how it sees itself in the life of its customers and neighbours.

For no overtly political company can better the Citizens' record in this latter respect. More people have flocked, over a longer period, and more cheaply, too, to the Havergal Citizens than they have ever flocked to anything written by Tom McGrath or Hector MacMillan. And the argument that the Citizens policy was keeping good new Scottish plays out of the public gaze was threadbare by 1980 as the new touring companies sprang up, the Traverse continued to prosper, and plans were in hand for a new theatre for Scottish playwrights in the old Tron Kirk near Glasgow Cross which materialised in 1982, two years after the bar was christened with lunch-time performances. By 1989, amusingly enough, McGrath himself, separately sponsored by the Scottish Arts Council, was working within the Citizens, as part of the Theatre Around Glasgow education unit, on a large-scale popular epic for the 1990 celebrations.

'A passion for beauty, a rage to love'

John Drummond came to the Edinburgh Festival in 1979 with good credentials in serious music (he is currently Controller, Radio 3, at the BBC and responsible, among much else, for the Proms) but was determined to redress the balance in drama's favour after years of comparative neglect under Peter Diamand. Drummond was, and is, an internationalist of almost rabid enthusiasm, and his impact on the Edinburgh Festival was of vigorous, whirl-wind proportions. He acted fast, and often furiously. When he received glowing reports on the Rustaveli Theatre of Georgia, he flew immediately to Tbilisi, and booked this astonishing company into the Edinburgh Lyceum for his first festival. In addition to the Rustaveli, he signed up the Bristol Old Vic, the Paris-based Argentinian Groupe TSE − and the Citizens.

As 1979 was the 50th anniversary of the death of Diaghilev, *Chinchilla* was appropriate, as was the other Citizens' contribution, a carnival confection of Goldoni, *The Good-Humoured Ladies*, for which Sue Blane recreated the costumes Leon Bakst had provided for a Massine ballet. MacDonald had adapted the show from two 1758 Goldoni comedies, one of which translated as the given title, the other, *Le Morbinose*, as 'The restless women'. Bakst was a jovially 'messy' designer who painted on heavy silks and cloths in bold, flashy colours. Sue Blane transformed the Lyceum stage into just such a riot of colour – orange, blue, red and green, the ladies' dresses heavily adorned with roses, and a Venetian backcloth in a state of near completion as indicated by the presence of ladders, a paint pot and a big blue splurge on the floor. Aunt Silvestra (Jonathan Hyde perfecting his myopic Martita Hunt act) was 'dressed to kill . . . well, maim' and her female harlequin, 'a malapert thing', instigated a plot to catch a count that involved masks and identification tags of pink ribbons in a coffee house. The whole delightful concoction came to the boil with people choking on pasta while bidding for marriage contracts and one suitor suspended by a rope and pelted with bread rolls.

Two years after its première, *Chinchilla* was better than ever, though not unattended by new controversy. The Citizens had been invited back to BITEF in Belgrade with the play, but the British Council refused to support the trip because Anton Dolin had gone on the radio and denounced the Citizens for stating that Diaghilev was homosexual. He also falsely claimed, in the *New York Times*, that he had been offered the lead role in an off-Broadway production of *Chinchilla*. He had turned it down, he said, because Diaghilev 'would never have ogled waiters on the beach' and neither smoked nor used four-letter words. Havergal did not care about what Dolin thought of *Chinchilla*, but he did mind very much that the British Council censored his invitation to Belgrade as a result. He was, and still is, 'jolly, jolly cross'.

The piece was never intended as an accurate representation of characters, any more than Shakespeare intended his plays about the English monarchs to be accurate historical portrayals. It was a peg on which the Citizens hung their collective hat, and the Edinburgh performance of Gerard Murphy as 'Chinchilla' Diaghilev had expanded incomparably to become one of the outstanding acting achievements in the British theatre of the 1970s. When, at the end of the first act, he embarked on Diaghilev's long speech of self-justification, he spoke not only for the actors and technicians of the Gorbals theatre, but also, and especially, for the three men who had been, thus far, its powerhouse and inspiration.

Chance, perhaps, threw us in the way of one another, and together we found a way to rid ourselves of a desperate inaction, as frustrating as it was futile, like nailing custard pies onto trees. And we work, we make revolutions, we make fashions, we make scandals. Many reasonable people are appalled, many despicable people delighted, but none of that matters. It comes from us. It is a passion, a disease, a lust. Art can rest on sinister foundations, and has the most intimate knowledge of sickness. They are both the product of excess, and there is nothing anyone can do about that. The single-minded concentration of an artist works like a cancer, and passion absorbs utterly.

Passion for reform, passion for power, passion for beauty, a thirst to show, a lust to tell, a rage to love. It is the only voice we can still trust in a complicated expensive world. And because it is all too ecstatic, absurd, miserable, happy, horrible and holy to contain within myself, I will show what I love, and tell what I love, with ardour, style and impeccable bad taste, whether it is Utopia, or the death of Kings, or simply those beautiful young men without whom my life is as dry as a nut: so that for a moment we can see them, created in our image, in the glare of arc lamps, as we should; beautiful, clever, wise, just and alive, and for that moment forget that we are ugly, crass, guilty, foolish and dying.

THE DIRECTORS: HAVERGAL, PROWSE AND MACDONALD

Now is the moment to turn the spotlight on the three directors themselves, three men of cultured, middle-class backgrounds, of individual talent and distinction, separate from each other in their private lives yet bound together, seemingly inextricably, in the fate of the Glasgow Citizens.

The actor Patrick Hannaway was bursting to define the differences between them: 'Giles is old-style, French's acting edition, and will spend two or three days blocking the moves then working methodically through the play. He says where the furniture is, and where you come on and go off, and once he has got the structure, he doesn't change very much. His great concern is diction and clarity, and can those little old ladies sitting in Row G understand what's going on.

'Philip is much more regimented, but if something doesn't work, he will scrap it and start again. If you're a foot out of place, you know it. He only ever says something three times to an actor, and then he stops. If the actor's just not listening, Philip doesn't want to work with him, and the same goes if he's too stupid to listen. He doesn't care what technique you use to arrive at what you do; you can prepare how you like. All he will say is that he wants to see you in that light saying that line in that position.

'David, on the other hand, is completely anarchic, lets it all roll over the stage before making selections and, at the last minute, usually at the first complete run-through, he will put in the music cues and you suddenly see everything drop into place. If you bring sixpence, he will give you half a crown. But you have to bring something; if you bring nothing, you get nothing.'

Angela Chadfield concurs, saying that a rehearsal with MacDonald is like a social event, a wonderful day during which he rambles on with so many ideas and nuggets of information that you have to go home and sit down to sort it all out. Laurance Rudic, who has been in the company on and off for most of his working life, says that the dominating aesthetic of the Citizens undoubtedly derives from Prowse, and agrees with Hannaway that Havergal is a much more conventional, and technically precise, director, while MacDonald is quite different from both of them: 'You could not call what he does directing in the usual sense of the word; working with him is like attending a very informative tutorial, and he's terribly funny and interesting.'

Giles Havergal

There is a lovely coincidence in the fact that Giles Havergal took up his appointment in Glasgow in the year of his father's retirement as principal of the city's Royal Academy of Music and Drama; father and son were leaving and joining the two great Glasgow institutions

James Bridie had fought for and fostered. Like his son after him, Henry Havergal (1902 – 1989) arrived in Glasgow at a crucial time in the life of one of those institutions; his post had hitherto been twinned with the Gardiner Professorship at the University, but now, in 1953, his task was to give the academy a separate and newly prestigious identity. In this, Henry Havergal is generally counted to have succeeded. He had taught music at four major public schools – Fettes, Haileybury, Harrow and Winchester – and was renowned as a champion of the music of Elgar and Vaughan Williams, and as an enthusiastic conductor of choirs and orchestras. He cut a familiar and much-loved figure in the city, one remembered at his memorial service in St Mary's Cathedral, Edinburgh, by Christopher Everett, a fellow teacher:

> Do you recall the red socks, the bow tie, the floppy broad-brimmed hat, that hurrying stooped forward gait, with piles of orchestral parts precariously carried in his arms, the wobbling chin – who would have thought that wobbles could communicate so wide a range of feelings? Do you remember the rehearsals taken in braces at which he would tug as he urged the music on, the occasional charge into the middle of the chorus to hear an individual sing, and the long walk down the aisle to listen while the orchestra and chorus played on their own?

Giles Havergal, born in Edinburgh in 1938, can claim Scottish antecedence from his parents, each of whom was half-Scottish. He was educated at Harrow and Christ Church, Oxford, and is a good deal taller than was his father, but he obviously inherited the precious ability to communicate with enthusiasm that characterises the born teacher. Eyes bright, features aquiline, hair now whitening and thinning, Havergal projects an unusual mixture of anxiety and perfect manners. One imagines him to be something of a worrier, while knowing him for sure to be considerate, hard-working and totally well-organised. He exudes a sort of steely diplomatic charm, and is known to lose his rag only very rarely and only when pushed just a little too far. The entire Citizens operation is held steady by his absolute refusal to put the theatre into the red:

It is a slight moral thing. We are paid by the State for doing what we want to do. We are given two thirds of our money and earn another third at the box-office. It is all too easy to be shut down because of bad management — oh, you know, they're artistic and they can't add up. We would never be so pathetic. If you balance your books, you buy freedom and you silence all criticism. I absolutely refuse to present the board with the only problem that really matters, which is a deficit.

After Oxford, Havergal's first job in 1961 was as an assistant stage manager at the Carlisle Rep, and it was given to him by Robert David MacDonald. Shortly afterwards he came to Glasgow where he appeared in an insignificant production of *Treasure Island* before joining the Old Vic as an actor in 1962, just before Olivier and the National Theatre moved in, whereupon Havergal took a Thames Television Trainee directorship at the Oldham Coliseum – in the same year, incidentally, as Trevor Nunn was similarly apprenticed to the Belgrade, Coventry. Havergal worked at the Barrow repertory theatre for six months before going to Watford in 1964, where he prepared to take over the Palace Theatre by working in the Town Hall for several months, getting to know the ins and outs of civic finance and the wiles of local politicians, a crucial experience.

His four years at Watford were successful both in terms of the calibre of repertoire presented and in putting the theatre on the map. The Watford Palace is the last surviving Edwardian house on the London periphery, a beautiful theatre of physical proportions very similar to those of the Citizens. Its social profile is more nebulous than the Citizens', chiefly because Watford is a far more nebulous place than Glasgow, but it does command a loyal bedrock audience, and it has a reputation for good pantomimes. In Havergal's time, national critics began to go there as a matter of course, much as they now go to Glasgow, and the theatre has thrived ever since.

Havergal has a firm view of the Citizens' place in the overall pattern of the arts in Britain; although his theatre seems geographically remote from the rest of the hurly-burly, Havergal himself is one of the more up-to-date and generally well-informed of artistic directors:

I suppose we do relate to such other regional success stories as the Welsh National Opera, or the City of

Birmingham Symphony Orchestra under Simon Rattle, only we're odder. We would not feel so out of place in mainland Europe, though we might get more money. The trouble with the National and the RSC is that they are intellect-, not emotion-oriented; their productions approach you through your knowledge of A-level English, and the acting is full of psychological realism which tends to mean a lot of actors just standing very still and gazing at you very firmly.

The logistics and planning of the Glasgow seasons have involved throwing the Citizens open to visiting companies. In the late 1970s, both Richard Eyre, as he retired from the Nottingham Playhouse, and Ruari McNeill, the administrator of the Edinburgh Lyceum, suggested it was easier for the Citizens to balance their books than it was for either of them because the Citizens only stayed open for half the year.

Havergal bridles at this and in so doing reveals his practical philosophy.

At Nottingham, the Playhouse is, or at least was, bound by statute to be open for forty-nine weeks of each year with their own product; which is a nonsense and indeed one of the reasons why we didn't go there. The point is that, if you can't fill all your dates, you get the visitors in, and they are all part of the cards in your hand. The Lyceum doesn't have to stay open; it can close if it wants to. And this is another card in your hand. Of course we all want to employ people all the year round, but there are ways of getting round that, too. We have simply been audacious in the way we have used time, as we have used space and people.

One of the things everyone says of Havergal is that his instinct for choosing and running a good team is second to none. He has a fine nose for talent as well as for the personal qualities essential for being part of a team. In this way the events on the stage extend right to the foyer, where the welcome mat is permanently out. I am told by Richard Eyre that when John Neville ran the Nottingham Playhouse in the 1960s, he was permanently visible to his audience, either on stage or front of house. And during the same decade, you were always aware of the hovering presence of Olivier whenever you went to the Old Vic, even if, on the street outside or in the foyer, his squatly sober-suited, bespectacled figure resembled an unremarkable bank manager or civil servant. Havergal is the opposite of this, an ideal host whose audience qualifies for friendship the minute they cross the portals. And in private, his friendships are many and fast; his 50th birthday party was a tumultuously populated affair, given in the London home of the writer and political commentator Ferdinand Mount, whose sister is one of his oldest friends.

At the same time, for all his affability, Havergal is painfully reluctant to take any credit for his success in Glasgow. When asked about it, he insists that the creative impulse derives almost totally from Prowse. It is Prowse, he says, who has the ideas for all their major shows: for Chinchilla, A Waste of Time, Anna Karenina, even though it is MacDonald who writes the scripts. And it is Prowse who advocates the equal wage, the non-billing of actors, the free sheet programme, the low price ticket, and who sets that particular tone of artistic haughtiness which characterises the Citizens' 'apartness' from London and indeed the entire British theatre.

But it is Havergal who makes all these ideas work, and who takes on the political responsibilities in the community. It remains to be seen whether the Citizens became more 'respectable' in the 1980s, but as the flak ceased to fly, and the company's fame grew, so Havergal, always a natural candidate for public recognition, received his well-merited due. In 1982 he was made a Doctor of Letters at Glasgow University, at the same ceremony as Maurice Lindsay, the poet and historian, was similarly honoured. And in 1987, he received the OBE for services to the theatre, twenty-two years after his father had received the same award for services to music.

Philip Prowse

Philip Prowse is a dangerous sort of person. His presence in a room, like that of many fiercely creative people, particularly directors, can be either electrifying or terrifying, and usually something of both. When he feels like it, he can be scathingly funny. He once told an interviewer that he only visited the London theatre 'in order to keep *au courant* with what is *déjà vu*'. When *Summit Conference* came to London in 1982, he gave a striking interview to Sheridan Morley in *The Times*. His most remarkable statement was picked out by the newspaper and highlighted in large letters:

Whether this works or whether it doesn't, I hope I'll have the courage to go back to Glasgow and leave the London theatre to die the death it so richly deserves – a death caused by directors who have not the faintest sense of design, actors who believe that a play can exist on a page instead of a stage, and audiences still willing to pay for provincial, parochial, puritanical rubbish.

He might have been a little less equivocal, perhaps, but you get the message. Prowse is a theatrical dissident, a contemptuous non-joiner and a free spirit. He is miserly of conversation except with his closest friends, by whom he is revered, temperamentally circumspect, and physically and vocally languid. He subscribes to no philosophy of design except the one forced upon him by both economics and a deep-seated loathing of all scene-changes: 'There is not a single play in the world that cannot be done on one set.' He rarely produces a model of his set for the actors, but is content just to mark out the exits and entrances with tape on the rehearsal floor. You do not meet many people who have worked with him who do not consider him to be some sort of a genius.

Once a heavy smoker, he has put on weight since he stopped, but his face bears the stamp of perennial youth, and a naughty boy twinkle hovers like a dangerous commentary around his eyes and mouth. Sentences trail off into the middle distance and hang limply on the air. Like Harold Pinter and Terry Hands, he quite often wears black, and there ends abruptly any similarity to anyone else in the British theatre.

121

One of his teachers at the Slade, Robert Medley, who
was in the Group Theatre before the war and who also
designed the original productions of plays by W.H. Auden
and Louis MacNeice, told Nicholas de Jongh of *The
Guardian* in 1985 that 'Prowse was an extremely
precocious, talented and self-willed boy. He was a very
good scholar too, but he was a sophisticated boy who
objected to getting his hands dirty scene painting. But
then after he left he buckled to.'

He was born in 1937 of a Devonshire family and brought
up in Worcestershire. He wanted to be a designer from
the age of five when he was taken to a pantomime. He left
his minor public school aged sixteen and went to art
school for five years, three of them at the Slade where his
teachers, as well as Medley, were Nicholas Georgiadis
and Peter Snow, all of whom remain good friends. He
rates himself a very bad painter, making a *Chinchilla*
connection for Barbara Newman in the *Dancing Times* of
April 1985:

You can't be taught to be either, actually – a painter or
a designer. You can only be put into an environment
which will allow you to expand. And if you're a painter,
you're really in quite another class from a designer.
This is one of my obsessive things. The only person
who ever used painters successfully for the stage was
Diaghilev. Nobody has really done it since. And all that
they really provided was backcloths, because those
are flat things which painters understand. But – and
this is what's always forgotten – when Diaghilev
used Picasso, Picasso wasn't Picasso. He was a

young painter, young-ish painter, who needed money. As soon as Picasso *was* Picasso, he never worked for the stage again.

After the Slade, Prowse worked for a year in the model rooms at Covent Garden, did a little teaching and then designed *Diversions* for Kenneth MacMillan to music by Arthur Bliss in 1961 ('The curtain went up, the audience applauded. What else could you want?'). Then came what he admits was a 'terrible' version of John Cranko's *Beauty and the Beast* which Margot Fonteyn took to Monte Carlo, and *La Bayadère* in 1963. His work on opera and plays started soon afterwards, and in 1967 he joined Havergal at the Watford Palace, moving with him to Glasgow two years later.

He feels uncomfortable with anything, such as the Mystery plays, set before 1500 and prefers to present even a medieval legend like *Swan Lake* in Gothic, nineteenth-century terms, as he did for a Sadler's Wells Royal Ballet revival produced by Peter Wright. His *Sleeping Beauty*, also for Peter Wright and the SWRB, was, according to Jane King of the *Morning Star*, set luxuriously in the court of the French kings, in the seventeenth century for the christening and Aurora's birthday, and in the eighteenth century for the Prince's vision and the wedding: 'the stage glows with gold and black, and deep, rich colour with magnificent period artefacts and fabulous costumes ... the Lilac Fairy is palely opaline, her fairies topaz, and Aurora a delicately blushing rose. The evil fairy Carabosse is in fiercely shimmering jet.'

This preference for a nineteenth-century visual language can also be seen in Prowse's two very different versions of Racine's *Phèdre* in the 1980s, where he moves from high baroque luxuriance in the Glenda Jackson production to a severe, dark Prussian formalism in the intimate Glasgow revival. That heightened quality of intimacy was apparent in his 1986 production for Opera North of Verdi's *Aida* where the very possibilities of intimacy were enriched, according to Max Loppert in the *Financial Times*, by updating the piece to its time of composition; in praising the liveliest and most intelligent account of the opera he had experienced in ages, Loppert further remarked that 'the richness and sophisticated colour sense of the female costumes (Winterhalter crossed with Delacroix-style orientalism) provide[d] in themselves a lesson in dramatically purposeful design'.

Prowse also isolated for journalist Barbara Newman the two major problems about designing for dance: the necessity of having to keep the stage floor entirely clear, 'a real bore', and of devising inventive costumes that can be moved in an unrestrictive way. 'Those are the two hardest technical problems, not only in dance but in any other form of theatre. It just becomes more rigorous in dance, where they are absolutely unavoidable.' But having risen to these challenges, Prowse has done less ballet as he has directed more of his own drama productions in Glasgow. A remark that exacerbated a good deal of comment was one he made to me shortly before his revival of *The Vortex* opened in London early in 1988: 'Dancers are just winged bimbos. Actors are bimbos, too, of course. But in theatre at least you are dealing with Hamlet and Phèdre. All you're dealing with in ballet is some girl who thinks she might be a fucking swan. And that's not worth dealing with on the long term basis.'

Fidelis Morgan, the writer and actress who was in The Vortex, spoke for many when she said that while the actors at the Citizens were always loyal to Prowse, she felt that he was never loyal to them. In her notebooks, Morgan jotted down that at the first rehearsal of A Waste of Time, the reduced Proust extravaganza of 1980, there were at least six academic degree-holders in the room. In The Vortex, the cast of eight included four published authors (Morgan herself, Maria Aitken, Stephen MacDonald and Derwent Watson, aka Derek Watson, a noted musicologist and 'Uncle Derek' in the pit at pantomime time). The Citizens simply does not employ bimbos, so Prowse's remark is either superficially flippant or carelessly derogatory. I suspect a bit of both, but this is all one with his own determination, perhaps need, to keep himself aloof and apart from his actors.

Directors perfect many variations on the tyranny they exert over actors. There is the screaming bully, the intellectual show-off, the avuncular guru, the feebly acquiescent chairman. Prowse belongs in none of these categories, for his activity as a director, and his attitude towards actors, is fuelled only by the overpowering vision he develops of the work in hand. He once told Cordelia Oliver that he starts work on page one, day one, and busks, though he does know what he wants, finally. He says he never works with people who are not his friends, and regards the chemical mix in the rehearsal room as more important than the presence of talent. He is less interested in actors' looks than he used to be: 'I now want to know if they have the gift of sounding as if they have just thought up what they are saying.'

As influences he cited for Barbara Newman Visconti's regular costume designer, Piero Tosi, collaborator on the film of *Death in Venice*, 'who set a standard which really has never been surpassed, on the historical level and for inspiration of what that character would wear in that situation. Just immaculate, always. Then there's that marvellous designer who did sets and costumes for Fellini, Danilo Donati. He was the greatest of the lot, a really inventive, spectacular designer. Those designers are in a class that we simply do not have − I don't know why. They're probably more literate − Italians are, as a whole. They dress better and eat better and live in nicer places and have better weather, so it probably goes through to the work they do as designers.'

This instinctive Europeanism is part of what attracts him, as a temperamental Anglo-misfit, to Scotland, where he likes the idea of the country negotiating, as proposed by the Scottish National Party, its relationship with the European Community independently of Westminster, although his pathological fear of flying ironically restricts his exposure to European performing arts. He did particularly admire Patrice Chéreau's production of Marivaux's *La Dispute* ('An English director would have done it in Watteauesque costumes and blue light') and Nuria Espert in Victor Garcia's trampoline version of Lorca's *Yerma*, and he counts Peter Brook's *Marat/Sade* in the early 1960s as one of the most exciting things he has ever seen in a theatre. More recently, he sat admiringly through Yuri Lyubimov's production of *Crime and Punishment* 'turning pale green with envy. Nobody in Britain could come up with anything so vigorous and achieved as that. Every problem was given an elegant solution. And when it came down to a show about what you can do with just a door, how it can be mobilised, well, it was totally wonderful.'

With Havergal and MacDonald he shares one absolutely crucial conviction. As he told John Clifford in *The Observer* in 1986, 'Our primary duty is to the audience, not to the playwright'. It sounds paradoxical that a theatre often accused of being arty, or 'irrelevant', is in fact the only theatre in Britain that can make such a categorical and unfashionable statement of its preferred allegiance. You are more likely to hear such sentiments from a commercial West End manager; except that a West End manager cannot possibly have as clearly defined a notion of his audience as does the Glasgow directorate. Their bond is their word.

Of his own work Prowse is reluctant to talk, being proudest of the fact that 'given the wonderful opportunity we had, we made the Citizens work. I would much rather talk about this social aspect. I believe in trying to make Socialism work in a practical way. We put on good shows and we balance our books. We employ a lot of good people and we entertain large numbers of even better ones. So it is possible, I believe, to be politically useful in a non-aligned, non-tub-thumping way.

'I do have a list of twenty great plays in English I still want to do, but I never say what they are because some silly redbrick university arsehole at the RSC will fuck it up and that puts paid to that for another ten years. The Jacobeans are really my forte. I was pleased with the Wildes; I managed to make them into dramas, not just comedies, and gave them a kind of depth they don't in fact have.

'We have a lot of wonderful texts but we tend to reduce them, not use them as springboards, which is what the Europeans do with their limited number of great plays. We tend to trap and diminish Shakespeare, instead of taking him and expanding with him. The RSC is greatly to blame for this. It's a great shame, really, that there are thirty-seven plays of Shakespeare extant. I would much rather there were thirty-seven by John Webster.'

The blowtorch intensity of these remarks is all the more disarming for being inflected through a silken, detached, slightly mannered conversational style. But for all his protestations of dissociation from the mainstream British theatre, the influence of Prowse has been enormous. No other theatre in Britain — except, you might argue, the Royal Court, Olivier's National, or Joan Littlewood's Theatre Workshop — has produced so many outstanding young actors for the film and theatre industry, ranging from David Hayman, John Duttine, Mike Gwilym, Gerard Murphy, Ciaran Hinds and Jonathan Hyde, Patti Love, Suzanne Bertish, Pauline Moran and Sian Thomas; right through to Pierce Brosnan, Gary Oldman, Tim Roth and Rupert Everett, Charon Bourke and Yolanda Vasquez (who has shown a marked tendency to live up to the exotic promise of her name). Prowse, if you like, has styled and nurtured these young artists, picked them in the first place for their propensity to dazzle. '*Étonnez-moi* ' was Cocteau's famous injunction to his fellow artists, and Prowse expects no less from his anointed novitiates.

Consider, too, the impact he has had on a whole generation of British designers. However much he may affect disapproval of their work once they have fled his clutches, he does admit to being inordinately proud of all his design protégés, and especially the first two he encouraged and employed at Glasgow, Sue Blane and Maria Bjornson, both of whom remain palpably Prowse-influenced. Blane is a particularly witty costume designer, but her large-scale, spaciously well distributed setting for the National's *Good Person of Sichuan* in 1989 also repaid a neo-Meyerholdian debt to Prowse in continuing the grim concrete architecture of the Denys Lasdun building onto the stage; she went even further by incorporating the tramps and winos of the South Bank's notorious 'Cardboard City', thus renewing Brecht's sardonic images of poverty for the self-help enterprise culture of Mrs Thatcher's Britain. Bjornson's work in opera is a variation on Prowse's nineteenth-century brutal lushness, but she reached an ingenious, technology-driven apogee with her designs for Andrew Lloyd Webber's *Phantom of the Opera* in 1986, a deftly conceived riot of swags, curtains, gilded ornamentation, the sensational materialising of the half-masked phantom in a dressing-room mirror, and the magical apparitions of the Opéra's grand staircase and its underground, candle-lit lake.

Both Geoff Rose, responsible for many of the most

delightfully atmospheric designs in the Bush Theatre, London, and Stewart Laing, recently Prowse's head of design at Glasgow (Prowse himself is now listed as a director), started out at the Citizens as scene-painters. As a place to learn the design trade, it is ideal. The theatre still has a fully operational painting gallery with a frame for hanging the stage cloths (in most theatres today, the cloths have to be painted on the floor); the last surviving Scottish wooden understage, ranked in the top half-dozen in Britain, where there are lots of perfectly preserved slots to project and contain painted scenery; the remains of two star traps (from the old pantomime days, when the demon and good fairy would shoot up on opposite sides of the stage) and of various thunder runs; and three full-width stage traps, or bridges, as well as a grave trap at the front that comes in handy for *Hamlet*.

Most sets, budget permitting, are built from new timber in the on-site workshop, and all costumes made in the wardrobe and, once used, stored in three packed draughty rooms nestling under the wooden eaves of the theatre roof. With the rehearsal room also situated at the top of the Citizens, a pleasant barn-like arena with views of the Clyde bridges only partially obscured by new building, the whole place is geared to the practical job of putting on theatre, and is therefore ideally suited to the training of budding backstage apprentices. As well as Laing, other talented new designers brought on by Prowse in this hothouse environment include Kenny Miller, who has revealed a penchant for the Gothic and monumental side of Prowse's work, and Kathy Strachan who, in her collaborations with Jon Pope towards the end of the 1980s, made some spirited, eerily atmospheric investigations into the structure of the stage area itself, designing right into the side and back walls, as indeed Prowse himself has done on occasion. We may expect many more design developments in the 1990s, as the last stage of the renovations has included the installation of a counter-weight system thus enabling designers to fly scenery in and out, something largely denied them to date: a large piece of scenery used to be pulled creaking into the roof by six people on the end of a rope; now the job can be done by one person.

Robert David MacDonald

Robert David MacDonald, playwright, dramaturg, director, translator and occasional actor, was born in Elgin in 1929 and educated at Wellington School, Oxford University and the Royal College of Music. His family were once well-known tobacco importers in the city – MacDonald's of Glasgow, est. 1840 – so his Glaswegian connections are, if not impeccable, certainly valid. He has worked professionally as both pianist and conductor. He did three years' National Service in the Army, before Oxford, and spent two years at the Conservatory in Munich studying conducting. After that he claims he spent a few years 'wandering around' before taking a job as a translator with UNESCO.

MacDonald told Cordelia Oliver in a 1979 *Plays and Players* interview that if, as a theatrical translator, you cannot get the letter *and* the spirit right then 'you ought to go back to the Berlitz or think about another career . . . I trained on reports about the wheat yield in the Argentine

131

where, incidentally, there *is* no spirit and if you get the letter wrong you are likely to upset the economic count of nations for years to come.' Dictionary and computer-style translation has its dangers, too, he continued, citing what happened when the Russians fed the line 'The spirit is willing but the flesh is weak' into a computer and the result came out as 'The whisky is good but the meat has gone off'.

A self-taught linguist, claiming fluency in at least eight tongues, he first met the German theatre director, Erwin Piscator, in 1957, while working with UNESCO. He became more intensely interested in theatre under the influence of this outstanding intellectual proponent of an engaged political theatre. His first, accidental, practical theatrical involvement was as a director of a production of Benjamin Britten's *Noye's Fludde* at the Berlin Festival for which he had been hired initially as the conductor. He later worked as an assistant director at both Glyndebourne and Covent Garden.

In 1962 Piscator was appointed director of the Volksbühne in West Berlin, a few months after the documentary dramatist Rolf Hochhuth had paid him a first visit. In the following year he directed Hochhuth's *Der Stellvertreter*, about the alleged indifference of Pope Pius XII to the fate of the persecuted Jews during the last war, and the play became a topic of heated argument and controversy all over Europe. MacDonald, who was now to become a close colleague of Hochhuth, prepared the English translation of the play we know as *The Representative*, first performed by the Royal Shakespeare Company at the Aldwych Theatre, London, in 1963; he

Opposite:
Gerard Murphy,
Ciaran Hinds and
Jill Spurrier in
Chinchilla.
Overleaf:
The dance goes on
in *Semi-Monde*.

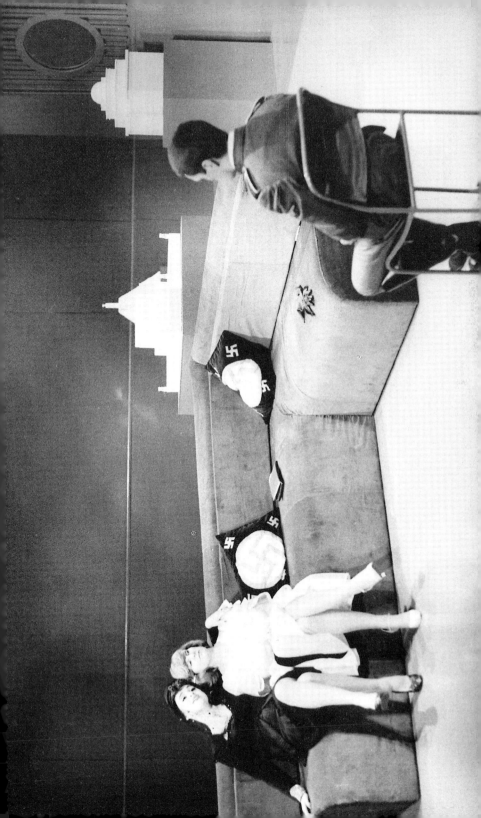

also translated the subsequent *Soldiers*, produced after Piscator's death, in which Churchill was tendentiously implicated in the aeroplane crash that killed General Sikorski. This led to a most enormous row at the National Theatre, where Kenneth Tynan, Olivier's literary manager, was keen to produce the play but was prevented from doing so by an incensed NT board; Tynan took the play to a commercial producer, Michael White, who presented *Soldiers* in the West End in 1969.

One of Piscator's most famous adaptations was of Tolstoy's *War and Peace*, which he struggled for many years to have produced in America and London. When he finally did so himself, in Berlin, he was heavily criticised for telescoping so vast and sprawling a novel into a single evening of theatre. MacDonald – whose own translation of the Piscator *War and Peace* ran for two seasons on Broadway and received an Emmy Award when shown on American television – was to prove just as ambitious, some would say just as foolhardy, in his work on such seemingly intractable material as Karl Kraus's *The Last Days of Mankind*, Proust's *A la Recherche du Temps Perdu*, and Tolstoy's *Anna Karenina*.

Overleaf:
Julia Blalock,
Ann Mitchell and
Garry Cooper in
Summit Conference.
Opposite:
Laurance Rudic
and Ciaran Hinds in
*Painter's Palace
of Pleasure.*

MacDonald had been based in England, where he was appointed director of Her Majesty's repertory theatre, Carlisle, in 1960 and went to America in 1967 as a freelance director in Chicago, Houston, Minneapolis and Atlanta. What he had certainly acquired from Piscator was the Brechtian belief in the collaborative nature of theatre, so he welcomed the chance to join Havergal's new venture when the call came in 1972; he had already worked on at least half a dozen productions with

Havergal at both Barrow and Watford. He retains not an iota of self-importance as a writer. He told Cordelia Oliver, this time in *Plays* magazine in 1984, that 'the author is not even *primus inter pares*; he is only part of the *pares*. There are only two essential elements, an actor and an audience, and it is the duty of everyone else to see that the actors are presented to the audience in the most interesting, advantageous and accessible light possible ... If every theatre fell down tomorrow I don't suppose that more than about two per cent of the population would be more than momentarily inconvenienced. Does that worry me? Not in the slightest.'

He wrote his first original play, *Dracula*, for the Citizens in 1972 and has since translated and directed for them plays by Goldoni, Lermontov, Chekhov, Racine, Beaumarchais, de Musset, Sartre, Cocteau, Schiller and Goethe. The German connection in his work culminated, perhaps, in his 1982 translation of Goethe's rarely seen *Torquato Tasso*, the only major contribution in Britain to the 150th anniversary of Goethe's death. And in 1984, in a ceremony held in Glasgow's City Chambers, he was awarded the Goethe Medal by the Goethe Institute in Munich, whose citation read: 'Robert David MacDonald has given new perspectives to the transfer of German culture into the English-speaking world and built bridges of understanding between our two peoples.' Cordelia Oliver supplied an illuminating monograph and Georg Heuser, director of the Glasgow branch of the Institute, complimented MacDonald on receiving the only cultural decoration awarded by the Federal Republic; his fellow recipients that year were two academic professors, one Russian and one Hungarian.

MacDonald's original plays include *Summit Conference*, *Chinchilla* and *Webster*. Like *Chinchilla*, *Webster* (1983) discusses the colouration of the creative life by the personal, and also the pain of authorship. It is much the most autobiographical of MacDonald's plays and portrays the stress on the dramatist's stable domestic life by his weakness for passing homosexual attractions. Hardly anything is known of the real-life Jacobean dramatist, but MacDonald's John Webster has a Dutch wife and a spastic son who does not speak all evening but sits in a climbing frame dribbling away and stealing the show. Webster is known to have received payments for a lost play, a comedy called *Guise*, and the incinerated script at the end of *Webster* is, you are led to believe, that reputed comedy. Half-way through the writing, MacDonald realised that the lead actor, Ciaran Hinds, was never going to be able to learn it all (the production occurred during a brief period of almost weekly rep), so he allowed Webster to talk like hell in the first act and contrived total silence for him in the second: he was shot in the jaw and wore a huge bandage around his face. Havergal recalls as especially moving a scene between the literally speechless Webster, his wife, Webster's old boyfriend, and his new boyfriend in a rival company of players.

MacDonald's erudition and his Europeanism mark him out as unique in the British theatre, but he masks these characteristics behind a flippant, frostily waspish exterior. Responding, at the time of *Webster*, to the implication that his work does not have any local Scottish

application, he told Joyce McMillan in *The Scotsman*:
'Here we are, supposedly living in an economic community bigger than the Roman Empire, and I just think it's
quite *grotesque*, at this stage in the world's history, to be
fiddling around with parochial concerns.' His repertoire,
he had unapologetically informed John Fowler of the
Glasgow Herald in 1980 is 'funny, dirty, long and
political'.

One of his rare film appearances as an actor was in
David Hare's *Paris by Night* in which he played the British
Ambassador (Sir Arthur Sanderson) in Paris ('a very tall
man with silver hair in his early fifties') who comes to
Charlotte Rampling's (Clara) financial assistance after
she has lost her handbag at the scene of a murder:

SANDERSON. I'm President of the Embassy's Amateur
Dramatic Society. We've rather a hit on our hands. This
is last night's take.

CLARA. How convenient.

SANDERSON. Well, we're doing *Sailor Beware*. The
French just love it.

CLARA. I don't know it.

(SANDERSON *signals the* CHAUFFEUR *to leave.)*

SANDERSON (*Quietly*). I have the best part.

MacDonald is indeed tall and imposing and slightly
alarming, with a good head of white hair enforcing a
resemblance to a gaunter, racier version of the poet

Stephen Spender. Like Prowse, he was once a ferociously dedicated smoker, but he too has now renounced the weed. One of our most substantial conversations took place in the administration offices of the newly refurbished theatre, where he was playing that night in Philip Prowse's adaptation of Dickens's *A Tale of Two Cities*, a production in honour of the bicentenary of the French Revolution. MacDonald played the aristocratic Marquis whose cruelty and indifference – qualities he conveys effortlessly on stage – assume a symbolic significance in the political upheaval. I have in this instance preserved the interview format, stitching together the hard core of several conversations, chiefly because I wanted fully to convey the aroma of MacDonald's talk, which corresponds almost exactly to the style in which he writes. This style he has described, with some justification, as a kind of 'gutter mandarin'.

MC. Of all the foreign plays in the Citizens' repertoire, it seems that only those of Brecht have not been translated by you. Why?

RDM. I don't translate him simply because the Brecht estate is so irritating. Living authors are all right, dead authors are OK too, as long as they have been dead a long time. It's the keepers of the sacred flame who are so intolerable. *A propos* of Pirandello, Marta Abba is, or at least was, a real case in point. And, today, there is Brecht's daughter, Barbara, of course, who is really like Bridget D'Oyly Carte crouched over her property; but it's not just her – there is also Stefan Brecht, the son, in New York. It's all rather like the division of the Roman Empire, with the Empress Theodora in Byzantium! But you just can't say, obviously, that Brecht didn't exist. Everybody has been influenced by him; the least you can do is step carefully around him. Having said that, I am translating *Mother Courage* because Glenda Jackson wanted me to. And it's becoming increasingly unusual for the estate to turn down a new translation.

MC. How did you meet Hochhuth and what is it that attracts you to his work?

RDM. I was introduced to him by Piscator and we did *The Representative* together in London, and then he asked me to work on the Churchill play. We have always got on well, and remain great and good friends. I like very much the hard, flinty centre of his work and admire the genuine Protestantism of it, a very rare quality in the theatre. There are difficulties: the immense over-length, the discursiveness, the fussiness about undeniable facts, if not the deniable ones. But you just slash and cut away at all that in rehearsal. We gave the world première of *Judith* in Glasgow, a play about the assassination of an American president; I don't understand why it hasn't been done more elsewhere. The point about all of his plays, and especially *The Representative*, which I regard as a major classic, and certainly the most interesting and important play since and about the last war, is that they get better as they get older. The same is true of *The Crucible* by Arthur Miller, which is richer as it gets further away from the immediate application of the McCarthy witch-hunts and becomes just a great play about an insoluble dilemma.

MC. Why is it that Hochhuth remains unpopular in Britain?

RDM. There is a terrible tendency in Britain to practise what I call Equity Socialism. This is a fairly vapid form of left-wingery, very immature and idealistic, and fiercely parochial. And of course with Hochhuth, you do need a grid of historical reference to understand him; most people in the British theatre are pig ignorant.

MC. But we do tend to be justifiably suspicious of plays that toy with historical accuracy and rejoice in tendentiousness.

RDM. Every fact is interpretable. I don't think Hochhuth can be accused of the falsification of history. He can, I suppose, be accused of selecting his facts to fit a thesis. But so can every single historian from Gibbon onwards. The central theses of *The Representative* and *Soldiers* had both been written about before the plays were done; in the case of *The Representative*, indeed, the issue had been aired on the stage, in a play by Armand Gatti. Hochhuth comes along and the issue explodes; which of course is very good to have happen in the theatre.

MC. Do dramatists have a time that comes again? Genet, for instance?

RDM. I don't think Genet's time is of this moment. We have done him, of course, but I, personally, have to confess to finding him most luminously silly. His metaphors are sensational and then everything is spoilt by over-writing of a kind which really even the French should fight shy of. I would never direct a play of his because I am not in sympathy with him; with writers I admire, I know I can take certain liberties — which are, I hope, automatically in the right spirit. With Genet I would merely do a competent, professional job. I find the working out of his metaphors flatulent and wearisome.

MC. Sartre has become even more of a closed book in British theatre.

RDM. I have only done *Altona* though I would like to do many more. It is perfectly true that a playwright can seldom write novels, or a novelist, plays. But Sartre, almost alone in my view with Pirandello, could do both extremely well. Sartre can do anything. He was attuned to all the echoes of his civilisation and was simply the biggest brain around. Rather like Goethe, he was, for twenty years, the cleverest man in the world. If you now compare him with other French dramatists who were done during my youth — Anouilh, Giraudoux, for instance — he is a giant. The others were dilettantes. I'm not against dilettantism (God knows, I practise it all the time), and Anouilh is not unsalvageable, but he does now come out pretty thin. Even Cocteau, God help us, comes out thicker than Anouilh. The thing about

Cocteau is his ideas; all the ideas people have now, Cocteau had around 1914, when they were all ludicrously out of place and out of period. But, like Picasso, Cocteau was endlessly fertile and inventive.

MC. Is your dramaturgy a systematic progress through the world repertoire, or simply a case of finding a play for ten people at the end of the next month?

RDM. Both. People of my generation regard that sort of pragmatism as part and parcel of the job, whereas the practical considerations of matching plays to actors' availability just wouldn't occur to anybody in what I would call a properly funded theatre, as in Vienna, where there are massed storm units of dramaturgs; I mean, there are more people in the dramaturgs' office there than we have on the stage in Glasgow!

MC. Would you prefer that system?

RDM. No. We work very informally here, and I prefer that. As a dramaturg I occasionally say 'You must be mad to cut that', but I don't sit around fighting for the purity of my text.

MC. How do you live as a dramaturg in Britain?

RDM. Precariously. Once you start, if you're any good, people ask you to do things, and you can suggest things, too. I've just lobbed a very interesting 1930s Serbo-Croat play at the BBC Radio Drama department.

That is an entirely unknown language in Britain. The bane of all translation here is that it is undertaken, like almost everything else in the theatre, by ignoramuses. It simply is not enough to get a big name and put it on a poster, as in 'Edward Bond translates *Three Sisters*'. Edward Bond is doing nothing of the kind; Edward Bond is actually having a very nice time with five literal or previous translations and may or.may not think he's got it right.

MC. Which language goes easiest into English for stage purposes?

RDM. It is not so much the language itself but the quality of the text. The better the literature, often the less satisfying the result. For instance, the last speech in Goethe's *Faust* does absolutely defy all attempts at translation; you can only ever get a version that suits the production you are doing at the time. Which is why I have always said that translations should have a radioactive half-life and an auto-destruct factor once the production is over. I don't mind publishing my work, because we all have to make a living, but I would never undertake a new production with an existing translation.

MC. What do you feel when somebody else uses your translation, for instance of your *Mary Stuart* by Schiller?

RDM. I'm not really interested what happens to it.

Children have to make their own way in the world, don't they? I did see my version of Beaumarchais' *Figaro* the other day and I could not believe the awfulness of what I saw, though it pleased me to see the translation standing up pretty well.

MC. Is Goldoni or de Musset lighter and therefore easier than Schiller or Goethe?

RDM. No, you just have a different set of problems. You always have to go for what painters call the *tinta*. If you take a good Teutonic, that's to say, heavy comedy, such as Kleist's *The Broken Jug*, you have to lighten it up, ironise it I suppose, because irony is not something the Germans go in for a lot. But you do have to respect the essential gravity of the piece, its specific density. The French go in for an awful lot of irony, which I often find I have to calm down. I think it's important to make sure that people realise that they are watching something foreign. The real mistake is to try and make something acceptably English. Dürrenmatt, for instance, would have had more success in Britain if only translators had acknowledged his 'foreign-ness', his 'non-Englishness'.

MC. Why is Goldoni such a favourite of yours?

RDM. Because he is the virtuoso of the superficial. In a theatre you can only judge people by what you see and hear ; it is not the point to watch them think, they must either say things or do things. Everything in Goldoni is

143

there in either action or word. This is a great skill shared by few people, of whom Raymond Chandler would be another. People never think in Chandler, they say or they do. It's absolutely marvellous: 'I lit a cigarette. I smacked him in the face.' This is nothing to do with the profundity or otherwise of the work; it's just that there is no subtext. I suspect there is no subtext in most things. If an actor asks of a character something for which there is no concrete evidence in the text, then he is probably obscuring the clean lines the author has provided. You never have this difficulty with Goldoni: the clarity is like glass, it's wonderful. The characters exist entirely in their situation.

MC. What if an actor comes along and wants to discuss what a character was doing in a previous scene or year, or what he might have had for breakfast.

RDM. You discourage him very firmly. It is utterly unimportant, and he will obscure the play. I've got many more Goldonis I'd like to do, in fact I'd like to do one a year until I drop, and that would still leave me well short of the entire canon. Something like *Villegiatura* is of course a complete masterpiece; the reason why people get Goldoni hopelessly wrong in Britain is that they do not realise that all the good qualities are on the surface, where they properly belong.

MC. Are you remotely sympathetic to the notion that novels should not be adapted for the stage?

RDM. Not at all. The bigger and better the book, the less the translation of it to the stage matters. Which is why it is a very good idea to adapt *War and Peace, Anna Karenina, The Old Curiosity Shop, Nicholas Nickleby* and Proust. Fiction is fiction, whether it's prose, drama or musical. They're all the same, they're all not true. If one is obsessed by what one is reading, and if one works in the theatre, then that's where it all comes out. But not always. The people I admire most (apart from Dickens) are Jane Austen and Thomas Mann, but they defy treatment in the theatre and I would never do them.

MC. When you adapted Proust, it was not a question of filleting the highlights, but rather of distilling the atmosphere of memory into an almost tactile sense of experience. How did you set about reducing a literary work of that length to four-and-a-half hours of rough-ish theatre?

RDM. You don't reduce it. You first of all have to be working with a lot of people who all agree with you about how great a writer Proust is. Once that's done, you are free to practise all sorts of insolences upon him, free to take gigantic liberties. The quality of our adaptation became indivisible from the expression of a particular company of actors and artists at a particular time. This is where the whole process becomes both interesting and intangible. This happened, too, with Coward's *Semi-Monde* and Kraus's *The Last Days of Mankind*, where there were thirty people on the stage. The essence of a company will take over the essence of a play and all plays will, sooner or later, tend to become plays about theatrical companies, rather like Chekhov. All Chekhov's plays seem to me to be about out-of-work actors, and certainly all of his characters behave like out-of-work actors.

MC. *Chinchilla*, your play about Nijinsky and Diaghilev, was very much a metaphorical piece about the life of a company. Do you always like to cut your suits according to the cloth you can afford?

RDM. Yes. *Chinchilla* was a metaphor for the company as then constituted, as well as a statement about why and how one does things in art. *Webster* was a sourer sequel. Lermontov's *Maskerade* I had wanted to do for a long time and when we had an actor here who could do it, Mark Lewis, and be twenty-five instead of, as is usual in Russia, forty-five, we went ahead. I often wait for the right actor. I am biding my time to do one of the Arlecchino plays, but will only do it when an actor called Rupert Farley is available again. I used to talk a lot to Kenneth Tynan, when he was Laurence Olivier's dramaturg at the National Theatre, about doing Karl Kraus's *The Last Days of Mankind*, but the time was never right until I came here.

MC. Tynan used to have a list of 400 plays he thought any National Theatre should be interested in putting on. Why is it that seventeen years after Tynan left the National, British dramaturgy is so insular and we remain, on the whole, so pitifully cut off from the world repertoire?

DM. It is pitiful, but it is changing. I very much admire the exploratory work done in the classical repertory by a small, flexible company like Cheek by Jowl (I should add that I regard the Citizens to be small and flexible too). In contrast, the National Theatre is like the Vatican, or a battleship that cannot turn round in its own length. Some of the young directors such as Steven Pimlott, who did Botho Strauss's *The Park* at the Sheffield Crucible, Nicholas Hytner, Declan Donnellan and David Freeman (of Opera Factory) are at least talking European. They tend towards the condition of Euro-snobs, which is preferable to that of the Euro-phobes. There is growing evidence of a widening of interest. The predominant dislike, though, of foreign work in Britain stems from one simple fact: our ignorance of the languages. You cannot have access to foreign work if you cannot read it.

MC. Are you in a position to do anything about this fundamental problem?

RDM. 'If I had world enough and time . . .' Richard Eyre, the new director of the National Theatre, did invite me to go there as controller of the foreign repertoire, but I said that if I do find something good that is worth doing, you will be the *second* person to hear about it! Anything I want to do will be done in Glasgow. I'd love to be able to take on a trainee dramaturg here, but you do have to be polyglot, and you do have to be able to read plays and understand the practical nature of theatre. Dramatic dialogue is an extremely difficult thing to render in a different language. Take Russian, a very accessible language. In Britain there is only one writer, apart from myself, who can do it, and that is Michael Frayn, and that is because he is a dramatist in his own right and he speaks very, very good Russian. He knows what he's doing. Edward Bond, a dramatist, cannot do it; Elisaveta Fen, a translator, cannot do it. You need that precious fusion of the two skills. When I did a version of *The Seagull*, I read all the dreadful translations we have and noted how tradition irons in all sorts of errors. The result is that I am the first British writer to actually get the last line of *The Seagull* right. The line is *not* 'Konstantin has shot himself', but 'Konstantin has finally managed to shoot himself'. Chekhov uses a perfective verb.

MC. That is a detail of some crucial importance. So you are a purist yourself on some matters.

RDM. On the matters that really matter. But, generally, I suspect that purists, people who like to think of themselves in such a way, have no business being anywhere near the theatre. Theatre is an extremely eclectic, vulgar, entirely modish form of art. It has nothing to do with anything except what people happen to want that evening, and if a political event can change those expectations, then we can say that the merits of a particular performance are changed, too. I remember seeing the musical *How To Succeed In Business Without Really Trying* on the night that President Kennedy was assassinated. The whole piece had changed, the merits and demerits toppled over and re-arranged by an outside event. Now a place where that can happen is no place for purists, is it? Nor should it be.

MC. What about the purity of a received text, a high comedy for instance, how free do you feel to tamper with that?

RDM. I used to think you should do every word of a play, but I'm not interested in that kind of purity any more. I cut one whole third of *She Stoops to Conquer* and I defy anyone to have spotted where. I just took out every third word. You have to. Our reactions to jokes are so fast now because of our ability to absorb so quickly a bombardment of images on television and advertising posters. The main thing, if you are going to have words in the theatre, is to have marvellous words. The wordsmith dramatists – Coward, Orton, Wilde, Shaw, myself to a lesser extent – all have a marked, mandarin style that goes down very well with our audiences. Like the Irish, the Scots dearly love 'a good crack', a pile of words, an extravagant flourish. They also quite like having buckets of blood thrown over them, but we don't seem to do that as often as we used to.

MC. You say plays end up as statements of a company ethos, but don't they have to be about something else as well?

RDM. All plays are about politics, sex and death. If they are not, they tend to be jolly boring.

MC. Do you enjoy going to the theatre?

RDM. I do not go and see other plays unless I have to. And if I do go and see a friend in something, I will always leave after half an hour if I have no evidence before me of an obsession in the production. On this subject, I rather go along with Brahms who, when asked about going to concerts, replied that if he wanted to listen to some good music he was more than capable of staying at home and writing it himself.

THE 1980s: NOVELS AND NOVELTIES

Much of the most significant work in the British theatre of the past ten years was in the field of adaptation from fiction. There was nothing novel in the transference of books to the stage, but the widespread phenomenon in the 1980s amounted almost to a substitute for the deluge of big new public plays that never arrived on the large stages.

Having pointedly withdrawn from the 'new writing' issue in British theatre, the Citizens nonetheless led the way in what was, after all, a European speciality: the staging of great literature. The decade opened with the theatre's most hubristic project to date, a version of Marcel Proust's *A la Recherche du Temps Perdu*, laconically re-titled *A Waste of Time*. Prophetically, the action was contained within an arrangement of gilded frames, a design feature imitated throughout the British theatre over the next ten years.

This was also the era when, in finally breaking the shackles of the new social and theatrical realism of the 1950s and 1960s, theatre returned to a sense of its own 'theatre-ness'. The need to do so was articulated most memorably by Richard Eyre when he took over at the

National Theatre; politics, social conscience and agitprop were out, or at least relegated below the determination to survive by emphasising the positive aspects of theatricality.

There was nothing new in such a manifesto at the Citizens. The theatre was the market-leader in theatricality. Its approach was more widely appreciated in the 1980s, not just because the Havergal regime had survived for so long, but because its style and priorities became more recognisably consistent with the ambitions of other practitioners.

In moving from the Proust to an important Genet retrospective, the Citizens unleashed a new gestural and theatrical energy when they turned to Shakespeare and the Jacobeans. Parallel with *these* explorations ran a gorgeously rich seam of work by Philip Prowse in the higher reaches of the literary theatrical repertoire of Shaw, Coward and Wilde. The Proustian wheel came full circle with another landmark production of the 1980s, a version of Tolstoy's *Anna Karenina*; and we shall see how the adaptation craze elsewhere informed, and indeed transformed, the directing career of Giles Havergal.

Memories of Proust among the blockbusters

On the last Friday of February 1980, the Glasgow Citizens, after two months' writing and three weeks' rehearsal, presented *A Waste of Time*, Robert David MacDonald's three-and-a-half hour version, directed and designed by Philip Prowse, of *A la Recherche du Temps Perdu* ; with a cast of eighteen actors, and at a cost (set, costumes, wages) of £10,406, it ran for just one week and won no awards, though it did return to Glasgow for three weeks in September 1981 after a short tour to Holland.

Three months after the première, the RSC presented, in June 1980, after a year's work, David Edgar's adaptation of Dickens's *Nicholas Nickleby*, directed by Trevor Nunn and John Caird, as a joyous exercise in third-person company narrative; the show was triumphantly revived within the year, won every award going, was filmed for television, and transferred to Broadway.

Both *A Waste of Time* and *Nicholas Nickleby* heralded the return of the spectacle, the renewal of the idea of 'theatre as event'. Andrew Lloyd Webber's creative decade began a year later with *Cats*, the most successful of all musical 'happenings', and *Nicholas Nickleby*, which in many ways apotheosised the RSC of the 1970s under Trevor Nunn, made possible the blockbuster RSC musical of *Les Misérables* in 1985.

With the Royal Court placed under increasing economic pressure, and the RSC seeking economic salvation in showbiz, new writing dwindled in the 1980s. The RSC presented David Edgar's *Maydays* on its brand new Barbican stage in 1983, but the company's best new oratorical and prophetic writing (notable seasons of Edward Bond and Howard Barker, two good Poliakoffs) was hidden away in The Pit, the RSC's studio theatre, and thus robbed of significance. Not until Terry Hands belatedly directed Peter Flannery's *Singer* in the Swan at Stratford-upon-Avon in 1989 was there a second big new RSC play worthy of the name.

The situation gave a new twist to Parkinson's Law: the audience's appetite for new drama contracted just as the theatre's own desperation for commercial survival intensified. The Arts Council wanted to see full theatres at any cost and believed (wrongly, as I'm sure will be seen at the end of the century, which may well coincide with the end of the repertory theatre system) that unpretentious, unambitious, non-risky programming was the answer. The Royal Court found itself unable to adjust to the new political climate and was forced to reduce its output by the end of the decade to as little as four major new plays a year.

Squeezed by economics, 'new writing' was also removed from the agenda by the artists themselves, in favour of 'new theatre'. There was a concerted upsurge of interest in new physical forms of design, dance, musical and narrative aesthetics, and in the psychology of performing: an overall sense of the need to re-create the theatre and, in so doing, to reclaim the past. The predominant metaphor was of a return to childhood.

This could be seen in the quasi-Victorian/Edwardian fantasies of groups like Hesitate and Demonstrate and Impact Theatre, where a mood of cultural dislocation and disenchantment was compensated for by comforting, but distant, images of infancy and adolescence, the nursery, the secret garden, Paradise before and immediately after the Fall. There were larger, more exhaustively combative precedents for these stage obsessions in the startling, physically expressive and deeply influential work of Pina Bausch, based at Wuppertal in the Ruhr valley industrial belt, and of Jan Fabre in Antwerp.

While critics in London bemoaned the lack of new plays at the end of the 1980s, they seemed unaware that many of the artistic criteria had changed. Quite simply, the goal posts had been moved onto another pitch, where extraordinary work was being undertaken by such experimental new diggers among the collective memory as Steve Shill and Gary Stevens. The latter's *Animal*, for instance, dallied with the literally unspeakable, the beast beneath the stairs, in its proposition that children are treated like cuddly toys and pets like children; the social comment was seamlessly entwined with its physical representation, the five humans emerging from a sea of fluffy nylon bears and bunnies before being finally displaced by a group of little wind-up toys running wild from their Hamleys paper bags. Gary Stevens, a curious, other-worldly Gene Wilder clone, stepped, goggle-eyed, possessed and daft, into the limelight. His hour had come.

Recollections of childhood, its fears and expectations, are one of the prime concerns of memory. And art has always found ways of formalising the tricks of memory. The Renaissance theatre utilised a complicated system of mnemonics that corresponded to both theatre architecture and an audience's knowledge. Partly thanks to Shakespeare, and certainly by the end of the nineteenth century, theatre had become fascinated by a more subjective use of memory in accounting for individual behaviour. The phenomenon of memory itself, its tendency to distort and reconsider the past in the harsher light of the present, became one of the great artistic subjects. And, in the case of Proust, the greatest subject of all.

A Waste of Time extended the principle of soliloquy

155

into a full-scale theatrical event, just as Eastern European directors like Andrzej Wajda and Yuri Lyubimov extended Dostoevsky and *Hamlet* into new realms of subjective *mise-en-scène*. The action was set at that moment in the last volume when Marcel returns to society and, surrounded by the ancient marionettes of the Guermantes salon, is given a terrifying peepshow of the years. This salon, a hauntingly doomed and flamboyant arena clearly related to such other Prowse playgrounds as the St Petersburg gaming halls in *Maskerade* and the mirrored Ritz in *Semi-Monde*, was contained within five great gilded picture frames, one inside the other, each providing an increasingly raised stage level. An actress recited from *Phèdre* among the evening-dressed 'audience' seated at small tables and was received with muffled applause.

Marcel, in the hunched, drained and stricken figure of Steven Dartnell, pivoted away from the scene and saw that Gilberte was in grey; his love for her had been but a habit, a dream. Over there was the dreadful Madame Verdurin, coarse and loud, hair bunched in a ginger mop. That wretched Vinteuil sonata would give her a headache, she screamed, and it was played, softly, while Marcel asked a prim little Andrée what exactly it was she used to do with Albertine – and how often. Dartnell's Marcel, passive and asthmatic, had his life recreated for him by the production as an act of memorial vivacity rather than, as in Proust, by his own determination to erect, at last, an artistic monument. A motto of Kierkegaard was quoted in the programme: 'Life is lived forwards but it is understood backwards.' The onion, memory, was peeled to the insubstantial centre. At the end, a chicken was chased, a church bell tolled by the garden gate, Marcel wrestled Gilberte in a fumbling, childish embrace.

A Waste of Time was as important a summation of the Citizens' work since 1969 as *Nickleby* was of the RSC's under Nunn. But the Citizens' task had been so much harder and so much greater, with less money and less time. And yet there was no need to make any allowances. It was an evening of stunning beauty and mesmerising enchantment. When, in 1955, Kenneth Tynan had reviewed Orson Welles's stage adaptation of *Moby Dick* ('which dwarfs anything in London since, perhaps, the great fire'), he suggested humorously that Welles might only be confined by such merely possible things as Proust or *War and Peace*. MacDonald, having tackled the latter in Piscator's version, had no fears about the former, even though the conception was, in the first place, Prowse's. The Citizens' Proust proclaimed a whole succession of 'merely possible things', ranging from the darker recesses of the Jacobean repertoire to more de Sade, Karl Kraus, de Rojas' *Celestina*, another great Tolstoy and the Grand Daddy of all supposedly unstageable projects, Goethe's *Faust*.

The point, though, was not to buckle wildly under the pressure of ridiculous tasks and score marks out of ten for effort, but to extend confidently, within the realms of their own possibilities, the company's indigenous range of aesthetic statement. Jonathan Miller has eloquently objected to the plastering of visible form on characters with whom a reader has already established an intelligible acquaintance, and he rightly derided the slavish and superficial film of *Swann in Love*. But the Citizens took a playful distillation of themes and ideas in Proust and created their own distinctive work on the back of it.

Harold Pinter has said that the happiest working year of his life was spent adapting Proust in a screenplay (which remains un-produced) for the late Joseph Losey; the Pinter version, brilliant in its own way, can bask in the luxury of voice-overs, instant filmic access to Proustian emblems such as hawthorn, steeples, the yellow patch in Vermeer's painting, and has the cinematic advantage of being able to establish mood through silent expression and contrasts of tempi.

The only real luxury available to the Citizens was their own imagination. The narrative was unspooled back-wards, with just enough non-chronological material inserted to keep us informed. Out of this, snapshot scenes sprang to life within the framework – the gaggle of girls on the Normandy coast, Baron de Charlus stalking his prey to the brothel, Swann's declaration of impending mortality, the shattering rejection scene, the invasion of the Faubourg St Germain by louche café manners. Albertine was androgynously split between two actors: the sexually inquisitive Angela Chadfield and the coy Cherubino Rupert Farley (in the 1981 revival, Chadfield was succeeded by Johanna Kirby, and Gary Oldman joined the cast as a dancer). At the centre, quietly painting at her table, sat the Marquise de Villeparisis chivvying Marcel towards a state of self-knowledge. Not only the working of memory, but also the very nature of obsession, was expressed in a jangling, theatrical manner that still did justice to Proust's uninhibited digressions. The discussion of anti-semitism in the wake of the Dreyfus affair was usurped by the critical nailing of salon snobbery; Di Trevis, for instance, a beautiful Odette, marked the ageing process by growing into an insufferably high-flown and vulgarian Madame Swann.

The poet James Fenton had recently started a three-year stint as theatre critic on *The Sunday Times* and was distinctly unimpressed. He regretted his inability to join in the praise elsewhere and, concluding that he found the piece incomprehensible, declared that the project was foolish, revealing more of ambition than of achievement. Fenton was alone, however. Christopher Small, who had become increasingly enthusiastic over the years, said in the *Herald* that the production was the company's finest to date. When he retired in May of the same year, Small had grown large in his praise: the Citizens, he said, were 'unquestionably the most distinguished company working in Scotland, and among the best-known abroad of any British ensemble'.

If the company had created a poetic statement of identity in *Chinchilla*, they had started the 1980s at an instant watershed. But not without a few feathers flying. The Proust had been scheduled for two weeks of performances, but the first week was cancelled after the actors cast to play Baron de Charlus and Swann (Alan Rickman and Paul Bentall, the first new to the company, the second a regular member), quite within their rights, withdrew from the fray at the start of rehearsals. Actors never see scripts of new plays, new translations, or adaptations, before the first day of rehearsal; occasionally, as in this case, the sudden revelation can be either too daunting or too disappointing. A touring company filled the vacant week while Havergal took over as Charlus, and Paul Blake came in as Swann. A disaster had been quickly averted, but the incident presaged the costly mix-up ten years later when Richard Harris, unhappy with the new translation of a play he had desperately wanted to do at the Citizens, withdrew from the opening production of the 1990 programme, *Enrico Four*.

There is a sad post-script to *A Waste of Time*. On 1 December 1989, Steven Dartnell, the hallucinating, asthmatic Marcel, died in Glasgow aged fifty-eight of tuberculosis in a recurrence of a childhood susceptibility. The Proustian echoes are poignant indeed. What was particularly interesting about the unassuming, dedicated Dartnell, as widely respected as a director as he was loved as a man, was that he had been a crucial member of three highly significant movements in the British theatre: George Devine's English Stage Company, Joan Littlewood's Theatre Workshop at Stratford East, and the 1970 Citizens in Glasgow.

Over the top with Genet, de Sade and the Jacobeans

The one speech for which Marlowe's *Massacre at Paris* is famous, encapsulating as it does the Marlovian heroic ethos, indicates the shift at the Citizens from a desire, in part, to shock and offend, to a deeper, wildly exploratory ambition within and beyond the familiar repertoire:

That like I best that flies beyond my reach.
Set me to scale the high Pyramides,
And thereon set the diadem of France,

I'll either rend it with my nails to naught,
Or mount the top with my aspiring wings,
Although my downfall be the deepest hell.

The pinnacle and the abyss, the Faustian polarities, were the temperamental compass points of the Citizens. And the extremes of critical reaction were sure proof that the policy was vital. At all costs, the anodyne and half-baked were to be rejected, and nothing was more despised than the conventional bromide of so much in the British repertory system.

Attacks on the policy were rarer now, but a renewed assault by playwright Donald MacKenzie in March 1980 in the *Glasgow Herald* only succeeded in inspiring an outcry in defence of the Citizens; other Scottish playwrights and the public rallied to the cause, as indeed did Ewan Hooper in his capacity as artistic director designate of the ill-fated Scottish Theatre Company. Thus was the *Hamlet* rumpus turned inside out. The pattern of this decade, in fact, was a growing political and artistic reputation at home, sustained acknowledgement abroad, while London remained sceptical whenever the company, or a related offshoot, penetrated the capital.

But in the rampant 'theatrical' mode induced by the Proust, *Hamlet*, a play of inexhaustible political danger, could still be a subject of scandal and concern. In Scotland, as in most of Britain, times had changed and the florid flouting of convention was no longer that big a deal. But two productions early in the decade caused minor flurries. MacDonald quirkily produced the First Quarto of *Hamlet*, the first professional version of this fascinating text since Ben Greet's in 1933 (although both John Masefield and Kenneth Tynan produced it for the Oxford University Dramatic Society), a counter-play which almost makes you hear the play proper afresh: 'To be or not to be; ay, there's the rub/To die – to sleep – is that all? Ay, all. No; / To sleep – to dream – ay, marry, there it goes.' The play proved short but still exciting, and MacDonald and Prowse set it in a white-walled institution of silent screams, surgical belts, strait-jackets and medical charts. The three inmates were Hamlet, Horatio, and Queen Gertred; Ofelia was a nurse dispensing drugs and sedatives.

What promised to be a piece of academic excavation was overtaken by a consistent vision (asylums had not yet become a design cliché). Andrew Wilde's rasping nutcase of a Hamlet was fiercely committed, a reluctant hero but a powerfully impatient patient. The old objection to loss of neutrality in the presentation of classics was raised in a reader's letter to the *Glasgow Herald*: 'I would not like to think that schoolchildren's first impressions of the play were to be permanently coloured by the experimental.' There did not seem to be so many takers for this point of view in 1980; after all, the world was filling up with resentful theatre-haters whose first impressions of Shakespeare had been permanently coloured by compulsory visits to Perth Rep, the Edinburgh Lyceum, Regent's Park or Stratford-upon-Avon.

The other flurry of controversy was caused by a second de Sade show, *Philosophy in the Boudoir*, which this time attracted attention from the Glasgow branch of Mrs Whitehouse's National Viewers' and Listeners'

Association ('Storm Over City Sex Play' ran a headline in the *Evening Times*). Letters appeared about degradation, the corruption of small girls and the time being right once again for Giles Havergal to go. *Philosophy* was certainly an adult entertainment, and a pleasurably serious one, too. Prowse took the Marquis' 1795 dialogue in which a fifteen-year-old virgin is confirmed in a school of libertinage. The intellectual force of de Sade's arguments is concentrated in the fifth of seven dialogues in which a Republican call to arms is issued by the host; Prowse threaded this treatise through the evening, so that de Sade's views on religion, murder, and family ties (or domestic bondage) are absorbed in the crescendo of young Eugénie's awakening.

The boudoir was inhabited by leatherclad punks dispensing cocaine and tuning up the hi-fi, concocting a world of contemporary coffee-table decadence at odds with de Sade's remote castellated Gothicism. The clash was deliberate and disturbing, but the scientific experimentation became downright hilarious when lights and cameras swung into action to record the simulation of inventive sexual activity enacted to the accompaniment of de Sade's precise clinical descriptions. Eugénie's initiation in, and delighted adoption of, these allegedly natural practices had the dream-like, fantastical quality of a giggling schoolgirl becoming chief whip in a bizarre parliament of members and standing orders. The overall impression was, quite literally, ravishing; when Eugénie's mother turned up, she was degraded by her own daughter, infected by a syphilitic slave and stitched up with a darning needle.

163

And yet, as Joseph Farrell insisted in *The Scotsman*, this was by no means a work of commonplace pornography, adding that voyeurs would be disappointed. This caveat was unnecessarily prim, I felt; after all, cheap thrills have an honourable place in quite respectable drama. But it indicated a response to an underlying seriousness of intent, something that the Whitehouse smut hounds could never acknowledge or understand.

The Genet retrospective of 1982 summarised these obsessional theatrics by extending, in the manner of Meyerhold, the architecture of the theatre into the design itself: the Victorian box designs on either side of the proscenium were reproduced in triplicate on the stage. For *The Balcony*, a decadent Parisian atmosphere was reinforced by red couches, hanging lights, inlaid painted figures, a plethora of sinks and bidets, gilt mirrors, and an assortment of boys in leather shorts, whips and chains. In *The Blacks*, the allegory of colonial power-shifts, Cordelia Oliver noted in *The Guardian*, was set in a stunning 'jungle of dead white trees against a star-studded black skycloth'. And without sacrificing any of the mirror-image sensationalism of the first two plays, the third, *The Screens*, found some pulsatingly resonant parallels between the French-Algerian crisis and the presence of the British Army in Northern Ireland.

As so often, but especially with Genet and de Sade, the company compelled us to consider many variations of pleasure while striking to the heart of a dramatic, perfervid literature that was itself concerned with the twin face of moral tyranny and the survival of the human spirit. Underneath the surface aesthetic lurked a high

Opposite:
Angela Chadfield
and Fidelis Morgan
in *A Waste of Time.*
Overleaf:
Di Trevis in
The Battlefield.

moral principle, and Philip Prowse was to make this crucial link between Genet, the artist-criminal, and Oscar Wilde, the master of masks and un-masking, whose three 'problem' comedies he directed to very high attendance figures. But first Prowse had business with Marlowe and Massinger.

When the RSC opened their third Stratford auditorium, the Swan, in 1986, the intention was to explore the repertoire the company was in danger of forgetting, the plays of Shakespeare's immediate predecessors, contemporaries and successors through to the Restoration. Already, within three or four years, that ideal has been diluted with the addition of Shakespeare himself and of familiar Jacobean and Restoration plays. In spite of some good Ben Jonson and a long overdue revival of Wycherley's *The Plain Dealer*, one felt by 1990 that the idea of contextualising, even revolutionising, the main thrust of the RSC's work in a systematic exploration of revelatory by-ways and hinterland had been too soon ditched. The Citizens' exploratory work in the Elizabethan and Jacobean repertoire would remain essential.

Overleaf:
John Breck,
Gordon Hammersley
(above),
Sian Thomas,
Ida Schuster,
Di Trevis and
Roger McKern in
Don Juan.
Opposite:
Julie Legrand in
The Screens.

As Robert Cushman said in *The Observer* when Prowse directed Marlowe's *Massacre at Paris* in 1981 (five years before the Swan opened its doors), 'No other theatre in Britain would have had the cheek to do this play so well'. The whole of *Tamburlaine* has only sixteen onstage corpses; *Massacre* has twenty (not counting the 100 Huguenots thrown into the Seine), which works out at one every sixty-three lines. The text, claims the Oxford editor, is 'shockingly garbled' and the play devoid of 'either coherence or artistic finish', a view corroborated by

Cordelia Oliver who reckoned the piece 'ought to have remained in the library'.

Prowse, however, was not to be cowed by academic strictures. His design rose by steps from the auditorium into the semblance of a Gothic altar prepared for a funeral, the edifice draped in black and dotted with bunches of candles. The actors arrived like Jacobean conspirators through the stalls, gargling and coughing and arranging their properties. They were to perform before the Virgin Queen, who particularly appreciated the downfall of the Duke of Guise and, by implication, all Papist infiltration sponsored by Philip of Spain. Prowse thus sharpened the proceedings with a keen sectarian edge, and achieved a turbulent farce enacted in a whirl of black and gold for the slaking of Protestant righteousness. There was sudden, casual horror in the molestations ('Come sir, give me my buttons and here's your ear ') that seemed second nature to the cast of just six, led by Robert Gwilym's swaggering black-lipped Duke. There were poisoned gloves, executions by blunderbuss, double stabbings, an accumulating pile of dummy corpses, great jets of blood squirting into the audience, and a murderous friar slithering across the stage to extract vengeance.

Steven Dartnell was in the cast, as was John Breck, a local actor who was to die of a freakish bout of acute epiglottitis in 1984, aged just thirty. He had appeared regularly with the company since 1976 and was remembered especially by Havergal in an obituary not only as various dying Kings of France in *Massacre*, but also as a pair of murderous twins in *Webster*. (Continuity of personnel on stage and off has characterised the Citizens since 1969; it is a fitting memorial to Breck that his younger sister, Roberta Doyle, has been the theatre's press and publicity manager since June 1986.)

Much of the verse in *Massacre* was indeed corrupt and broken-backed, but the weaknesses were subsumed in the gestural magnificence of the whole. And after rare Christopher Marlowe, what better than rarer Philip Massinger? *The Roman Actor*, with which Prowse opened the 1982–83 season, was popular in its day but remembered in the middle of the nineteenth century only for its famous defence of the stage speech. There had been no record of a professional production for 100 years. Prowse reconstructed the barbaric world of Domitian Caesar's Rome in terms of the cinematic killer thriller: the acting area was a sordid dump of wooden platforms, abandoned motor bikes, rotting corpses and a heap of old chairs. The company assembled in flowing raiments and half masks to witness Caesar's abduction of Lamia's wife. Massinger enriched a scenario faithfully based on Suetonius by using the theatre itself as a context for the chilling sequence of murders and revenge motives. Prowse cut one of the three plays-within-the-play while creating an inventive havoc of lust and jealousy with the other two. Simultaneously, he blurred even further Massinger's distinctions between 'reality' and illusion. Once again, the front stalls were awash with blood which squirted out from concealed capsules and a highly visible throat-stabbing. In one extraordinary scene, two cultured senators were subjected to torture by electric drill; the victims laughed in the Emperor's face, providing a Black and Decker comedy of resistance to sadistic vandalism. The soundtrack throbbed with a metallic grinding that represented now the Emperor's mental instability, now the application of torture, now the buzzing of flies in a grotesque charnel house.

The exotic and the sensuously macabre had never been more emphatically done, yet I can report no furious expressions of outrage. Perhaps people now knew what to expect; perhaps the methods of presentation were more refined, mellower. As usual, Prowse achieved an unarguable stylistic consistency, and we must assume that, after ten years or so, the audience had learned how to read his work. The inevitable upshot would be an air of increased sophistication on both sides of the footlights. A contrasting Massinger production by MacDonald put paid, fleetingly, to that.

Although *The Custom of the Country* is collected in the works of Beaumont and Fletcher, it is more probably a collaborative effort between Fletcher and Massinger, a picaresque study of lust and love set in the stews of Lisbon after two brothers and a virgin have left Italy to preserve the latter from the custom of the country, i.e. the *droit de seigneur*, by which a nobleman can sleep with any new bride married on his territory. MacDonald adopted a Hollywood analogy for Lisbon as a centre of decadence, a ruse that was more fun than reverberative. The Jew Zabulon, for instance, who introduces the Italian trio to the low life, was played by the mountainous Ron Donachie (one of several Scots actors who were notable acquisitions throughout this decade of assimilation and consolidation) as none other than Sydney Greenstreet.

His mistress was translated by Fidelis Morgan into Jean Harlow, a slinky bare-backed platinum blonde first seen taking the stage brandishing an Oscar. Gloria Swanson and Mickey Mouse were in there somewhere, too. MacDonald's wackiness was really a diversion from the more serious Citizens business with the Jacobeans. Whatever the agreed priorities on theatricality in the British theatre of the 1980s, the best way to summarise the polarity of approach that existed between Glasgow and mainstream British theatre throughout two decades is to consider two revivals of John Ford's *'Tis Pity She's A Whore*, which opened within a month of each other in early 1988.

At the National Theatre, Alan Ayckbourn's revival was old-fashioned, traditionally costumed, timid and without venom. At the Citizens, Prowse thinned down the sub-plot, transposed the action from Parma to the interior of some great European cathedral, possibly at Toledo or Milan, and imposed a ritualistic acting pace of sinister slow motion. Regrettable cuts included an idiotic suitor's exclamation in his death throes of 'I am sure I cannot piss forward and backward and yet I am wet before and behind.' The difference was that Ayckbourn – who did not cut that line, or anything else – was probably horrified by the play whereas Prowse was gleefully delighted by it.

In Glasgow, bells chimed, thuribles spewed incense, the idiotic suitor became a crippled religious inmate of the cathedral, a mute penitent in the train of the Cardinal, gibbering wordlessly at the Stations of the Cross. A team of hooded sacristans continuously carted coffins and catafalques across the stage as plague and battle took an unseen toll on the life of a ravaged city. Into this fiery furnace were plunged the doomed incestuous couple and their hapless accomplices. The production ended with the gossiping Putana of Fidelis Morgan being incinerated on a bonfire next to the pupil she had betrayed. The intimate scenes were played with furtive blasphemy by Tristram Wymark and Yolanda Vasquez between white traverse screens in the church, as if we had removed merely to the sacristy. The hypnotic imposition of a director's vision both liberated the actors and redoubled the visceral, horrifying quality of the play, with all due regard to its ghastly cackle of laughter when the naked hero turned up with his sister's heart on a sword: one skewered kebab, medium rare, chips optional. Callous, tart, consistent and ferocious, Prowse's production was in a different dimension to the literal, polite doggedness of the London version. The two productions opened within two weeks of each other but might have come from different planets.

The art of artifice, the height of high comedy

Framing devices, whether derived from Prowse's gilded decoration of the Proustian snapshots, or from new responses to Genet and the absurdists, were all part of the new atmosphere. The artifice of form extended to the vernacular of expression. Havergal had shown his own literary nous in his interleaving of *The Importance* texts in 1977; a similarly ingenious process was adopted in his production of John Dryden's *Marriage à la Mode* in 1981, from which he jettisoned the inferior heroic plot while incorporating into the supple prose comedy that remained a condensed version of Dryden's Antony and Cleopatra epic, *All For Love*. This resulted in an intriguing play-within-a-play in which the quartet of lovers became actors performing the tragedy.

This cinematic toying with the reality of perpetrating illusion had been reactivated in the 1980s in the wake of such films as Truffaut's *Day For Night* and *The French Lieutenant's Woman*, which Pinter had scripted from John Fowles. The high-tech renewal of interest in the old illusion/reality axis would lead to some fantastic deconstructions, in Paris and Moscow, of Pirandello in the 1980s, and to Giorgio Strehler's sumptuous interconnected trilogy of Corneille's *L'illusion comique*, Shakespeare's *The Tempest* and Strindberg's *The Storm*. Even British play-wits like David Hare and Michael Frayn, in *A Map of the World* and *Noises Off*, would write plays-within-plays, the first time as comedy, the second time as farce.

So the Citizens can be seen as part of a movement which, while nothing new in itself, was very much to do with this reassertion of the 'theatre-ness' of theatre. Such a campaign was one they had waged anyway since 1970. You never saw in Glasgow a realistic set, a kitchen interior, a character in a cardigan or carpet slippers (except when a touring company came to call). Television could do that; theatre was an event, something different.

Only the Citizens extended this campaign to Brecht, who had been commandeered, in Britain at least, by the po-faced socialist fringe brigade. In Glasgow, the political appeal of Brecht always took care of itself. But the appeal to Havergal, when he directed *Puntila*, lay in the play's craft and dramatic richness, its blatant theatricality. This comic fable of schizophrenia — the eponymous alcoholic landowner is reasonable when drunk, unbearable when sober — was given the perform- ance context of Brecht's own flight to Finland, where he wrote the play on a country estate in 1940 while the Battle of Britain raged far away. Brecht and his family were seen marching through the auditorium with bags slung over their shoulders; the author's guilt and helplessness (cowardice and escapism, cry the anti-Brechtians) were poignantly contrasted with the light, summery playing of the comedy within which Patrick Hannaway as Puntila nonetheless made some precise, double-edged inves- tigations into the nature of tyranny.

The repertory theatre backbone also needed surgery in this context. As the British theatre in the regions resorted to West End re-heats and the admirable, but suburban, modern-dress *œuvres* of Alan Ayckbourn and Willy Russell, the class acts of Shaw, Coward and, especially, Wilde, were subjected to some outstandingly imaginative interpretative readings.

Most suited, perhaps, to the by now renowned Gorbals style of apocalypse in the gardens and salons of the West, was *Heartbreak House* from which Prowse insouciantly expunged in 1985 all regard for Shaw's stage directions, its ship-shaped house (and poop) on the Sussex downs, its nautical and scientific instruments. The design was achingly beautiful even by Prowse's standards: the shadow of the Great War shivered in his forest of suspended red and green discs, creating the effect of an inverted poppy field through which Gerry

Jenkinson's exquisite lighting shot a glimmering sheen of rose and magenta and beyond which could be glimpsed eight lace-curtained windows. Shaw's ship of fools heading for the rocks became a Chekhovian gathering on a dappled lawn, where Rupert Everett as Randall Utterwood was descried in a preliminary mime nicking the family silver off the table. The usual way to play Captain Shotover is as a dominating old mystical sea dog (*vide* the late Rex Harrison and the late Colin Blakely); but MacDonald, whose repertoire would not extend anyway to all of Shotover's seven dimensions, offered a tousle-haired and dyspeptic old cove in garden wellies, an approach that cut the play's more pretentious airs of sonority down to size and left plenty of room for all the other points of view to emerge. Everett's languidly toffish Utterwood was definitive, Patrick Hannaway's bullish Boss Mangan a blood relation of his Brechtian Pierpont Mauler, Jane Bertish (Suzanne's younger sister) and Robert Gwilym (Mike's younger brother) admirable as Lady Ariadne and Hector Hushabye.

There have been other productions of the play where intimations of the Great War were directed into *Heartbreak House* even before the heated anxieties of the antiphonal last scene – Nancy Meckler, for instance, had a soldier in battledress sitting around throughout the action in her 1989 Shared Experience revival – but only Prowse in the British theatre would have designed in the premonitions of carnage so poetically, and then incorporated the regular irruptions of four Tommies who ran, marched and finally staggered diagonally across the stage. Meckler had an idea and left it to thrive as best it may; Prowse thought on a higher inter-connecting plane of design, orchestration and choreography.

After the ecstatic rarity of *Semi-Monde*, it seemed dangerous of the Citizens to fall back on the familiar cut ˙ and thrust of Coward at his very best. *Private Lives* opened on the night a state of emergency was declared in a snow-bound Glasgow in January 1984. A state of euphoria was more like it inside the Gorbals theatre, where the proceedings were supervised around two long pink sofas by the outrageously funny Amanda of Roberta Taylor, who exuded exactly that refined sense of impulsive vulgarity I always imagine Coward responded to in Gertrude Lawrence. Such a play in the Coward canon, a popular war-horse, would not have been countenanced ten years earlier; and it would certainly have been done, if at all, with very young actors. The actors here were middle-aged, but the production still refreshingly out of kilter: Elyot and Amanda played the big row scene through a variety of archly delineated physical poses; the morbid chat sequence about the after-life was played lying flat on the floor, feet propped up on a sofa. Elyot was Robert David MacDonald ('Come and kiss me darling, before your body rots, and worms pop in and out of your eye sockets' has never sounded so lightly macabre); the pedantic Victor, first seen executing a deep-breathing knees-bend routine, Giles Havergal.

Coward here was not a soft option, but a flinty alternative voice, at once modern, clipped and deeply theatrical. But Coward retained the ability to provoke and astonish, as Prowse proved with his brilliant production of *The Vortex* in January 1988. *The Vortex* had been Coward's first play to be produced with any success; it won the playwright overnight celebrity in 1924. Prowse hit a chord by realising that it was, as he said, 'a yuppie piece then, and it's a yuppie piece now'. The listless Nicky Lancaster, a new European, returns home from studying music in Paris in a mood of feckless irritation; Rupert Everett as Nicky, stoned and damned from the moment he entered his mother's boudoir, gave new meaning to the line 'I'm a little beyond aspirin'. The performance injected a study of the pathology of addiction into a play that toyed with the subject of drugs without confronting it directly; the miracle was that the production also sustained the genuine Coward style, its brittleness and fizz, its perennial decadence, while imparting a sense of absolute modernity.

Coward had described the colours and decorations of Florence Lancaster's London flat as 'on the verge of being original'. Prowse covered his own stark black walls with paintings redolent of Juan Gris and Kandinsky (one of them now hangs in the Citizens backstage canteen), adjusting the locations with white sofas and gauze screens, vases of white flowers and, for the final traumatic Oedipal bedroom encounter, a tilting mirror above the silk sheets and pillow-cases. Maria Aitken gave the best performance of her career as Florence; the production was remounted in London, at the Garrick Theatre, at the start of 1989, a delay ironically caused by Aitken's appearance in court to defend, successfully, a charge of cocaine smuggling. She played a woman fighting off loneliness and despair with a hectic determination to stay in the swim, and Prowse supplied her with a stunning array of dresses in pink and black silks, satins and taffetas, as well as a plunging backless white gown for the country house dance. Coward shared with Wilde a delight in dissecting the moral shams and hypocrisies of a society he had gone out of his way to adorn, and Aitken projected an exact and critical sense of being both symptom and victim of the enervating social charades.

Oscar Wilde's decade in London was the 1890s; in Glasgow, the1980s. In more ways than one, the Citizens provided a perfect *fin de siècle* synthesis of two centuries. Prowse's productions of the three problematical melodramas were given at two-yearly intervals, and in reverse order of composition.

Wilde had first read the first three acts of *A Woman of No Importance* to Beerbohm Tree in Glasgow in 1892, when the latter, who had commissioned the play, was on tour there. So you might say that Prowse was completing the job, and he did so in the grand manner, setting all four acts in a great semi-circular walled garden, with gilded pots, banks of daffodils and narcissi, a 'real' lawn. The childhood scars inflicted by absentee or deceptive parents and the question of true identity are themes in all of Wilde's writing, and Prowse found a uniquely resonating way through these areas while doing full justice to the jewelled, aphoristic language. In this respect, there was an electric connection made with his work on Proust. And instead of trying to disguise the weakness of wit vying with melodrama, Prowse's treatment was evenly gesticulated, with full weight on the

New Woman question which boils down so often, even today, to a choice between embroidery and emancipation. 'Children begin by losing their parents. After a time they judge them. Rarely, if ever, do they forgive them.' The vengefully repeated maxim ran like a chill wind across the garden.

There was some consternation over the fact that Prowse cut the last line of *An Ideal Husband* so that Sir Robert Chiltern received no positive reassurance from his wife on the query 'Gertrude, is it love you feel for me, or is it pity merely?' But Michael Billington in *The Guardian* found 'a dazzling and unified production' in which Prowse had brought out the spiritual squalor behind the chiselled phrases: 'Elegant women pass out dead drunk on the sofa, evening-dressed men parade in front of them as in a sexual meat-market, and when the blackmailing Mrs Cheveley finds an incriminating bracelet caught on her wrist, she utters a four-letter expletive and then, in attempting to stuff a letter down her dress, sees her breasts nakedly revealed.'

Nudity of any sort had become a rarity at the Citizens, another reading on the barometer of how much things had changed in ten years, so perhaps it was this incident that persuaded Mary Brennan of the *Herald* to suggest that Roberta Taylor's Mrs Cheveley was too markedly common to pass in polite society. But the same critic responded to her own point by saying that while the production was impertinent about the period, it was certainly pertinent for today and our own fragile principles. For John Peter in *The Sunday Times*, the show established Wilde 'as the missing link between the

Congreve of *The Way of the World* and the political chamber dramas of Granville Barker'.

In spite of all protestations that the Citizens is not a writers' theatre, Prowse, in completing his Wildean trilogy with the author's first great success, *Lady Windermere's Fan*, adjudicated in the author's favour (and against the first producer, George Alexander) by reverting to his original intention of withholding from the audience until the last act the nature of the true relationship between Lady Windermere and her mother, the woman with a past, Mrs Erlynne. Alexander had insisted on hinting at the information in the first act and revealing it in the second, and Wilde, exhausted by the argument, had complied with his wishes and been drowned in success. But this, above all of Wilde's comedies, is one of determined concealments and deceptions. As Richard Ellmann pointed out, three secrets, at the end, are left undisclosed to the parties most affected: Windermere will never know that his wife was on the verge of running away with another man; a daughter will never know who is her mother; and Lord Augustus will remain unaware of having been hood-winked by Mrs Erlynne. Prowse restored dynamic bite and tension to the piece by honouring Wilde's first instincts, and took up the sweeping rhythms of the action in a procession of magnificent costumes, as beautifully paraded as the clothes in *Semi-Monde*. The stage swished with a predominantly gold and black array of brocaded lace taffetas and weighted silks. In a miraculous transformation, the Windermeres' airy London salon of gold and slate-blue Louis Seize chairs, satin cushions, candelabra, and cream and lace curtains was replaced by red sofas, a great hanging Persian carpet and wall-to-wall Fragonard. Clearly, and as the plot demanded, women were criminal intruders in such a sublimely louche and crimson hell-hole.

All the great stiletto one-liners, pungently antithetical, were discharged with flashing precision: 'I can resist everything except temptation'; 'Crying is the refuge of plain women but the ruin of pretty ones'; 'We are all in the gutter, but some of us are looking at the stars'; and 'Scandal is gossip made tedious by morality'. But, more importantly, Prowse had captured in his Wildes an ambiguous social climate shot through with drained but glittering decadence, where the world of truth was held at bay by the displays of an ultimate dissembler whose knowledge of that truth, and keen moral sense, transformed art into glorious life.

Wilde usurped Genet in the Citizens' pantheon; homosexuality was a common drive and, well before he had found success as a playwright, Wilde had, like Genet and Joe Orton, worn his heart conspicuously on his sleeve. Also, the badge of the outsider-artist suited the Citizens as well as it did Wilde and Genet, and Wilde had even anticipated the fundamental Genetesque credo by noting the social affinities between art and crime in the late 1880s. Prowse's voyages on the high comic seas had two important consequences: a definitive appraisal of period comedy in terms of rich moral purpose and contemporary delight; and the relocation of our greatest literary-theatrical stylists in the right and proper rank of wizard artificers.

Tolstoy and the fictional imagination

Prowse punctuated his Wilde exploits with *Anna Karenina*, described in the programme as 'dialogues by Robert David MacDonald after Tolstoy'. This 1987 production was another major piece of interpretative adaptation, which told the story through the viewpoint of Anna's abandoned son, Sergei, the child of the loveless marriage she exchanged for her love-affair with Vronsky. Sergei, in MacDonald's treatment, had been reduced to the position of doorkeeper at his ancestral home, now a post-Revolutionary Soviet museum, where he tore tickets as the proletariat wandered through. Anna was played by five actresses, each of whom played other characters in the story; each Anna wore black, reverting to grey when relinquishing the role. There were 132 quick changes in a production that played for just fourteen performances to 93 per cent capacity business. Havergal's three abiding priorities – good work, balanced books, full audiences – were all achieved on this production, to which he simply refers as 'game, set and match'.

Randall Stevenson in the *Times Literary Supplement* admired the mixture of memory, dream and illusion in a staging both 'provocatively multi-layered and multi-dimensional', while Joyce McMillan in *The Guardian* noted a 'brilliant emphasis on Anna's emblematic role as an embodiment of all women's potential for passion'; a nineteenth-century heroine victim had been expanded into a 'powerful, adult, responsible and infinitely complex female presence'. Martin Hoyle's 'three hours of deadly dullness' in the *Financial Times* was almost as lonely a response as had been James Fenton's to the Proust, although John Peter in *The Sunday Times* did ask after Tolstoy's piercing sense of individuality and regretted the loss of the brilliant marriage portraits in 'a sense of shallow but solemn theatrical excitement'.

But in welcoming one of the most original stage adaptations he had seen, Michael Ratcliffe vividly preserved the ephemeral excitements in *The Observer*:

Prowse sets the play in a large neo-classical box decorated by relief friezes and dominated by three towering cenotaphs with draped bowls on top. It is a space both oppressive and open which serves for a variety of locations from aristocratic salon to the grander kind of railway waiting room, with the opera, the races, a park, a street, a theatre in between. The social choreography of the Annas and the other men in their lives, behind the cenotaph and along the narrow red carpets dusted with falling snow, is as ritualised as the manners prescribed by nineteenth-century sexual convention and Christian teaching. The lighting (Gerry Jenkinson) and the sounds tighten the thread of the narrative, and sustain its harmony and pulse – the seductive tug of the slow, minor key waltz from Rachmaninov's 'Symphonic Dances', the rumble and shunting of trains, the persistent two-note clink of the level-crossing bell, like the tap of a leper's stick warning of plague and catastrophe to come. It is the density of these images rather than the acting itself – which is discreetly and perfectly at one with them – that gives the show its power.

The Proustian texture, reinforced by the decrepit figure of

old Sergei watching his own younger self, brought the company full circle to its obsessive, reflective, poetic and thoroughly integrated mode of adaptation in *A la Recherche du Temps Perdu*. What the Citizens had anticipated at the start of the decade turned out to be true. Fiction was a prime source of mainstream theatrical innovation, whether the director was Lyubimov, doing *Crime and Punishment* and *The Possessed* with British actors, or Declan Donnellan of Cheek By Jowl ripping joyously into Thackeray's *Vanity Fair*, or Christopher Hampton elegantly disembowelling Laclos for his RSC version of *Les Liaisons Dangereuses*.

The RSC's *Nicholas Nickleby* had been anticipated to a large extent by Mike Alfreds' quadruple-evening production of Dickens's *Bleak House*, a tumultuous bare-bones adaptation for the company he founded, Shared Experience. Havergal's extra-curricular activity now took him to Shared Experience, where he directed two novel adaptations as a guest in Mike Alfreds' absence. Just as Prowse and MacDonald had pipped the RSC to the blockbuster post in 1980, so Havergal was first to the tape in early 1985 with his stage version of a fictional compilation of letters, Samuel Richardson's 1740 *Pamela* (Hampton's *Liaisons Dangereuses* opened at Stratford that October). Like Hampton, Havergal and his co-adaptor, Fidelis Morgan, dropped the letter convention and invented a new eighteenth-century play which they set within the controlling physical metaphor of a rehearsal room in a subsidised theatre. Two years later, in 1987, with Alfreds himself on extended loan to the National Theatre, Havergal, working with the writer

Felicity Browne, produced another novel adaptation, of Elizabeth Bowen's 1948 *The Heat of the Day*.

Apart from charting another stage in Havergal's directorial evolution, the two Shared Experience productions were notable for blistering performances by Charon Bourke, who was to make such an impact, later in the same year, as Schiller's Joan in Glasgow. As Richardson's Pamela, Bourke avoided all hint of simpering virtuousness in wittily covering a full range of helplessness, resentment, humility and pride; as Elizabeth Bowen's dithering factory girl Louie Lewis, she was a brilliantly comic and heart-breakingly doomed single mother.

Havergal brought his Shared Experience work to bear on the Glasgow stage in late 1989. A cheap show was needed to counterbalance the demands on the budget already made by *The Crucible* and *Macbeth*. For many years, at policy meetings, Havergal had threatened the ultimate in low budget productions: himself, in his own polo-neck sweater, reciting the Gospel According to St Mark. Although he was aware he might attract unflattering comparisons with Alec McCowen, who had done it already, he sensed his time had come. MacDonald welcomed the solo Havergal, and his polo-neck, but angrily censored any suggestion of an official religious text. Prowse suggested one of his favourite books, Graham Greene's *Travels With My Aunt*, and the budget was juggled to allow for three actors in addition to Havergal. The latter set about his task of adaptor, actor and co-director (with Jon Pope).

The result was a graceful and witty experiment in

theatrical third-person narrative at the opposite end of the Proust and Tolstoy scale. There had been five Anna Kareninas; there were now four Henry Pullings, Greene's timorous retired bank manager quadruplicated in the spinsterish trio of Havergal, Derwent Watson and Patrick Hannaway, plus the younger, shadowy Christopher Gee. This latter represented the potential hedonist in Pulling, while the other three, mustachioed, in matching grey-suits and maroon V-necked sweaters, were at once all of Henry and various aspects of him: Havergal, tall and fussing; Hannaway, squat, square and suburban; Watson, primly twinkling, almost demure. The other characters were then assumed by rote, without costume changes, Havergal concentrating on the imperious Aunt Augusta and Hannaway on various shady police chiefs and the loyal black valet Wordsworth.

The delayed loss of childhood, the search for its renewal and the ultimate transformation of innocence by experience, linked this beautiful, imaginative distillation (every sparkling word was Greene's) to the predominant theatrical mode of the decade, and its Proustian harbinger. The production was such a hit that it returned to the Citizens as part of the 1990 Strathclyde Summer Season. On the home front, the scene was set fair. But as the Citizens of Glasgow knew better than anyone in the British theatre, there was a world elsewhere.

7

THE 1980s: HOME AND AWAY

Although the status of the Citizens in British theatre remained alien throughout the Havergal years, it must by now be apparent that there were channels through which the theatre related, however slightly, to the rest of the kingdom. Its importance in the Scottish theatre became incontestable, as we shall see later, while its reputation in London, always fluctuating, and subject to a peculiar death-wish emanating from the Citizens' own directorate, was itself a fascinating theme of the 1980s.

Britain posed problems. It was far easier to see the Citizens in an international setting, where theatre communities in mainland Europe responded with a mixture of pleasure and surprise to the productions that came their way. The hitch, and something of a scandal, was that the productions ceased to go Europe's way after 1983. The money ran out, and the British Council, which is instrumental in handling invitations and funding travel requirements, was less than well-disposed towards the Citizens in the wake of the *Chinchilla* fracas.

Italian connections

Even so, the Citizens' reputation had taken hold abroad, and it thrives there still. No more so than in Venice, spiritual home of Philip Prowse, where the company scored a huge hit at the Biennale festival of 1981 with Goldoni's *La Guerra* (translated by MacDonald as *The Battlefield*). The production, although premièred in Glasgow in late 1980, had in fact been commissioned in Venice, partly on the advisory initiative of John Francis Lane, an English critic resident in Rome. The Citizens' production was one of many representing different European approaches to Goldoni; it was acclaimed as the best of all the entrants.

Goldoni was one of the Citizens' most productive European connections. MacDonald had seen a production by Visconti of *Mirandolina* in Trieste just after the war and had remained, as we have seen, entranced. His post-Strehler conflation of the *Villegiatura* trilogy, translated as *Country Life*, in 1979 had been a high point of the company's work, and this Goldoni decade, which started with *The Battlefield*, was followed by *The Impresario from Smyrna*. This latter piece cross-referenced back to *Chinchilla* by dealing with another impresario hanging around the great city for which Goldoni wrote countless festival pieces. The Turkish impresario knows nothing about opera, but everything about the role of stage-door Johnny and consequently inveigles himself into the absurd aspirations of a group of Venetian prima donnas. Goldoni's satirical points were embellished by the flimsy, cheap-looking scenery (the flats literally, at one point, fell flat) and by costumes which disintegrated; the ridiculous upstage-facing singers were caught with their pants down and their parts, or at least some of them, hilariously exposed.

Il vero amico (translated as *Friends and Lovers*) was MacDonald's eighth Goldoni. It was also a transplant, from Bologna to less sunny but more affluent Hamburg. The revelation, for Michael Ratcliffe, was that Goldoni was thus considered as a fully paid-up member of the European Enlightenment; his quartet of lovers were much nearer the world of Diderot's letters and Goethe's *Elective Affinities* than to anything south of the Alps . . . 'the entire piece breathes and sighs to the music of Schubert and Schumann and sustains a marvellous balance between the enthralling and the absurd.'

Viennese waltzers and German jeremiads

The last genuine international showing of the company was at the Edinburgh Festival of 1983, and it is an alarming thought that an abiding internationalist reputation is sustained on so distant a practical bid for it. John Drummond, who had presented the company in 1979, his first year as festival director, found an ingenious way of threading the Citizens into his fifth and final bonanza, which had a double related theme of the Vienna Secession and the centenary of Wagner's death. Moving from their 1979 berth of the Lyceum, the Citizens occupied the Assembly Hall with two lush, poisonously romantic spectaculars derived from Karl Kraus and Hugo von Hofmannstahl.

Kraus's *The Last Days of Mankind* was one of the Citizens' most spectacular 'impossible' undertakings.

187

MacDonald, who adapted the 800-page epic to a four-hour entertainment set in a Viennese coffee shop, told Sarah Hemming of *The Times* that Kraus experts would be horrified; but any purist outrage, a limited commodity in respect of Kraus, would have been overshadowed by Kraus's own acknowledgement of the difficulties: 'The performance of this drama is intended for a theatre on Mars. Theatre-goers of this world would not be able to bear it.' Hence the apocalyptic conflagration at the end of MacDonald's extraordinary production in which a disembodied voice from – yes – Mars terminated relations with our planet and left us to stew in our own rancid juice.

This was the outbreak of war and catastrophe confidently predicted by Kraus the Grouse (biliously impersonated by Giles Havergal as 'a Thersites in evening dress' according to Michael Billington and 'a Diogenes of the flesh pots' in Irving Wardle's estimate), while the Viennese *beau monde* sat around with their noses in newspapers and heads in the clouds. Images of war, prostitution and disease were overlaid in a nightmarish correspondence with the disintegration of Viennese intellectual and artistic life. Yet another version had been wrought of the Citizens *fin de siècle* salon style, while introducing British audiences to the authentic voice of one of Europe's master satirists.

An even older, more vanished Vienna was conjured by the interesting experiment of seeing how well a Hofmannsthal libretto stood up without Strauss's music. John Fowler described Prowse's beautiful setting for *Rosenkavalier* as 'a wedding cake canopied by swaths of white drapery and seeded with flower-favours and a myriad candles'. Most critics missed the music, and John Higgins in *The Times* said frankly that MacDonald was both too old and too slim to play Baron Ochs.

But, once again, the company made a real impact in Edinburgh and served convincing notice to the outside world of continuing animation. There remained plenty of room for disagreement on the true calibre of their work, but not on its adventurousness. The festival offerings were merely representative of MacDonald's work in the German-speaking repertoire at home base; Goethe, Schiller and Hochhuth were each twice represented in the Citizens seasons of the 1980s, and all the productions were of value and significance.

In 1982, MacDonald used Goethe's own cut version of *Torquato Tasso* as the basis of his own blank verse rendition of a play largely constructed, as Cordelia Oliver said, of conversations between two or three people. Michael Levine's split setting struck a grave contrast between the hay-strewn, sheep-infested fantasy world of the summer palace and, on the upper level, a serious debating chamber. The romantic spirit of the artist was endangered by his own patron, leading to many varieties of resentment and insecurity. The very least you can say of *Tasso* is that it was worth doing, while most accounts of the production suggest that the Citizens had here unearthed a crucial text of the European experience.

The point would not even have to be argued about *Faust*, three years later, which MacDonald cut until it lasted just three-and-a-half hours: 'Public transport dictates.' Four-fifths of the original went, I guess, which did not best please Michael Ratcliffe in *The Observer* : 'MacDonald has cut Goethe to the bone and very nearly right through him. "The pruning knife? Zounds! The axe!"'

The intention was itself Faustian, and the action started and ended not in heaven, but in that great rehearsal room in the sky where Havergal was discovered as the Divine Director. Kenny Miller's extraordinary design was brutally white, its brash ruined classicism fitted out with Anglepoise lamps and bookshelves for Faust's study and a white traverse curtain which conveyed both the presentational theme of the plays and the flashing, magicked aspect of the narrative. Mark Lewis as Faust, who shared a protean quality with his spiritual adversary, was transformed from grizzled, bearded intellectual, to lover, man of action and powerful businessman benefactor. Andrew Wilde's devil was a fancy-dress chameleon, a tireless master of ceremonies whose ministrations were finally rejected by the celestial director.

The translation was almost relentlessly witty. It is worth recording that when Simon Callow led a full-length production (by David Freeman) of MacDonald's text at the Lyric, Hammersmith, in 1988, the concert pianist and German-speaking Goethe student Alfred Brendel is reported to have declared it as good an English version as he could hope to hear. The fabled coarseness of Goethe's rhyming couplets was well caught, as well as his trick of switching from four stresses in a line to iambics. And many of Goethe's erudite references were sharpened up in the process; Mephistopheles, off to 'resettle' Baucis and Philemon, says 'Not for the first time in history it's been done/See Naboth, Kings One, twenty-one' – chapter and verse exactly.

Part Two of *Faust* is rarely performed in Europe, never in Britain. But without it you can never see *Faust* as, in George Steiner's words, 'a sublime melodrama', with the hero getting the better of Mephistopheles. He may not win the wager struck in Part One, but he does not lose it, dying on a vision of an affluent society in a free country. Mephistopheles, dazzled by the angels, declares he has been swindled by God as Faust is quietly transported to heaven. The social comedy of this was particularly marked at Glasgow; you understood the point of Faust's enslavement, and there was a sharp echo of the inflation-infested economies of Europe as his material rise was achieved by literally printing tons of money for the Emperor, then reclaiming stretches of land from the sea.

The Hammersmith marathon was a marvellous, exhausting event, but in doing everything of *Faust* it omitted to make any points of its own as a dramatic event. The diversionary nature of the stage action, especially in the fountain-splashing nude rudery of the classical episodes, implied that an amount of silliness was inherent in doing *Faust* at all; the Citizens aimed in its *Faust* for concision and coherence, as in the presentations of Proust and Karl Kraus. And while Simon Callow in Hammersmith unwisely adopted an old man's wig and bent posture for the final scenes, Mark Lewis, playing straight down the middle, left us with a much firmer impression of a man who has mortgaged his soul to the ideals of sexual fulfilment and political power;

such a man may not lose out to the devil but, as Goethe knew from bitter personal experience, happiness would remain elusive and at a premium.

MacDonald's two Schiller translations, *Mary Stuart* and *Joan of Arc*, have been equally interesting, if not without contentious interpretative slants. In the first, directed by Prowse, Schiller's two young queens were restored to a more marmoreal middle age by Ann Mitchell as a devout, French-accented Mary Stuart, and Fidelis Morgan as a crabbed and shrewish virgin Elizabeth; in the second, MacDonald, directing, updated the disturbing case history of a national heroine to the Occupied France of the 1940s. The crucial thing was that Schiller was seen, for the first time in Britain, as a blood and thunder dramatist who wrote scenes of historical and poetic complexity that do stand up without their various operatic settings and are bettered only by Shakespeare. The point was reinforced by a successful production, during this same period, at the Royal Exchange, Manchester, of *Don Carlos*, directed by Nicholas Hytner, with Citizens alumnus Ian McDiarmid as a testily insomniac King Philip of Spain.

Prowse designed *Mary Stuart* on a zero budget for the set; nonetheless, when the black drapes dropped to the floor in a domino effect as Mary goes deliriously free for a while in Fotheringay castle, he achieved one of his most memorable coups. The lighting of Gerry Jenkinson, a constant creative component in Citizens productions, was masterly, picking out figures in a succession of embracing spots and deliquescent cross-fades, characters looming from the back or rising sedately through a centre-stage trap. A sense of ghostliness extended to the unscripted apparition of the murdered Darnley, whose bloodied head Mary cradled with distracted affection in her lap; the gesture was echoed by Elizabeth's fondling of Leicester.

The small design budget was reserved for costumes, which were sumptuously magnificent. In a final dress reversal, Mary went to her death, transfigured and at peace, in a replica of Elizabeth's Gloriana gown. This rich emblematic use of costume is a typical Prowse touch; there was no way that the dressing of the male courtiers in modern grey suits seemed incongruous. Rather, it explained a great deal about the relations between men at court who allowed regal patronage to include sexual privileges.

The *Joan* was a less grave and stately affair, but an astonishing revelation as a play. John Peter declared in *The Sunday Times* that he had always believed it to be unperformable. But he found instead 'a series of harsh, unforgettable stage images', which created a sense of high, florid, romantic theatricality combined with muscular intelligence. In the lead, Charon Bourke, the latest in a long line of outstanding young discoveries, played with uncouth swagger and no trace of sentimentality a country girl who first accepts and then rejects her historic role. She appeared to be the inmate of a sanatorium, dressed in a baggy, striped suit, uniform of madness and criminality. Captured by the English, the Maid of Orleans donned a brown overcoat, on which was stuck a yellow Star of David; she was transformed from Resistance heroine to scapegoat of the Occupation.

The update worked because it simultaneously dissolved all objections to the historical inaccuracies of Schiller's play while exploiting to the full the nationalistic potency of the Joan legend. Schiller's Joan is not burned at the stake, but MacDonald superimposed a brutal execution on the battlefield expiry of the text, and resurrected his dead heroine to breach the celestial rainbow ('The pain is short, the joy is everlasting') as a group of gawping tourists reached for their cameras. The play attracted wide interest but little controversy beyond the complaint of a letter-writer to *The Scotsman* about excessive onstage cigarette-smoking; this was deemed an unfortunate gaffe in the context of Glasgow's rather unlikely ambition to become a cigarette-free zone by the year 2000.

At one stroke, MacDonald introduced to the British repertoire a play which, having been written when Joan's reputation was in abeyance and before the quest for historical truth about her was under way, Shaw had pompously derided as the tale of a heroine drowned in a witch's cauldron of raging romance. Instead, we had a modern, vibrant strain of psychological anguish among the war games, nowhere more pronounced than in the second act sequence where Joan disregarded the desperate pleas of a homesick English soldier and butchered him for being a blasphemous invader. Subsequent battle experience was a grim learning process, in which bloody exchanges became a livid nightmare for a girl whose faith, not in God, but in the truth of her own cause, had simply collapsed.

The issue of historical truth in drama has been

notoriously raised this century by Rolf Hochhuth, and as his regular translator into English, MacDonald set about both reviving his most famous play and directing the world première of his latest. The biggest surprise about *The Representative* was that you could hardly credit the furore it once caused, although, on the Sunday before the Glasgow opening in 1986, the play was preached against from the city's Roman Catholic pulpits. Pope Pius XII was presented not as a collaborationist anti-semitic cold fish (which is what the Church's propaganda alleged the play had proposed in the 1960s), but as a subtle, anxious politician convinced that Communism and Stalinism formed a much bigger long-term threat to the Catholic Church than did Nazism and Hitler. As Cardinal Pacelli, Pius had been instrumental in formulating the 1933 Concordat with Hitler and he was shown not wishing to violate that treaty while washing his hands of responsibility for the Jews going to the death camps. Ciaran Hinds as Pius was trembling but hawkish behind severe, protective spectacles, papal with dignity, whiter-than-white. A young Jesuit, who represented in the play the spirit of guilt and inquisitive conscience felt by Hochhuth and his post-war German contemporaries, was based on a real character who protested against the Pope's silence by adopting a yellow star and boarding a train to Auschwitz.

Guilt was rampant at the start of Hochhuth's *Judith* (1984), too, with a Nazi commissar in Minsk in 1943 deciding to censor a play about the Jewish biblical heroine who murdered Holofernes. The switch to contemporary Washington introduced us to another

Judith, the sister of a Vietnam veteran. She decides to assassinate the President while planning a visit to Minsk to make a television programme. The piece was unwieldy to put it mildly, but it did raise a vital issue of the ethics of extermination. Do you have a just cause in killing a political figurehead because you believe that you will thus undermine more catastrophic political interventions? An individual act of violence strikes many people as the only way of registering disapproval at greater suppressions. The justice and folly of this were examined, and the great lumbering edifice of the drama, while breaking rules and disappointing reasonable expectations of 'an evening in the theatre', did constitute an angry lament for the genocidal atrocities that have disfigured this century. But the structure was a serious problem. Joseph Farrell thought that watching *Judith* was like watching some hustler trying to build an imitation Parthenon with *papier-mâché*.

Still, it was hard to find any other theatre in the 1980s that entertained the idea of theatre's function as a moral tribunal. Hochhuth, and his fellow countryman, the documentary dramatist Peter Weiss, were severely out of fashion. They had been adopted by the British theatre of the late 1960s, or the long since defunct radical RSC wing of it, as part of the protest movement. Hochhuth in Glasgow has at the very least demonstrated how lamentably bereft of challenging ethical and moral discussion our theatre has become, with the sole exception, perhaps, of Wallace Shawn's *Aunt Dan and Lemon* at the Royal Court in 1985.

Opposite:
A scene from
The Roman Actor.
Overleaf:
Laurance Rudic
(above) in
*Philosophy in the
Boudoir.*

Fascinating curiosities in foreign climes

There was no let-up in the unveiling of fascinating curiosities. MacDonald did Sartre's *Altona* in 1984 (its second Citizens production; the first one had been in 1962), a bulgingly talkative piece about modern capitalism, the generation gap, authority, power, free will, incest, torture, morals and politics, while Prowse responded to such fluffy triviality with a brutalised, quirky version of the libretto to Offenbach's *La Vie Parisienne* called *French Knickers*, a sort of 'Second Empire Strikes Back' with the score bashed out on a tinny piano in what looked like a recreation of the Gare du Nord. It was salutary to recall that, as in Glasgow, Offenbach's own company were actors first, singers second. This was a less po-faced deconstruction of a popular opera than was Brook's *Carmen*, and had the great virtue of inviting an audience to reconsider the work afresh, if not aghast.

Even more recherché was *Oroonoko*, revived in 1983, a Restoration tragi-comedy by Thomas Southerne, popular throughout the eighteenth century but long since forgotten. The story of an Angolan prince enslaved on the British colony of Surinam was based on a novel of Aphra Behn. It proved a mixture of low comedy, high tragedy (à la Dryden or Otway) and fortune-hunting mystery, presented by Prowse as a Maughamesque idyll on a remote beach littered with old cans and skulls, backed off by a grey façade of a dubious shanty town. Prowse also compressed characters and rendered others dumb. But the central conflict of mercenary and frustrated love, of dignity in chains and of a revolutionary outburst when the

Overleaf:
Giles Havergal in
The Last Days of Mankind.
Opposite:
Yolanda Vasquez
and Jane Bertish in
Rosenkavalier.

royal prince Oroonoko was stirred to action, all this was urgently and sensuously projected and fully justified the play as a remarkable dramatic essay on colonialism.

Jeffrey Kissoon returned to the company he graced in the early 1970s to play a lithe and lissom black panther converted from monarchichal totem to champion of the oppressed, while his beloved Imoinda, an Indian sired by a white father, was a figure of haunting, lobotomised power, according to Johanna Kirby. And the comic plot involved the tricking of a rapacious old widow by a girl who has fled, *en travestie*, the degenerate foppishness of London. So the slavery theme expanded, fascinatingly, to embrace the business of arranged marriages. There were attempted strangulations, bloody immolations and an extraordinary suicide pact for the noble lovers which drove the play on to a bizarre conclusion. *Oroonoko* was a very good example of a wonderful rarity brought to pulsating life, cheaply and briefly, for an admittedly smallish audience.

But such efforts were never high-minded sops, nor were they occasional. They were vitally endemic to the enterprise supported not just by the grants, but also by the box-office income for the pantomimes, the Shakespeares and Brechts, the visiting native companies. Goldoni always performed respectably, but not brilliantly, at the box-office. The German classics did well, and there was extensive coverage in the European Press for an event like Hochhuth's *Judith*. The persistent adventurousness of the repertoire during the 1980s, building on the iconoclastic reputation of the 1970s, ensured that the Citizens stayed fresh in the minds even of people who never went there. And plenty of them missed *The Spanish Bawd*, Prowse's poorly received and poorly attended 1986 version of *La Celestina*.

La Celestina by Fernando de Rojas was written around 1500 in sixteen acts and is one of those impossible projects that theatre companies never quite get round to. The National had a production planned, with Joan Plowright in the lead, but the death of her husband, Laurence Olivier, in 1989, moved it on to the back burner, where it has since fizzled out altogether. The Citizens had got there first anyway, turning up a splendid prose dramatisation by James Mabbe which dates from 1631, the year of Donne's death and of Dryden's birth. The text came across, suitably enough, as a sort of rude compromise between Shakespearean comedy and Websterian excess.

The bawd Celestina manipulates the affections of two doomed lovers and of her adopted son, while various servants indulge in deceit and double-dealing that makes your average Restoration plot sound simplicity itself. Prowse directed a cast of just six on a whitewashed maze of streets and corners with an upper level cut off from the sky by a great torn and hanging yellow canopy. The company van driver, Dennis Knotts, led a quartet of extras as the hit-man Crito, required to respond to such callous instructions as 'I would have him beaten but not slain'. The actors forged a sinister visual world from Rojas and Mabbe, studded armlets and great robes in browns and blacks contributing to that distinctive Prowse 'look' of fantastical contemporaneity. This allowed for the various diagnoses of Celestina's craft to prosper in a convincing way – was she a witch, a procuress, a freak, a sorceress or an agony aunt trying to earn an honest bob?

In fact, she was Robert David MacDonald in a tent-like heap of scarlet robes, headbands, brass medals and gold chains, not to mention a frankly errant Glaswegian accent. The dark pattern of the play, its cumulative violence and bizarre Jacobean plot twists, all were meat and drink to Prowse who pulled off a series of wonderful tricks and stage pictures, not least the final, heart-stopping revelation of Celestina as a bereaved Renaissance *father* stalking the stage, comfortless and alone in a valley of tears. Celestina's posthumous identity was a typically outrageous elaboration on Prowse's part; the mother proved the necessity of invention.

Meanwhile, home on the Scottish range . . .

The Scottish theatre was a vibrant and going concern throughout the 1980s, and the Citizens comfortably slotted into an overall picture of booming activity. The company participated in Mayfest for the first time in 1988 with *Lady Windermere's Fan*. Mayfest had been launched in Glasgow in 1983 and had played, immediately, in all venues, to an overall audience capacity of 75 per cent. 1983 was the year Provost Michael Kelly launched the 'Glasgow's Miles Better' campaign, and, for all the cheerful abuse hurled at the yellow Mister Happy figure who danced across the slogan, it was a symbol of the gathering confidence, what Joyce McMillan called 'a strange exuberant life after industrial death'. Any remaining pressure on the Citizens to dig up good local work was eased by the opening of the Tron Theatre in 1982, and there was yet another attempt to revive flickering nationalist ideals in the launch of the Scottish Theatre Company in the same year.

Mayfest went from strength to strength, in spite of discontinuity of artistic management. By the end of the decade, the event had become Britain's second (to Edinburgh) largest theatre festival and, for many, the most interesting. The ambitious William Burdett-Coutts, who had run the Assembly Rooms in Edinburgh during the Festival weeks since 1982, expanded his empire to include Mayfest in 1988 and promptly scored a significant internationalist coup by presenting the Maly Theatre of Leningrad in *Stars in the Morning Sky*, a stunningly performed Soviet post-glasnost play about Moscow prostitutes who had been moved out of the city centre during the 1980 Olympic Games. At the same time, Peter Brook, having failed to find any takers in London, brought his best production for many years, *The Mahabharata*, to the Old Transport Museum in Pollokshields; its triumph there ensured the future of an important new Glasgow venue, now rechristened the Tramway. And Brook promised to bring all his work, when he could, to Glasgow in future.

Leaving London during the 1980s, where subsidised art was on the defensive and under fire, and coming north to Glasgow, was to enter, even more so than usual, a different world. The place was buzzing. In 1985, Joyce McMillan wondered out loud if cultural independence was not now seen as an alternative to the political independence Scotland had been denied. In March 1986, the Citizens Theatre was nominated a listed building and thus officially, and finally, preserved.

In October of the same year, Glasgow was designated the European City of Culture for 1990. Richard Luce, the Minister for the Arts, had no hesitation in making the decision after Glasgow District Council had brilliantly co-ordinated the campaign and rounded up the city's various arts groups to put their arguments directly to Luce's committee from the Office of Arts and Libraries; that left Edinburgh (whose councillors had presented the city's case themselves, on behalf of the arts organisations), Liverpool, Leeds, Bristol, Bath, Cardiff, Swansea and Cambridge — the other contestants — panting in its wake. The final humiliation for Edinburgh was that, out of those cities, it came only fifth in the reckoning.

And in the very next month, the legal services centre, the Scottish Development Agency's £6.4m Gorbals project on the corner of Ballater Street, next door to the Citizens, was given the official go-ahead. One major condition was attached by the Glasgow District Council: that the SDA must carry out all remedial work to the exterior of the Citizens, and rebuild the landscaped area on the other side of the road.

Meanwhile, the Scottish Theatre Company was in deep trouble within a year of its launch. Ewan Hooper had started the enterprise shortly after leading an Arts Council survey that identified a potential need and market for such a company. The need and market soon evaporated, although Hooper defiantly told Joyce McMillan, in the Sunday Standard in March 1983, that he still believed in a Scottish theatre to compensate for what he called a preponderance of Theatre in Scotland, an extension of the English rep system.

But Hooper's problems stemmed directly from an insistence on stirring up old classics from a not very important theatre literature. Sir David Lindsay's *The Thrie Estaites*, which had been famously revived by Tyrone Guthrie after the war, and again in the 1970s by Bill Bryden, was done with some success at the Edinburgh Festival. More adventurous was the touring production of a fine new play by Marcella Evaristi, *Commedia*, which drew profitably on the author's Italian family background. But an appearance at the 1985 Edinburgh Festival with a truly appalling revival by Tom Fleming of Sydney Goodsir Smith's *The Wallace* featured a lot of solid Scottish actors trooping on and off looking in vain for something to do. A would-be festive dwarf capered dolefully before the interval, at which point I abandoned the Scottish Theatre Company for ever. The company tried to change tack and appeared at the Citizens during the 1986 Mayfest with Joe Corrie's 1930s play, *Robert Burns*, directed by David Hayman. For a few years, the STC had staggered on, trying to service the large theatre circuit of Glasgow, Aberdeen and Edinburgh, as well as the MacRobert Centre near Stirling, but its inevitable demise coincided, one feels, with that of the whole idea of a National Theatre in Scotland.

John Fowler of the *Herald* put the predominant view, which was also the official line at the Scottish Arts Council by the end of the decade, when he said in 1987 that the national theatre of Scotland already existed: at the Citizens, at the Lyceum and the Traverse in Edinburgh, in all the touring companies, and indeed, for as long as it existed, in the Scottish Theatre Company. In other words, it existed in the sum of its parts. The same is true in England, in spite of the establishment of a National Theatre, after a century of agitation, in 1962. National Theatres invariably become shrines to idealism or reputation or literature; it is one of the modern theatre's less remarkable discoveries that they sometimes start off well but end up miles from where the action is. And Scotland, even after James Bridie and Bill Bryden, still had to find this out the hard way. The STC was way off beam right to the end. Tom Fleming, who had succeeded Ewan Hooper at the helm, averred wrongly, as late as June 1987, that 'Any country with a head and a heart has to have a National Theatre'. In this, he was supported not by the native theatre profession, but by the director of the National Theatre of Iceland, and by Frank Dunlop of the Edinburgh Festival. The STC expired in late 1987.

The post-Bryden Edinburgh Lyceum had become a middlebrow repertory theatre with a bill of fare indistinguishable from any other middlebrow repertory theatre in Britain. In 1984, Leslie Lawton, who had been there for five years and done a few Scottish plays (by Donald Campbell, Hector MacMillan, Sue Glover and John Byrne) among a plethora of West End comedies and musicals, was succeeded as artistic director by Ian Wooldridge, who had, in turn, for six years run Theatre Around Glasgow, TAG, the educational wing of the Citizens. Wooldridge has had his successes and is building slowly towards a new and regular audience. But the process has been painful, not least because of the misguided attempt to ape his former home theatre in the west of Scotland. Designs have been sub-Prowse-ian, sometimes executed by Prowse protégés; a policy of pale imitation includes the opening of new productions, as at the Citizens, on a Friday night, with a free preview on Thursday. The context of Edinburgh is somehow wrong for this, and after five years one cannot say that anything decisive or indigenous has been achieved; nothing, certainly, to give the Citizens any sort of run for their money.

The Edinburgh Traverse, after a quarter century as a club theatre, has gone public and courts sponsorship. It remains, fitfully, a powerhouse, and invariably produces work of integrity and significance for the Edinburgh Festival each year. Never quite adjusting to the 1970s, its fortunes revived in the 1980s under Peter Lichtenfels and his successor Jenny Killick, who mixed imaginative new plays from abroad with some notable new Scottish playwrights – John Clifford, Simon Donald, Chris Hannon and Peter Arnott. There is every indication that the Traverse will continue to prosper under the direction of Ian Brown, who first made his name, like Ian Wooldridge, as director of TAG at the Citizens.

Vital new work emanates still from the touring companies, from the energetic, rough and raucous off-shoots of 7:84: Wildcat, Borderline and Communicado. 7:84 itself lost the popular theatre initiative to these companies and fell foul of the Scottish Arts Council who threatened to withdraw funds in 1989. Before then, a powerful rearguard action was mounted by John McGrath, with support from Labour Party MPs and the Scottish Trades Union Council. But none of the company's work had made the same impact as in the mid-1970s, and there was talk of mismanagement, talk which McGrath eloquently insisted was a veiled excuse for political disapproval. From the outside, this looked unlikely, given the high esteem in which McGrath as an artist continued to be held, and the continuing uncompromised left-wing stance of the other groups. McGrath left 7:84 in a flurry of acrimonious bickering, and David Hayman took over as artistic director in 1988, a rather curious appointment if the objection to McGrath had been partly on the grounds of his absenteeism from Scotland; Hayman was, if anything, by now even busier than McGrath as an actor and director in films and television.

Michael Boyd took over at the Tron in 1985, building on the work of its first administrator, Linda Haase, and its first artistic director, Faynia Williams. The Tron came about largely due to the voluntary work and enthusiasm of many former supporters of the Close at the Citizens, who wanted a new studio space for Glasgow and were prepared to spend their Sundays up ladders, painting and distempering the interior of the old Tron Kirk, in order to get one. Boyd is of Irish descent and thus averted a clean sweep of English directors running Scottish theatre operations: Ian Brown at the Traverse, Clive Perry at Pitlochry, Joan Knight at Perth, Alan Lyddiard at TAG, Ian Wooldridge at the Lyceum, Frank Dunlop at the Edinburgh Festival, William Burdett-Coutts at the Assembly Rooms and Mayfest.

I can find no satisfactory explanation for the comparative dearth of good Scottish theatre directors beyond the tenacious inferiority complex diagnosed by

Andrew Leigh. Havergal is less surprised, pointing out that Scotland is a very small country, and it is hard to gain experience of running a theatre within its boundaries. Iain Cuthbertson at the Citizens had been a notable exception to the rule of English importation. At the very start, when James Bridie had hired Jennifer Sounes as his director of productions, all the Citizens directors were English. As Jan McDonald rather brutally put it in 1984, there simply were not any Scottish directors of distinction, 'and that state of affairs has not markedly improved in the last 40 years'. The trend may soon be reversed, though, with the recent arrival on the scene of Gerry Mulgrew with Communicado; and, of course, Wildcat and Borderline, like 7:84, have Scottish directors in charge.

Nationalism, anyway, had been eclipsed by internationalism at the Citizens, and the nationalist opposition, embodied in the Scottish Theatre Company, routed by the sustained calibre of the Citizens' operation, while other companies and personalities re-grouped around them. The palpable sense of a political and spiritual intensification in the arts in Scotland in the 1980s was undoubtedly reinforced, you might even say led, by the continued artistic vitality at the Citizens.

Honouring the founding father

Given the extent to which the Citizens had gone out of their way to play down the Scottish heritage, it was a surprise to find them marking the centenary of Bridie's birth in 1988 by performing one of his plays. The fact is that Havergal, the most traditionalist of the three directors in his theatrical taste, has a deep-rooted admiration for many of Bridie's plays, and believes that several of the less whimsical of them will stand the ultimate test of time.

The choice for the centenary was the 1947 *Dr Angelus*, first played in London by Alastair Sim and George Cole. This was a compelling murder mystery with a pertinent discussion of ethics in the medical profession; Havergal's production opened with a recital of the Hippocratic oath, a speech dislodged from the second act and shared among the play's three doctors. The story is based on the notorious Glaswegian case of Dr Pritchard, who murdered both his mother-in-law and his wife in the 1830s. Bridie updated the incidents to 1920, creating a double-bind on Angelus of Victorian marital repression (he is sexually unfulfilled) and a more modern hypocritical licentiousness (he is in physical thrall to the sluttish maid).

The diagnosis of gastric tuberculosis and syncope is a false trail; murder is committed by antimonial poisoning, and the new, earnest young doctor in the practice is awoken to his sleuthing destiny in a central dream sequence after he has signed a death certificate. The set at this point split apart, and the other characters floated through the interrogatory dream, before the young doctor departed in a magical, mystical echo of that same scene, and of Priestley's *Johnson over Jordan*, the play with which Bridie's Citizens began their first season at the renovated, re-named Royal Princess's Theatre in 1945.

Images in London, alarums and excursions

The profile of the company in Britain outside of Glasgow was not so much high as constant. People continued to have an idea of what the Citizens was like without seeing all that much evidence of the work. The company itself paid its first visit to London with MacDonald's *Don Juan* in late 1980, at the Round House. (The Round House presentation of Keith Hack's *Titus Andronicus* in the early 1970s was not a Citizens production, though many of the actors in it had been in Glasgow.) The delayed arrival was also a prompt adieu: *Don Juan* was a disaster of such proportions that the company has not even entertained the idea of going to London since.

The effect was to compound the distaste for London theatre values with an anxiety over what unfriendly critics might say. The fear was not one of being attacked, but of a knock-on effect which might lead to the forfeiture of political credibility at home. As a result, the theatre was (unnecessarily, as it turned out) meticulous in dissociating itself from the commercial West End re-heat early in 1989 of Prowse's production of *The Vortex* with Maria Aitken and Rupert Everett.

The critical reaction to *Don Juan* concentrated on the inherent inertia of MacDonald's play in which a group of fancy-dress gun-toting revellers entered a monumental library and held the residents hostage to a revolution plotted by the old seducer. It was the anniversary of Bastille Day, and MacDonald's relentlessly aphoristic script, an acid variation on the Genetesque theme of illusory political transformations, was directed by Prowse as a Parisian re-run of his *Threepenny Opera* salon riot. The element of invasion and hostility also carried with it echoes of the post-war Teutonic theatre of Peter Weiss's *Marat/Sade* and Günter Grass's *The Plebeians Rehearse the Uprising*, itself a satire of a revolting theatre company preparing a text of revolt, *Coriolanus*.

John Elsom in *The Listener* described the MacDonald literary style as 'Shaw pulled through a hedge backwards and colliding with Ivy Compton-Burnett on the other side', an insult that could just as easily be construed as a compliment. Elsom was adamant, though, that the script was more forgettable than the design. Most other critics concurred in this evaluation, though Michael Billington in *The Guardian* was much taken by the cross-cutting of period costume and silky lingerie, a case, he said, of Louis XVI meets Janet Reger.

Nonetheless, in these middle years of the decade, Prowse sharpened his own London profile and the image of the company in the capital. All three directors accepted outside commissions, but the creative base remained the Gorbals address. They took out what they had developed not as a market commodity but as a visiting card; landing again was bumpy but usually welcome and it is my impression that outside experiences only reinforced the conviction that the Citizens was, in Prowse's phrase, 'the heart of the artichoke'. There was no intention of trying to impress anyone; if, like the old vaudevillians at the Empire, you succeeded in Glasgow, you had done the business. But the capacity to irritate remained.

The reception afforded the first two London outings, as

has already been seen, was decidedly mixed. *Don Juan* had been a resounding flop and *Summit Conference*, though not without admirers, was generally berated. Prowse had been teamed on the latter revival with Glenda Jackson by the fairly new London producer Colin Brough. Jackson's screen performances under the direction of Ken Russell, and her abiding friendship with him, testify to her preference for working with risk-takers of vision rather than wilting violets. After *Summit Conference*, her next London stage appearance had been in Eugene O'Neill's *Strange Interlude*, directed by the Citizens alumnus Keith Hack. Her Citizens connection was to be consummated during 1990 by her appearance in Prowse's Glasgow production of *Mother Courage*. But it was *Phedra* (as MacDonald called it) at the Old Vic in November 1984 that established the connection.

The English-speaking theatre fights shy of Racine on account of the twin problems of his language and his classicism. Even Robert Lowell, who did a very good version of *Phèdre*, considered the rhyming alexandrines untranslatable, while the newest way of doing Racine and Corneille discovered by Declan Donnellan and Nick Ormerod's Cheek By Jowl company was deflationary, conversational, ironic, anti-classical. Prowse and MacDonald went for baroque broke, matching where possible Racine's metre, that extended rhythmical tread which is almost invariably rendered in English as pantomimic pentametrical, with a stage composition of swagged curtains, tarnished gold, standing pillars and burning urns. This was a suitable frame for Jackson's Phedra, and in many ways the performance was the

Cleopatra she never delivered at Stratford-upon-Avon under Peter Brook's curiously misfired direction in 1978; it was tragic on the large scale, using every part of her voice – its hard, cackling timbre and mellifluous dulcitude, its fishwife flare and soft embrace. She painted an entranced portrait of a woman, and mother, who was on the rack. Gerard Murphy was a grizzled, growling Theseus, Tim Woodward a tremendously impassioned Hippolytus.

Prowse himself preferred the later production he did of the same translation in Glasgow during the enforced onstage studio season of 1988 (during the final period of the renovation), which was much more severe, concentrated and Prussian. But there was a magnificent clamour about the Old Vic version, and a rich gestural and emotional texture to complement the visual finesse. An even richer tapestry of European interconnections would be sewn in 1986 when, at the Lyric in Hammersmith, Jackson appeared, along with Joan Plowright, in MacDonald's specially commissioned translation of Lorca's *The House of Bernarda Alba*, directed by Nuria Espert from Spain and designed by Giorgio Strehler's regular collaborator in Milan, Ezio Frigerio.

Phedra punctuated two other important invitations Prowse accepted in London, from Greenwich and the National Theatre. Alan Strachan, then in the middle of his ten-year stint as artistic director of the Greenwich Theatre, gave Prowse *carte blanche* while he took a five-month sabbatical at the start of 1984. Prowse directed *The White Devil* and *The Seagull*, and invited Havergal to chip in with *The Way of the World*. The first production was an inflamed, imaginative elision of a great and notoriously difficult play with an amazing set of two great walls, containing hinged doors, evocative of city streets, secret gardens, domestic interiors and nightmarish corridors. The murderous Brachiano (played by Gerard Murphy) chased a panting victim through this sinister labyrinth and ran straight into Irving Wardle's crunchingly well-organised attack on the Prowse method in *The Times*:

> ... here we hit a rock. The victim is Vittoria's servant Zanche; and, when Brachiano catches up with her, it is to enlist her aid in poisoning his wife, a task to which she readily agrees. This contradiction is not Webster's; it is the result of Mr Prowse's decision to eliminate the scene of the dumb show and the conjuror assassin, and substitute Zanche in their place. It is the old Cits [*sic*] story. Story-telling and theatrical logic are butchered to make way for an arresting flow of stage pictures ... The atmosphere of a terrible dream certainly grips the stage, but it is thanks more to stage management, camp-baroque costume, and Bond-like additions (such as the translation of murder victims into ghostly spectators) than to Webster's verse rhythms or intended climaxes.

There is no way round this sort of objection to the Citizens' textual impertinence unless you find what they do preferable to, and more imaginative than, the docile literary interpretative traditions of the English theatre; and the majority of drama critics do not. Their mission is

213

to defend classic texts against the interference and tampering of directors. I have never understood this when it is known that the texts themselves were cobbled together from various versions and based, in the form we have them, on a manuscript prepared for the printer, not the actor. This was certainly the case with *The White Devil*.

There was more uniform approval of Prowse's Greenwich revival of *The Seagull* in MacDonald's translation. The most inspired idea was to postpone the only interval until after the third act, thus gaining maximum dramatic charge from the two-year gap in the narrative; Prowse replaced his iridescent garden with a funereal study, the stuffed seagull in pride of place, and the white bentwood chairs with black ones. We thus saw how an incipiently dipsomaniac Masha (whom Julie Legrand paired with a sulphurous, flame-haired Vittoria in the Webster) had been reduced in the passage of time by marriage to the pathetic schoolmaster; and, even more vividly, how Johanna Kirby's abused and abandoned Nina had descended from a promising ingénue to a full-blown, haunted tragedy queen.

This Greenwich season gathered together many stalwarts of the Citizens, and also initiated Maria Aitken, who had worked previously at Greenwich with Alan Strachan, in the Prowse style; she would later renew the collaboration here forged with the director, and Rupert Everett, in *The Vortex*.

There is a myth that Prowse the director gives actors a hard time because they have to handle his re-writes of classic texts, and cope with his sets and costumes; Paola

Dionisotti certainly found it difficult to cope with Prowse's heavily adapted treatment of *The White Devil* when she turned up on the first day of rehearsals ('All the preparatory work I had done as Isabella was absolutely useless'). But that was the first time she had worked with Prowse as a director.

It was the first time, too, for the National Theatre actors who joined the newly formed company within the NT led by Ian McKellen and Edward Petherbridge; they chose to do *The Duchess of Malfi* in 1985 and invited Prowse, the seeming antithesis of an actors' director, to direct it. The Glasgow connection was honoured in the presence of Jonathan Hyde, switching from the Cardinal to Ferdinand, and of Laurance Rudic as the emblematic hooded figure of Death. The production was strong and stately, apparently placed in a limbo-like grey mausoleum, where the air was heavy with the cawing of crows and the pealing of bells. It imposed an intriguingly morbid uniformity on such disparate ingredients as McKellen's blank Bosola, Eleanor Bron's drained Duchess and the distinguished comic trio of Sheila Hancock, Hugh Lloyd and the late Roy Kinnear.

I thought it very fine; but Rudic, looking back, thought it failed because the actors in the first place were insufficiently prepared to submit to the visionary context. A traditional, humanist way of looking at *Malfi* did not coincide, he reckons, with Prowse's unblinkingly dark, extreme and cruel conception. For Prowse, as for the Soviet Constructivists and the German Expressionists and their successors in the contemporary European theatre, acting is but one element in the theatre, where many elements (text, design, lighting, costume, sound effects) have equal sway, and the confusion arises when different assertions, equally valid, are made by others — actors as often as critics — who disagree.

Looking forward in hope with Pope

Havergal's assistant on *Travels With My Aunt*, Jon Pope, embodied a hint of the future, and may yet prove, if his association with the Citizens prospers, a key figure in the continuity of personnel as the three main directors approach the end of the millennium and, dare one say it, later middle-age. When Havergal and Prowse went to Glasgow, they were young men in their thirties, and most of their actors were ten years younger. Twenty-one years on, the age gap between the directors and actors remains, on the whole, about the same, ten years. Which now makes the acting company itself middle-aged.

Jon Pope (b.1958), who studied theatre in Poland, and was a finalist in the 1986 Young Directors competition sponsored by BP and organised by the Battersea Arts Centre, runs his own company, Shadow Syndicate, a cross-disciplinary outfit specialising in gestural performance, systems music and the sort of cool, crop-haired, black-garbed designer post-Modernism that characterised much contemporary art at the end of the 1980s.

His main-house debut for the Citizens, directing his own adaptation of Mary Shelley's *Frankenstein*, was one of the most promising in our theatre, metropolitan and regional, for a very long time. Contemporary performance manners were excitingly hitched to the intellectual star of

Romanticism: the story was set in some snow-swept Arctic tundra where the blasted Victor Frankenstein interrupted his pursuit of the Creature to tell his tale to a fellow explorer; the congealed veneer of the horror film industry was peeled off to reveal the work's richly attractive surface of scientific and philosophical adventurism; and, in going beyond the book itself, Pope dramatised a reverberative commentary on the Promethean legend that obsessed both Shelleys, brother and sister, as well as Byron, whose spirit underpins many Citizens productions from Lermontov right through to Wilde.

Pope went on to direct a *Richard III* in 1940s' costumes in the enforced studio (on the stage) season, during the final phase of renovations, in 1988. Havergal's generous susceptibility to Pope's influence could be seen in his own chilling, uncluttered, modern dress production of *The Crucible* a year later, in which the firm denial of all the consolations of a period drama – leather jerkins, white-bibbed smocks, Cavalier hats, flowing locks and knee-high boots – ensured the atmosphere of an eerily modern chamber babble of guilt, accusation, and adolescent freak-out (was it an acid party the girls had attended in the woods?).

There were no significant outbursts of hostility towards the Citizens as these fundamental artistic shifts at the end of the decade – the grandeur of Prowse's work on Wilde, the toughening of MacDonald's Teutonic creativity in Goethe and Schiller, the spare flintiness of Havergal's productions, and the post-Modern input of Jon Pope – were underway.

A lone voice on the *Glasgow University Guardian*

(where the novelist William Boyd had contributed some outstandingly perceptive notices of the Citizens' work when a student in the mid-1970s) proclaimed, in 1986, that the artistic innovations had dried up and that the company was now stuck in a camp slapstick rut: 'Critics who once savaged, now bow in agreement. Havergal has now come full circle and is faced by a posse of sycophants where once stood a group of hangmen. Their support for his panto-camp style is leading to the slow asphyxiation of the theatre.' This entertaining but misinformed outburst by Ian McKay also diagnosed an entrenched apathy towards the local community, the most haywire of all his allegations, as we shall see in the next chapter.

There was, however, a lurking charge to answer here: the regime had now acquired a seeming respectability, regular serious coverage in the national Press, and it had inevitably grown up as it had grown older. But I don't think the policy had become smug or moribund, nor was there any one style even resembling 'panto-camp'; the whole point, as I have tried to demonstrate, was that the 1980s, even more so than the 1970s, had seen a deepening of in-tellectual purpose in the work, and an absolute refusal to become bogged down in trademarks or production clichés.

Pope's emergence was just one example of this, and he promptly weighed in with a mangled, heavily cut and outrageously designed *Macbeth*, which stirred some familiar tones of resentment that now sounded positively antediluvian. The play was set in a post-nuclear war-zone of dry ice and wind machines, with benighted warriors in gas masks staggering around in heavy-duty protective clobber and luminous lemon fatigues. They hacked at grilles with pick axes, a cadre of Antarctic firemen in cold pursuit of King Sweno of the Norways. Mary Brennan of the *Herald* was outraged ('Reducing *Macbeth* to a load of old cobblers' ran the headline to her review) and her arts editor, John Fowler, followed up angrily, revealing an odd Bardophiliac loyalty to 'the Scottish play', which had been defiled in, of all places, a Scottish theatre:

> "This castle hath a pleasant seat . . ."? Oh no it hath not. This castle hath a seat deep in the permafrost of Ice Station Zebra . . . Its starting point is *Macbeth* as myth, not the specific *Macbeth* created by Shakespeare, though what has been retained of the text is more or less what Shakespeare wrote. It is Shakespeare gutted on the principle that a work of art can legitimately be divorced from the intention of its creator, and that an interpreter has free flight.

We were back to square one. All the old, worn-out objections to interpretative direction could be reactivated at the touch of a nerve button. Even some of the regular Citizens actors were scathing about someone of a younger generation daring to tread paths they themselves had trod fifteen years earlier. The verse-speaking was imperfect, one or two younger actors all at sea. But perhaps it was high time to see rough execution and bold ideas all over again. The women who waited for these snow-bound warriors were strange, veiled North African creatures among whom Charon Bourke's Lady Macbeth was an ambitious reader of signs and portents swathed in veils and bazaar beads. Stewart Laing's design covered the entire stage in silver paint and Bacofoil, the theatre's structural innards exposed as on a Richard Rogers construction. Simon Tyrrell's ranting, skinhead Macbeth screwed up the poetry but almost compensated with his haunted, headlong portrayal of a murderous psychopath. The witches patrolled the scene with clipboards and walkie-talkies, their magic an agent of control, and doubled as doctors, women, adversaries and invisible knife-bearers.

It must be embarrassingly clear by now that I like very much the idea of a production that jostles against received notions of a text, especially a well-known text. The audience for *Macbeth* was primarily composed of schoolchildren, just as the audience for *Hamlet* in 1970 had been. They responded to Pope's *Macbeth* in exactly the same way: with delighted surprise at liberties taken and with pleasure at the clothing of a sacred cow in unexpected raiments. The production's images of terrorism and heroic struggle were culled from cinematic clichés and television reportage in the Middle East. What may be difficult for some critics is not difficult for children; they find excitement in the poised retention in the memory of a cultural artifice and the simultaneous counter-play of its vital and conflicting representation.

Pope's vision had flaws, but ambition was not one of them. A letter to the *Herald* in defence of the production placed Pope alongside creative visionaries who had been applauded by Scottish critics, including Mary Brennan: Ninagawa, Peter Sellars and Johann Kresnik (whose blood-boltered dance *Macbeth* was a sensation of the

1989 Edinburgh Festival). The correspondent, James Mavor, might have added the names of Prowse, Havergal and MacDonald. And if the correspondent's name rings a bell, here was the loveliest, most final irony of all: the grandson of Doctor Mavor, aka James Bridie, founder of the Citizens Theatre, was not talking nationalist or even 'new Scottish plays', but defending that theatre's right and duty to be in the internationalist vanguard.

There was no clearer evidence that the oppositional crusade of the Citizens was still thriving. The theatre was now widely recognised as the most European of all British theatres, at one with a growing community of artists in opera and theatre who seemed certain to set the pace in the 1990s. But perhaps the real secret of the Citizens' success lay in the extraordinary manner in which reputation abroad had been based on a deepening affinity with local political aspirations.

George Devine's Royal Court had lasted, according to Lindsay Anderson, just about twenty years and had then, in the mid-1970s, changed its colours completely. Peter Cheeseman had remained in Stoke for over twenty years, but it would be difficult to make out any sort of case for his work or influence over the last ten. The only comparable operation to the Citizens in the modern British theatre outside of the National and RSC had been Alan Ayckbourn's tenure at the Stephen Joseph Theatre at Scarborough. And that was mainly renowned as a springboard for Ayckbourn's own plays; there was nothing particularly radical or distinctive on the production side, although the atmosphere at the Stephen Joseph has a similar friendly informality to that of the Citizens' foyer.

221

Havergal, Prowse and MacDonald had turned round a famous but doomed theatre, presented the most challenging repertoire in Britain, in the most interesting variety of styles, had produced countless young actors, and many designers, of talent and promise, had secured a reputation and yet remained a subject of heated critical, if no longer public, argument. But all three would say that the most important achievement, apart from survival, had been the salvation of the theatre building and their success with the local community. How had they done it?

8

POLITICS, FINANCE, SURVIVAL

The cornerstone of the Citizens' survival plan has been not so much the artistic policy as good management. No one who knows anything at all about the arts in Britain disputes that they are underfunded by the State. But although many fine theatres have many reasonable excuses for running into deficit, it does come as a shock to learn that the Royal Shakespeare Company is running at a loss, announced for April 1990, of £3m, or that the Leicester Haymarket, which at the end of the 1980s boasted of internationalist aspirations, and indeed had realised a few of them, is nearly half a million in the red. Whatever these theatres' arguments for increased subsidy might be, it is certain that they are trusting to political authorities and sponsors to bale them out while they pursue policies both unrelated to realistic and coherent planning and wildly in excess of their economic means.

Paul Bassett, the Citizens' general manager since 1979 (he recalls driving up for his job interview on the day that Mrs Thatcher was elected Prime Minister), says that in approximately only one out of ten meetings with the artistic directorate does the subject of art crop up. All the talk is of money. The constant discussion, confirms Giles

Havergal, is of 'matching the plays we want to do to the money we have got'. Philip Prowse is unlikely to volunteer a Wilde production if he is told that £3,000 is available (*Lady Windermere's Fan* was done on the unusually high, top-whack budget for sets and costumes of £17,500); but the average budget, excluding wages and permanent overheads, is usually about £4,000 or £5,000. If something goes wrong, adjustments are rapidly made within the same financial year so that the annual figures are squared.

There are two examples of drastic action being taken. In preparation for the 1983 Edinburgh Festival, *Rosenkavalier* was disastrously overspent by £20,000. This meant that the following spring season had to be pared to the bone. The two home-grown productions were Toller's *The Machine Wreckers* done with five actors, and Sartre's *Altona*, its cast list reduced, with no great loss, from ten to five. These plays were even more cheaply complemented with the import of a one-man show by Jack Klaff.

A second crisis loomed when industrial action by school-teachers at the end of 1985 had the knock-on effect of hitting school party bookings for the Christmas show; nineteen performances were cancelled with an estimated net loss to the theatre of £34,000. In this instance, the Scottish Arts Council made a special contribution (as they did to other theatres similarly affected) of £9,500 in the following April. But, before then, the main repair job was done in the programming of three exceedingly cheap productions, all with small casts: *The Spanish Bawd*, *Friends and Lovers* and *Entertaining Mr Sloane*.

There are several points here. While saving on wages, the repertoire remained adventurous. Toller, Sartre, de Rojas and Goldoni are not authors with whom you would normally expect to play safe. Indeed, the average attendance for those six productions was just over 47 per cent of capacity, with Orton top-scoring with 64 per cent and the Toller registering a disappointing low of 35 per cent. But the clever trick was that, even without filling the theatre, an overall economic balance was restored, and the reputation of the theatre for doing interesting work was sustained, while costs were savagely controlled. Ian Ribbens, the production director, who co-ordinates the building and technical operation, recalls that Prowse produced *The Spanish Bawd* on a budget of £1,000 and indeed came in at something under that figure; he simply went into the workshop and used bits of old sets and scaffolding boards, any old junk lying around. The miracle is that, in performance, the design appeared deliberate, consistent, evocative, memorable.

The ruling idea, finally, is to balance the books. The figures for the 1980s show four years of small surpluses (£4,927 the maximum) followed by four years of small deficits (£4,217 the maximum), with one year, 1982–83, of absolute balance. In twenty-one years under Havergal, the deficit has never exceeded £5,000, and the theatre's reserves remain intact.

This is music to the ears of Donald Frame, of McLachlan & Brown, the chartered accountants who have monitored the theatre's books throughout this period. Frame's vigilance is constant, but only at Havergal's insistence. First of all, Frame hives off the fixed charges (heating, lighting, rates, rents, etc.) from the total income of grants and projected box-office. The rest is handed over to Havergal, and budgets for each production are prepared on cost sheets which are pre-set, having been worked out with the production team and heads of department. Frame says that the exactness with which these procedures are followed is rare in his experience of dealing with artistic enterprises. The books are computerised and maintained by his company outside of the theatre; there is a method of reporting that derives from the theatre, and, built into that, are controls. The minute anything goes wrong — in budget variation, bar sales, box-office receipts — he hears about it almost immediately.

People backstage and pictures in front

Havergal once said that he did not believe in under-paying the wardrobe mistress so he could afford to air his socialist conscience on stage. Donald Frame is struck by the fact that in Havergal's book the cleaner is just as important as any actor on the stage. Similarly, the theatre's canteen costs something in excess of £20,000 each year. Frame argues that the actors could go out and buy their own food; Havergal insists on making good hot food cheaply and readily available to his staff. He also points out that, once in the Citizens, there is nowhere locally to go and eat without crossing back over the river, or risking a new, expensive (for actors) restaurant with table-cloths by the Sheriff's Court. The issue is often keenly debated, Havergal's arguments invariably accepted, although by February 1990, with costs soaring, an outside firm was given a catering contract by which the company hopes both to improve the choice on the menu and to keep the annual costs within £15,000. (One or two redundancies in the kitchen have been necessary, but not that of the ebullient and long-serving Rose Cull, who presides over the cheap and cheerful, unlicensed-for-alcohol canteen, with its television, pool table, well-filled ashtrays and decaying furniture.)

Frame was first put in the picture by George Singleton, whom he describes as a hard businessman. At the end of the Cuthbertson regime, the finances were not in order. The bars were not balancing and a lot of money was disappearing on travel and entertainment. Frame's remit was to take a cold commercial look at the theatre and to revise the controls. The new system did not produce satisfactory results, Frame says, until Havergal arrived. But the crucial difference was probably made by the appointment of William Taylor to the chairmanship in 1970, in succession to George Singleton, who had remained an avuncular and powerful presence on the board since the company's inception in 1943.

William L. Taylor (b.1917), a formidable Glasgow politician and lawyer, and a partner in the firm of solicitors Rosslyn Mitchell, Taylor and Ramsay, had been on the Citizens board since the mid-1960s. He had served on the council, formerly the Glasgow Corporation, since 1952, eventually becoming leader of the Labour Party group. He retired, undefeated, from the Corporation in 1969, retaining (until the mid-1970s) his chairmanships of the new town of Livingston and of the Scottish special housing association. He liked Havergal from the beginning, although the new director's dealings with Singleton and other board members were proving sticky. It was in the spring of 1970 that he was invited to become chairman, and he has been an exemplary and supportive one ever since. On the odd occasion when he neither likes nor even approves of the work, he will defend his artistic directorate to the hilt against all attacks. He never disputes with writers who air critical differences of opinion or well-argued hostility. In fact, he rather enjoys such articles. But he is alert to any attempt on the part of critics to call for resignations, or stir up political trouble under the guise of a theatre review. In Havergal's first ten years, Taylor regularly invaded the letters columns, courteous but firm, the minute his directorate was taken to task and the call sounded for heads to roll. The need for him to take such action in the succeeding ten years has been much rarer. He has steered the board into granting Havergal a succession of long-term contracts, four or five years at a time, and it is understood, with no need of further ratification on paper, that for as long as Havergal stays, so do Prowse and MacDonald.

From this solid basis of understanding between the board and its appointed artists stems everything else at the Citizens. It is worth elaborating on the continuity of the theatre's personnel. Ian Ribbens was with Havergal and Prowse at Watford, and has been production manager and technical director at Glasgow for the entire period, with a two-year gap halfway through; he went off, not to another theatre, but to be a self-sufficient farmer, living off the Scottish land for a while with his family. Gerry Jenkinson, who was also at Watford, does the

Opposite:
Jill Spurrier and
Paul Rhys in
*A Woman of
No Importance.*
Overleaf:
Fidelis Morgan and
Robin Sneller in
French Knickers.

lighting design for most productions, and has done for twenty years, justly acquiring a national reputation as a freelance thanks chiefly to his symbiotically creative work at the Citizens, especially with Prowse. Tricia Biggar has only recently left the wardrobe department after fifteen years, but the two present heads of wardrobe have been at the Citizens before, gone away, and returned. Ribbens sees this ability of the theatre to retain key people as the clearest measure of its success, and the fact that everyone knows how each of the directors works means that corners are cut and valuable time saved, an essential factor when the average rehearsal period is three weeks.

Some staff have been in place for even longer. The chief maintenance electrician, Fred McGowan, will soon have completed a thirty-year term, as will Mary Sweeney, the brisk and efficient staff supervisor at front of house. The latter, always smartly attired in a fresh white blouse, black skirt and cardigan or jacket, with never a hair out of place, can tell many a tale of checking the theatre in the old days for interlopers from the adjacent tenements.

The self-effacing Lyn Pullen, the production and company manager, who came to the Citizens as a secretary to Robert Cartland just before Havergal's arrival, describes herself ungenerously as 'a skivvy support system for the artistic directors'. Pullen, born in Aberdeen, worked part-time in the Citizens' box-office while attending Glasgow University. After teachers' training college, she decided she hated the idea of teaching and returned to her beloved theatre. She speaks for all the backstage staff when she says that 'We all feel

Overleaf:
Ann Mitchell and
Ciaran Hinds in
Mary Stewart.
Opposite:
Harry Gibson and
Yvonne Orengo in
An Ideal Husband.

part of something here; it's not just another job'. She is entitled to six weeks holiday, but Prowse simply will not tolerate her absence when he is either casting or directing. 'I usually only get a script from him two days before we start. David [MacDonald] has improved slightly in this respect, now that he gives us discs that I can print out from. And Giles gives me a script all cut to pieces and stuck together again. They are all different. But it's really special here. Everyone who works here knows that.'

The non-acting staff often find themselves thrust into the limelight. Pullen herself was cast as an on-stage dresser in *Chinchilla* because she was the only person around who was smaller than the actress in need of the attendant, Anna Keaveney. She hated the experience and will not be repeating it. Others are not so retiring. The day-man and van driver, Dennis Knotts, a bulky, jolly Glaswegian father of seven children, has 'walked on' several times, most notably in *The Spanish Bawd*, and he was also the chosen spokesman for the theatre in a series of TV advertisements on Channel Four in which he more or less said 'It's good, and it's cheap: get there'. This was in 1984, and the attendance figures for the 1984–85 season show an 11 per cent increase on the previous year (142,000 people came, compared to 127,000). Knotts repeated his 'oyez' in a series of community service announcements on Scottish Television in early 1990.

Another fixture in the building, resident since 1955, is Sheena Dickson, a misleadingly sour-looking woman, now just turned eighty, who mans a desk in the foyer every night on behalf of the Citizens Theatre Society, a pleasantly anachronistic social set-up which organises raffles and sherry evenings to recall the great days of the past and, presumably, such sad issues as the rotting away of the Alfred Wareing portrait shortly after Havergal & Co. were installed. The Society does still have two seats on the board, and one of them is now occupied by the very same Tony Paterson who resigned as the suddenly superfluous literary manager in 1969.

One would like to imagine an off-shore band of Bridie loyalists cursing the present incumbents in obscure Scottish verse, whipped to a frenzy by the crazed and furious exhortations of Miss Dickson. But Miss Dickson is not the mournful nostalgist she might appear, any more than she is a fawning pushover. Indeed, she is known around the building to be something of an intellectual. And she has firm views, positive and negative, on all the productions. Her praise, even when qualified, is not to be sniffed at. She once waylaid MacDonald as he drifted through the foyer: 'David!'; 'Yes, Miss Dickson?'; 'I enjoyed *Camille* . . .'; 'Oh, thank you, Miss Dickson'; '. . . much more than I expected to.'

Miss Dickson's lugubrious visage is her natural mask, her best face forward, and indeed very probably not a statement of sorrow at what has happened to the Citizens, but a defensive flourish of regret at the intrusion of a paying public in the temple of her private dreams. For Miss Dickson, too, has trod the boards. She did so as the non-speaking Queen of Naples in *A Waste of Time*, alongside Mary Sweeney and Agnes Rhodie, the long-serving barmaid in the now regrettably obliterated circle bar (up the stairs and on the right, a real cosy nook it was), who were card-playing denizens of the Guermantes salon. All three ladies were splendidly attired; in a Prowse production, even the extras are dressed to kill.

(Agnes Rhodie, who also once worked in the Citizens box-office, used to work for Jimmy Logan at his Metropole Theatre and, in earlier days, was a world champion highland dancer. Moreover, it was a likeness of young Agnes Rhodie who danced patriotically on tins of tobacco produced and traded by Robert David MacDonald's family firm, MacDonald's of Glasgow, thus forging one of the most extraordinary Citizens links in the whole story!)

These are just small outward signs of the integrated nature of the operation, but they explain a lot. All posters, announcements and display advertising tend to be matter-of-fact, and the theatre feels hard done by in the local press where there is little news or feature coverage that is not prompted by a whiff of puritanical righteousness. To this day, news coverage is still skimpy; but the poster information was not always so low-key. In the 1970s, an advertisement campaign in the theatre magazine *Plays and Players* toyed with glistening images and icons of the counter culture daubed provocatively on a dilapidated Gorbals background: Jill Spurrier and Rupert Frazer sat at tables on which was laid out the apparatus of cocaine consumption ('Still by courtesy of Twentieth Century Fix'); Suzanne Bertish leant against a graffiti-covered peeling wall in a striped suit and Homburg while Di Trevis, wearing just patched jeans and a fox fur, stood by her side; David Hayman and girlfriend repeated the pose, but this time he wore the jeans and bared his torso. This jumbling of sexual identity, as much as the juxtaposition of glamour and poverty, was an outrage and an irritation to some, a sure indication of the theatre's individuality to others. The campaign softened at the end of the 1970s when Adrian George provided some delightfully ghoulish line drawings: a youthful Arlecchino holding a severed head, an androgyne in a suspender belt executing a hand-stand beneath a curtain dripping with blood. Finally, even these deft evocations gave way to the brute reality of the environment when the bleak landscape of the Gorbals in 1977 – 78, with close-up photographic studies of local kids aggressively challenging the lens, was deemed a sufficient visual statement of an artistic counter-presence.

These images still resonate and define the essential identity of the Citizens for many theatre professionals and critics who rarely venture north of Watford. They were not exactly misleading, and they certainly indicated the sort of bravura and insouciance endemic to many productions of the time. Even the pictures of deprived young local boys avoided the sentimentality of the Bert Hardy photograph of Gorbals street urchins that is reproduced every time somebody writes a magazine article on Glasgow. They also declared a lack of middle-class guilt or political hang-up about the theatre's position in the community. But the truth, which could never be gleaned from the advertisements, was that the Citizens Theatre, for the first time in its history, was irreversibly establishing itself in the changing political climate of the city. By the 1980s, there was no need to make a song and dance about it. The critical coverage was more regular, money for advertising much scarcer, and *Plays and Players* itself a much less significant magazine than of old. Also, the renovation programme was fully underway.

Renovation, cheap seats and subsidy

This renovation programme has been completed in four phases. The first two phases, in 1978 and 1979, were undertaken by the owners, the Glasgow District Council. The building had survived without major repairs since 1878, and Phase I, costing £250,000, improved the backstage area and upgraded the heating system and ventilation with all necessary concomitant rewiring and plumbing. An extra £4,000 came from the Scottish Arts Council towards refurbishing the dressing rooms. In Phase II, also costing about £250,000, the auditorium was recarpeted and redecorated, the front of house areas were improved and the upgraded plant (the heating and ventilation) was extended to front of house. In 1985, Phase III was undertaken by the theatre itself and consisted of structural repairs to the main roof, the cleaning of the stone walls of the exterior, the provision of toilets for the disabled and a new ramped area near the stalls bar and an upper circle bar. This cost £280,000 and funding came from the Scottish Office in the form of Urban Aid of £140,000, matched by the same amount from the SAC (Housing the Arts Fund). In addition, in the spring of 1988, Glasgow District Council replaced the south side roof at a cost of £30,000. Phase IV, comprising the new façade, foyers, bars and general re-design at the front of the theatre, was funded, as we have seen, by the Scottish Development Agency as part of a deal with Glasgow

District Council for the construction of the neighbouring commercial development. The cost was £800,000. To coincide with Phase IV, the Citizens undertook its own improvements to the auditorium and adjacent passages, the stairway to the upper circle, and the stage itself, including the installation of a new counterweight flying system. This work was funded by the District Council (£100,000), Strathclyde Regional Council (£100,000) and the SAC (£42,000).

Thus, over £1.8m of public money has been spent on the theatre building while ticket prices have remained conspicuously low and concessions to certain members of the audience increased. I remember a talk given by Peter Brook in London, under the auspices of the RSC, at which he was asked what was the single most important factor in the future of a healthy theatre. There was a short pause to allow for the collective intake of expectant breath before the twinkling guru crisply responded: 'cheap seats'. While the RSC has not been able to follow its own advisory director's advice, the Citizens has maintained the lowest seat prices of all Britain's permanent theatres.

There has always been a free preview on the Thursday night before the Friday opening of each new production. Thereafter, seats were 50p each for nearly six years, rising to 75p in 1975. In 1982, the price was 90p, rising in the same year to £1.50. In 1984, the cost of a ticket was £2, and by 1986, £3. For the season 1988 – 89, the full price was still £3, with concessions of £1 for students, and free tickets for Old Age Pensioners and the unemployed available on the door. That pattern of pricing, in place for several years, was altered in 1989–90 to a full price of £5, with concessions still of £1 for students and free seats available both on the door *and* in advance for unemployed and senior citizens.

This is a far cry indeed from the West End of London, where a top-price ticket can be £25, and the cheapest £10. The National Theatre offers student standby tickets for £5, weekday matinée tickets for £7. Otherwise, the NT tickets range in price from £6.50 to a £16 top.

The new Citizens policy is still under review, for the 57 per cent of the audience who paid full price over the three years from 1986 to 1989 dipped to below 40 per cent in the year 1989–90, partly because *Macbeth* had 66 per cent of the total audience comprising students or schoolchildren paying £1. And there is a difference of opinion within the administration over the single-price ticket. Prowse, supported by Paul Bassett, unwaveringly advocates the single-price £5 ticket, whereas others, Havergal included, would be happier with a £4 ticket for the large upper circle which now incorporates the old gallery; all seats up there are separately numbered places on newly upholstered and comfortable wide benches. But the back rows are very high up and, while it is exciting to sit there, you are not as intimately involved with the proceedings as you are downstairs. However, for 1990, all tickets will probably remain at £5.

The total annual subsidy from local and national sources at the end of the 1970s was £300,000. By the end of the 1980s, this total figure had risen to about £650,000. Even by the parsimonious standards of British arts funding, this is still not very much, placing the Citizens at the lower end of the big range of subsidised houses and almost level with the Royal Court (an unexpected 17 per cent increase from the Arts Council has boosted the Court's grant to £672,500 for 1990−91). The funding bodies in Scotland have responded as well as they could possibly have done over the years, although there was a slight brush with the Scottish Arts Council in 1980. The SAC failed to increase the grant by £10,000 in line with similar increases to other theatres because they disapproved of the low seat-price policy. In his 1985 lecture to the World Congress of the International Federation for Theatre Research, Havergal referred to the incident and said that the shortfall had not yet been made up. He had buried the hatchet with the SAC, but had also marked the spot.

The Citizens constantly plays cleverly to its strengths. They know, for instance, that if they announce a play by Schiller or Goethe, then the very supportive Glasgow branch of the Goethe Institute will contribute a sum of about £10,000. Thus, as Paul Bassett admits, *Joan of Arc* was done partly because the theatre knew that extra income (in that case about £12,000) would be made available; the cash from the Goethe Institute pushed the theatre over the edge and made a reality of the lurking intention to do such a piece. Bassett says that even on an annual turnover in excess of £1m, the issue of five or ten thousand pounds is a crucial one. There will be haggling over items of set or costume decoration, even if it is just a piece of glitter costing £25. I think this is fundamental to the calibre of the work and the survival of this regime. There is no conspicuous waste, and thrift is a matter of not just economic necessity, but of moral responsibility. You can say that of very few other theatres in Britain. In the age of the subsidised whinge, the Citizens has been able to secure its funding increases by working in the first place within meagre budgets and thus convincing politicians that money will not be wasted. And, following on, comes security of status and the loyalty of an audience. This attitude has been unique and its consequences apparent.

Playing a role in the community

The assumption in the early days that the Havergal Citizens would prove to be an alien force in the community has been entirely squashed. The theatre, as it stands, is a part of local life; but it also infiltrates the community in the work done by Theatre Around Glasgow, TAG, in schools and arts centres. TAG's reputation is high, and many fine young actors and directors have come from its ranks. Its main job, though, is to service the community.

In January 1979, I was stranded in Glasgow thanks to a British Rail strike and a snow-bound airport. I made virtue of necessity by following TAG to Woodside Secondary School in the Charing Cross district of the city. Ian Wooldridge had just taken over as director, and had produced a short programme of nine plays written by schoolchildren (sixty-eight submitted). The subjects ranged from parents stuck in front of television, to unemployment, a community's preference for a welfare centre to that of the council for a flower bed, and punk animosity when a returning native denied his background. The audience of pupils, many of them Asian, sat riveted throughout an energetic performance.

Formed in 1967, TAG was one of the first theatre-in-education groups in Britain, and it has been doggedly preserved through thick and thin by Giles Havergal. Although its administrative base is at the Citizens, and Havergal and Paul Bassett take final responsibility for it, the operation is entirely separate from the Citizens company, and is funded separately, too. In 1989–90, TAG received £83,000 from the Scottish Arts Council, £65,000 from the education department of Strathclyde Regional Council, and £18,000 from Glasgow District Council. It also received a special grant of £25,000 from Glasgow Health Board to fund an anti-smoking show.

In the shape of TAG, the Citizens goes out to the people. But who are the people who come to the Citizens? The free Thursday night preview, according to Ida Schuster, is a vigorous, and often raucous, ritual for the locals, which triggers for her memories of the old days. At other times the audience seems very mixed, with a smattering of students, university types, professional couples, young lovers and quietly appreciative, rarely sullen, Glaswegians. An audience survey once reported, recalls Havergal, that 47 per cent of them came from outside the city, a crucial figure in his negotiations with Strathclyde for equal funding from the region. 51 per cent were found to have come from within the city, and the remaining tiny percentage from Edinburgh or further afield.

In 1984, Jan McDonald averred in her monograph that 58 per cent of the audience was between the ages of fifteen and twenty-four. But a survey conducted for the

Policy Studies Institute in 1986 revealed that only 15 per cent of the audience was in that youngest age group; 24 per cent were aged between twenty-five and thirty-four, and the largest proportion, 27 per cent, were between thirty-five and forty-four years old; two age-bands covering mid-forties to the mid-sixties accounted for 26 per cent of the attendance, while 8 per cent were over sixty-five.

The audience overall, however, was significantly younger than at those theatres canvassed in Ipswich and Cambridge in the same PSI survey. And there was a 62 per cent dominance of women, as well as a very high, 82 per cent, representation of middle-class, or ABC1, customers. Such a survey does indicate an acceptance of the theatre in the community, though it obviously does not reflect the special role of its catering for schools and pantomime audiences, or its work outside the building in the TAG department.

How does the oddball work perform at the box-office with such a constituency? Until August 1984, the seating capacity of the theatre was 831. In March 1984, Sartre's *Altona* played to an average attendance of 353, or 46 per cent of capacity. The wacky Offenbach deconstruction, *French Knickers*, presented six months later when the capacity had been reduced to 641, played fifteen performances to an average of 475, or 60 per cent. Hochhuth and Schiller both did well in this same first season of the reduced capacity, playing fifteen perfor- mances each to 55 per cent and 72 per cent respectively. But obviously such comparatively recherché work was only possible when, in the same season, Wilde played to

90 per cent capacity and *Arsenic and Old Lace* (the murderous ladies played by male actors) to 96 per cent during a longer run of twenty-seven performances. This illustrates how Havergal has cannily used the repertory system to subsidise the risky work. Each year, the Christmas show fills the theatre to capacity for about sixty performances and makes possible, for instance, a piece like *Oroonoko* (just nine performances playing to a total paid attendance of 2,435, an unpaid attendance of 1,032, at a total average of 385 a performance).

Jean McFadden, deputy leader and treasurer of Glasgow District Council, used to go to the Close with her mother before she was married and became embroiled in a political career. Through her work on the Labour Party-dominated council (she was leader from 1979 to 1986, when she was succeeded by the present incumbent, Pat Lally) she claimed a place on the board of the theatre. She admits that she is surprised that Havergal and Co. have stayed so long, but detects no deterioration in the freshness of their approach. She pinpoints an interesting and surprising fact of Scottish political life in remarking that, following the first round of local Government cuts in the mid-1970s, the feeling then engendered, under a Labour Government, that the arts should be shelved in favour of other priorities, did not take hold during the next ten years of cuts under Mrs Thatcher.

A lot of people in the Labour Party still hanker after the good old days of ship-building and so on; they can't let go. But Glasgow is becoming an important financial centre as well, and the tourist business has been booming, so there is no significant political difficulty in keeping the arts going. There is much more political difficulty in respect of subjects like the sale of council houses and the poll tax. The arts just jog along.

As for the tag of European Capital of Culture 1990, that is just one big item in a regeneration programme that has been underway for fifteen years. No one wants to dispense more urgently with the old mythologies of a violent, hard-drinking, dangerous Glasgow than do the politicians: Pat Lally told *The Sunday Times* in 1987 that 'being given the European City of Culture award is the funeral service for the *No Mean City* image'. Mrs McFadden acknowledges that the continued presence of the Citizens under Havergal has been a factor in winning the honour, but she is far more interested in looking at ways of translating the short-term benefits into long-term improvements. The same goes for the Labour-dominated Strathclyde Regional Council, whose support of the arts is unequivocally related to social objectives. Councillor John Mullin, chairman of the Finance Committee, regards the political body's support of the Citizens as an integral part of a comprehensive strategy to support the arts in the region. In representing the interests of 1.7m poll tax payers, Mullin regards the arts as crucial to their well-being; indeed he expresses great concern over the ambivalent attitude towards arts funding not only in central Government but also in his own Labour Party leadership. He is despondent that some of the main figures in the party do not seem to spot the link between the regeneration of the conurbation and the regeneration of the individual; in his view, they go together.

In this context, the Strathclyde Regional Council regards the Citizens as a crucial political tool in their aims. They admire the low seat-price policy, the TAG operation, the concern for access to the theatre from the community, and they know full well that these are not suddenly adopted criteria. By first demonstrating its commitment to the city and neighbourhood, the Citizens has won the reciprocal co-operative response of the regional authorities. But the theatre had to adjust carefully to the surrounding political situation. When the old Corporation was divided between Glasgow District Council and the regional authority in the mid-1970s, the region maintained its support and indeed continued to match that of the district. When legislation relieved the regional councils from any funding responsibility for the arts, Strathclyde nonetheless continued its support with a core grant, which remains at about £80,000. The district council's support has obviously far outstripped this figure, but Strathclyde has kept up and kept faith, not only with the capital grant towards the refurbishment, but also with the £100,000 for each of the last two Strathclyde Summer Seasons. This is a contribution not automatic- ally available, but subject to the region's discretionary powers each year, which ensures that the Citizens provides the audience with the very popular work of companies such as 7:84 and Wildcat, and chimes with a policy of making the city attractive to tourists in the busiest months of the year.

The interesting thing here is that neither the audience nor the Strathclyde politicians make any significant distinction between the Citizens' own programme and that of their visitors. George Thorley is an unelected assistant chief executive at the Regional Council and he is adamant on the subject of why the Citizens is politically approved. It has very little to do with the quality of their work, and nothing at all to do with what they say. It is because of their perceived sense of social responsibility, their concessions, their facilities for the disabled, as well as the fact that they keep reassessing their artistic aims and coming up with fresh proposals. The same give-and-take characterises the council's relationship with Scottish Ballet, the Scottish Jazz Orchestra and the Scottish Chamber Orchestra (leading to the commissioning of Peter Maxwell Davies's series of Strathclyde Concertos).

This binding of the artistic enterprises into a quality of life policy is rather more than making concrete a pious hope. The cultural programme is seen clearly as a method of reinforcing the commercial trends in investment and the consequent material and educational improvements in the city at large. In 1990, over £2m is earmarked by Strathclyde for the development of the curriculum in schools and tuition for the handicapped. For the arts as a whole, the regional council's investment for 1989–90 was £2.4m, leaping in 1990 to £12m. The high profile, Thorley says, is not the point: the razzmatazz of 1990 is regarded as 'a nice wee boost' to a campaign that has been underway for fifteen years.

If you raise the subject of the Citizens' international reputation with these officers, you receive a cool counter-assertion that Strathclyde Regional Council has a

European reputation of its own to maintain, and that an association with the Citizens will enhance it. They would not wish to be seen mixing with failure, and Mullin admires the fact that the Citizens 'really are tuned into the real world; it is useful to us to have them as an example to hold up to other theatres. I am sure that their importance will only increase because they are prepared to give so much. And when youngsters go there, they feel that the theatre is alive, not just there for a performance, but as part of their community.'

From being a group of controversial outsiders, Havergal and his associates have skilfully manoeuvred themselves into a unique position of both local political importance and national significance. The stability is also due to the fact that nobody who works there regards the place as a stepping stone to somewhere else. This philosophy runs like a filament through every aspect of the work, and I believe it stems in large measure from the healthy artistic and intellectual arrogance of its directors. What is good enough for Glasgow is certainly good enough for them. And this, surely, is where the objections to 1990 and to the so-called yuppie culture boom, levelled by John McGrath and the more cynical nationalists, disintegrate entirely. The Citizens' success is not a flash in the pan. Nor could it have been achieved in an environment hostile towards the idea of slow and painstaking improvement. On the subject of the 'new' Glasgow there will always be areas of disappointment and disagreement, but you simply cannot write off the cultural boom, and the story of the Citizens, as a sop to yuppies or a dastardly reinforcement of the Act of Union.

245

Local commentators such as John Fowler are still liable to under-rate the Citizens, perhaps because, while aware of the great civic struggle that has been endured, they do not see how brilliantly the Citizens has prospered in this respect, through a combination of high cunning and tactical nous, compared to theatres in other British cities. There is also a pervasive reluctance to admit that there is anything special about the Citizens, and all the more so if London critics keep saying there is. In a *Glasgow Herald* anthology of writing to celebrate 1990, Fowler almost parenthesises the Citizens in his chapter on the arts in Glasgow, commenting on its fame achieved beyond the city by innovative staging of the classics and remarking that what shocked prudes in the early Havergal years is now acceptable because tastes have changed: 'Glasgow has become more sophisticated, and the Citizens has become respectable even in the eyes of those who never go near it. Judging from recent productions, the standards have never been higher.'

The corollary reaction to this is very much part of the novelist William McIlvanney's anti-1990 line, which is unashamedly suspicious of cultural bonanzas that seem to glorify a city still up to its neck in problems. Ever the romantic champion of the local underdog, 'the quizzical starers, the cocky walkers, the chic girls who don't see a phoney accent as an essential accessory of attractiveness', McIlvanney prefaces Oscar Marzaroli's superb photographic historical documentary of the city by distancing himself from more formal expressions of art. May the Citizens, he says, and the Tron, and the King's, and Scottish Opera, 'always find among their audiences some of those perennially disgruntled faces that could be captioned: "They ca' this art?"'

This insistence on not being over-impressed by anything is a likeable local trait that often obscures the reality of achievement. Humane irreverence, McIlvanney calls it, in a good phrase. But the Strathclyde politicians are surely entitled to point out that the so-called yuppie binge only began as a result of the major urban renewal programme in the West of Scotland dating from the mid-1970s. New town growth, along with Green Belt development, was curtailed, and an urban housing market created. *The Mahabharata* and Pavarotti concerts may be objectionable, plush-trendy intrusions on the granite political sensibilities of a certain number of the engaged local artists. But the majority of ordinary citizens regard them, dispassionately or enthusiastically, depending on circumstances, as visible signs of fundamental civic renewal.

The continuing presence of the Citizens is part of that profound recognition of a process of change and improvement. Strathclyde has pathetically high unemployment figures, and a concert by Pavarotti, or a firework display in George Square, or even Glenda Jackson playing Mother Courage at the Citizens, is not going to do very much about that. But all things are relative, and a political community which failed to attempt to balance material improvement with educational and leisure opportunities would be both irresponsible and philistine. George Thorley protests that he and his Strathclyde colleagues are under no illusions about the task ahead: 'We have twenty more years hard

247

labour.' The Citizens, one feels, will play an important part in those coming years, and is thus implicated in the life of a city to a far greater extent than ever James Bridie could have envisaged.

It is because of the inclusive way in which they have assessed the contribution they might make that the Citizens have survived thus far. It is not a question of art on one hand and politics on the other, actors on the stage and audience in the stalls. This is why there is, as yet, no sign of commercial sponsorship. The pressures are mounting on all theatres in Britain to attract financial support from the private sector. Havergal, typically, is not against the idea, but he is against having a little bit of sponsorship tucked away in the corner and feeling he has to apologise for it. If the Citizens decides, after 1990, to enlist sponsors, it will almost certainly do so with vigour and enthusiasm. Any serious qualms about sponsorship would abort the process. But if and once the process is instigated, all qualms would themselves be aborted.

Everything interconnects, and so would sponsorship. The theory, in so far as it is a theory, smacking so strongly of practicality, was best summarised by Havergal in his concluding remarks in the 1985 lecture to theatre researchers from which I have already quoted:

Whether the show is chosen by an actor, director, writer, witch-doctor or priest, whether the expectation of the audience is to see a big star on Broadway or to make local maidens fertile, whether you have to please Louis XIV, the Central Committee, the Chrysler Corporation, Glasgow District Council or the local rain god, whether it takes place in the Royal Shakespeare Theatre or in a clearing in the jungle, I suggest that the creative choices will be conditioned in some way by money, by where the play will take place, by what the staff structures are, who the audience might be, who the actors and directors are, what external political forces are at work and finally by the creative abilities of the people making the decisions.

9

ACTING UP AT THE CITIZENS

It has been noted already how many very fine actors have
made their first mark at the Glasgow Citizens in the past
twenty years. But while the notoriety of the theatre has
given way to a general recognition of its achievement,
there remains one issue on which feelings run very high
indeed: the issue of the acting. Acting at the Citizens
made Tom McGrath's flesh creep and led Allen Wright to
declare that there must be another acclaimed south side
Glasgow theatre, where good acting was to be found,
besides the one he had been visiting for so long.

The first thing to be said is that there is no such thing
as empirical proof of good acting. One senses greatness
in the air when Olivier, Gielgud, Richardson or nowadays
Michael Gambon is on the stage. There is danger and
surprise to be gleaned from the performances of Antony
Sher, Jonathan Pryce and Simon Callow. One cannot
easily resist the notion that we have lived through a
golden age of actresses, of Peggy Ashcroft and Judi
Dench, of Maggie Smith and Vanessa Redgrave, of
Glenda Jackson and now Fiona Shaw. But for every
hurrah, there's a boo, for every impassioned celebration,
a hint of disapproval and of doubt. This is not simply a

251

matter of critical response. It is a common fact of ambivalent human reaction to the efforts of those who are vocationally hell-bent on two interestingly contrasted, sometimes conflicting, missions: the expression of personality; and the communication of a dramatic text. The balance of effect lies precariously and indefinably between self-indulgence and artistic purpose.

Gerard Murphy has told me how it is even more complicated than that. Like David Hayman, he rates the *Macbeth* directed by Havergal as the most exciting production he has ever been in (he played the title role), and declares that one of the major attractions of the job is 'getting inside' the director's head. The vanity side of acting means nothing at all to Murphy, a performer of headlong emotional intensity and a fine musician. A blazingly intelligent Irishman from the border town of Newry, Murphy says that acting is like a drug, and the doing of it an inexplicable fusion of need and possession. One of his first roles on joining the RSC was in *Juno and the Paycock* opposite Judi Dench. He was astonished to find that Dench was terrified before each and every performance; she told him this terror did not lessen with the passing of years, but, if anything, increased. There was something addictive, too, about the nature of company life, not as a substitute for domestic stability, but as a complement to it. Murphy seems as genuinely enthusiastic and fulfilled at the RSC as he was at the Citizens.

This security within an ensemble, which compensates for the individual perilous acts of performance, is what makes the whole business of acting interesting. Theatre is dirty, Howard Brenton used to say. It is also ephemeral, and long may it remain so. There are no rules, not even much agreement, on what constitutes a good play or a good production, let alone sound acting technique, in the way that such ground-level consensus informs all musical performance. As Kenneth Tynan once said, 'For 99 out of every 100 of us, the score must provide an absolute yardstick for measuring the Eroica; there is no similar standard for *Macbeth*'. G. H. Lewes, in a brilliant essay on the latter play to mark the retirement of Macready in the title role in 1851, remarked that a test of an actor's genius lay not in his fidelity to Nature, but simply and purely in his power to excite emotions in an audience respondent to the situation. He defined greatness in acting as a tripartite summary of conceptual intelligence, representative intelligence and physical advantages, concluding that while Macready was undoubtedly great on all three of these counts, his talent was untouched by genius.

But even within those definitions, who can agree on what is the concept and what the representation? The actor himself might know, but the audience, even a critical one, is not easily able to spot the distinction. There has been a great surge of actors' lib in the British theatre of late, partly as a reaction to the theatrical institutions, partly as a defiant stand against the encroaching fame and influence of what are seen as the parasitical functions of the director and designer. But the phenomenon is also surely something to do with the assertion of dignity in a job it is all too easy to perceive as thoroughly silly. Symptomatic indications of this serious

253

trend include the Actors' Company, of which Paola Dionisotti was a key member, democratically led by Ian McKellen in the mid-1970s (a set-up partially reinstated within the National Theatre in the mid-1980s, led again by McKellen, with Edward Petherbridge, for which Philip Prowse directed and designed *The Duchess of Malfi*); the actor-oriented informal fringe companies of Joint Stock and Shared Experience; Simon Callow's blistering handbook, *Being An Actor*, in which he proposes that actors should first organise their own productions and only then hire a director; the reactionary critical backlash against 'conceptual' theatre to which I have already referred; and that backlash's favoured touring group, the Renaissance Theatre Company, led by Kenneth Branagh as an unapologetic new-style actor manager.

Rights and responsibilities of a vagabond

We know from politics in the real world that democracies are not always what they seem. At the time of the Actors' Company, one well-travelled joke was: 'Isn't it marvellous, you can see McKellen as Hamlet one week and as a waiter the next!'; 'Yes, what's the second play called?'; '*The Waiter*.' But as Patrick Hannaway says, in the early years of the Havergal Citizens, there existed, without any artificial pressure, an ideal of role-sharing, because all of the actors were of a similar inexperience. There is a hierarchy of function at the Citizens only to the extent that everyone is clear as to what his or her job entails; there is absolutely no insistence upon special status or privileges within the company.

The vagabond nature of acting is renewed in Glasgow,

and the difference between working there and, say, the National in London, has been vividly noted by Laurance Rudic. Everything at the Citizens, says Rudic approvingly, is less domesticated, more bohemian; when working at the National (in the Prowse *Duchess* and Mike Alfreds' production of *The Cherry Orchard*) people would rush off home at the end of a day to their houses, their cars and their families. He also discovered that if you were a small actor in the company, you were treated as one. 'In Ian McKellen's *Coriolanus*, Peter Hall didn't even talk to the extras. He sent them his assistant. That is totally disgusting. What you always get at the Citizens, as an extra, is as much dignity as the principal players, you are well choreographed and you get a very nice costume. So who is talking about respect for actors and acting? Glasgow has more respect for the actor than any other theatre in Britain.'

That point is less contestable than the one about the quality of the Citizens acting. London-based directors concede the gorgeousness of Prowse's designs, the adventurousness of the repertoire, and then add dolefully, 'but there is the acting'. At the Citizens, technique is regarded as something for which the actor himself is responsible. Motivation is not a matter for discussion in rehearsals, certainly not with Prowse and MacDonald. Ian McDiarmid tells of an actress in the early days, Carol Drinkwater, who has since become well-known on television, who prepared each night for the role of Olga in Chekhov's *Three Sisters* by cleaning out both her dressing room and the entire backstage area before she felt ready to go on; nobody minded, least of all

Prowse, who said 'If that's what you wanna do, fine. We may all have a good laugh about it and say that you probably gave a better performance in the dressing room than on the stage, but that's your business.' Rudic, too, has an elaborate system of preparation and always invents a back-up emotional world and past life for the character. On the morning of a performance, rather as Callow relates in his book, everything is geared to the moment he hits the stage at night. The interesting thing is that he has no idea how his colleagues prepare. There are no formal warm-ups or technical sessions, although Steven Dartnell used to hold such classes in the early days for those who wished to attend. David Hayman, too, went into rigorous training for each role, keeping fit and swimming regularly, as Rudic still does.

The upshot is that one is often aware of different levels of concentration and effort among the actors on stage. There have been consistent and appalling lapses in articulation in a theatre building where there really is no excuse not to be heard; it was unforgivable, when Prowse embarked on his Wilde ghost chase with *A Woman Of No Importance*, to miss many of the best lines, including, can you believe, 'Nothing succeeds like excess', and the definition of the English fox-hunting craze as 'the unspeakable in full pursuit of the uneatable'. Other critics disagree with me on this, but the articulation record is really no worse at the Citizens than at the National or the RSC in recent years. And that is not to excuse it. The defence of such slovenliness at the Citizens would be that words and meanings are only one element in a theatrical philosophy which, along the lines of the modern European theatre of Strehler, Chéreau and Peter Stein, often subsumes sharp-edged clarity of diction and indeed facial visibility in chiaroscuro lighting effects and the overall composition of the design. I think too much can be made of this. The unevenness is undoubtedly what is intended. Patrons who prefer even, clear, no-nonsense and straightforward productions uncluttered with ideas and drolleries have many other options, if not in Glasgow, then certainly elsewhere in Britain. But, as has been noted, all three directors have different ways of working. Charon Bourke says that Havergal does actually talk about acting a good deal more than either Prowse or MacDonald; one of his rehearsal exercises is to run through the play in hand at which the imaginary audience is either completely blind or completely deaf. Bourke professes admiration for Havergal as a teacher and claims that he encourages actors to think quite deeply about how they present themselves.

Style, personality and the wearing of frocks

The propelling desire in acting at the Citizens is to avoid work which falls within the received notions of interpretative mannerism. John Gielgud is often quoted with approval as saying that style in acting is a matter of knowing what kind of play you are in. Fidelis Morgan rejects such a definition as 'utter trash', suggesting that style is playing the truth of the lines as they come, whatever the play, and sifting them through your own personality as an actor; that, she says, is exactly what Gielgud himself does anyway. Morgan sometimes gives acting courses, 'primarily because I hate going to the theatre so much that I want to do something to change it', with the avowed aim of breaking down the idea that there is one way of carrying on in Restoration drama, one way of speaking in Noël Coward, one way of cringing tragically in the Jacobeans.

The idea of the personality itself defining the nature of performance is at the root of the Citizens style. Charon Bourke says that most actors who work there a lot, or at least the best of them, have three things in common: they know how to wear a costume, how to use a light, and how to reach the back of the gods. The capabilities of actors are taken for granted in the way they are treated, and in the costumes with which they are supplied. Paola Dionisotti recounts how, as Madame Irma in *The Balcony*, she had to pour her performance, and herself, into a skirt with a ten-inch diameter at the bottom, and then cope with nine-inch heels on a stage with little steps all over it. She thinks these restrictions in fact defined her performance.

Fidelis Morgan goes further, declaring as hopelessly wide of the mark the idea that the Citizens in general and Prowse in particular are uninterested in acting, or even theories of acting. While acknowledging that their approach is entirely different, she insists it is also full of subtlety. 'Philip will order you to come in the door, be cross, sit down on a particular word, bang your stick on the floor, and so on. There emerges a very strict set of rules and you have to try and squeeze your performance through the holes of various instructions.' This rigour extends to the treatment of language, so that in *The Vortex* there were a lot of unnatural stresses, in unexpected places, but as the method was consistent in all the playing, the stage became a specially created world for the play and its people. Morgan says that working as an actor with Prowse is like playing chess; it is interesting because of the complexity of the rules. She cites a scene in *Lady Windermere's Fan* where, as the Duchess of Berwick, she was told by Prowse not to move at all while delivering her vast speech of about five pages. The job was to command attention even though the audience was likely to be distracted by Lady Windermere, who was allowed to move around during the speech. 'It was a challenge to wrest the audience back. It was terrifying, but also creative; the scene worked very well, every single night, and I got a round when I went off.'

Some actors would deny that a director who sets such obstacle courses is collaborating on an equal basis. Sian Thomas says that Prowse's costumes are both incredible and impossible:

In *Vautrin* I had a huge Parisian agglomeration of skirts, 1840s style, with crinolines and beautiful sloping shoulders. It had a great heavy fringe, which kept catching on the furniture, so I would develop this sort of Ariadne web behind me. I was so heavily corseted that I thought I was going to have a heart attack, and indeed I went to hospital suspecting (wrongly) that I had suffered a thrombosis. So you have to be physically strong to wear Philip's costumes; he is also very keen on high heels, which lends another element of strain on a raked stage – it's murder on the calves. On the other hand, I loved *Semi-Monde*, which was easier, and I adored my costume in *Chinchilla*: at the fitting, Philip just sort of looked at me and picked up this fake fur and with this one movement wrapped it around and put it on my head. It looked absolutely brilliant, and of course I had wonderful jewels and things. I was playing a rather grand prima ballerina, and they knew just what to do with me.

It is a curious paradox at the heart of the Citizens that this visible sumptuousness is so casually contrived. Rudic denies that there would be any improvement in having more time to prepare, a sort of creative purdah of three months, for instance, as is the European habit. Rudic likes a short rehearsal period because he enjoys knowing that he then has four or five weeks of the run itself to continue working on the play. He contrasts this with the experience of Mike Alfreds' *Cherry Orchard* at the National, which exhausted all the possibilities during an extended rehearsal period, leading, in his view, to a rigid, repetitive type of performance, squeezed of all juice and any sense of interpretative danger. There is no in-depth discussion about acting at the Citizens for the simple reason that there simply isn't time for it: 'You get on with your job, get on the stage and get off.'

Indeed, you might say that what the Citizens specialises in is paying attention to the actor, as opposed to the acting. Actors are made to feel proud to be working there, and this surely informs the quality of the performances they give. Fidelis Morgan emphasises the efficiency of the backstage operation, noting that everyone working in the theatre has the same goal, of

Opposite:
Fidelis Morgan,
Alan McCullough,
Tristram Jellinek,
Jill Spurrier and
Robert David
MacDonald in
Anna Karenina.
Overleaf:
Maria Aitken and
Rupert Everett in
The Vortex.

getting the play on as best they possibly can that night and every night. In most theatres, actors have to mime their properties until at least the technical rehearsals. Not at the Citizens. Most properties and accessories are available on the first day of rehearsal. Morgan cites in contrast the more typical experience of working at the Birmingham Rep and needing attention one Saturday on her costume. No such luck; the wardrobe was shut on Saturdays. And Paola Dionisotti recalls how, in her Glasgow days, while having to work extremely hard (the Close operated from Tuesday to Sunday, the main stage from Monday to Saturday, which meant most actors were rehearsing all day and often playing seven nights a week), the actors were none the less treated like stars: 'It was utterly different from anywhere else at that time. You had the whole business of the first night, the whole Noël Coward bit, with absolutely nothing tacky or fringey about it. There were bouquets everywhere, and champagne, and it didn't half go to everybody's heads, actually!'

Rupert Everett, when he returned to the company to play Randall Utterwood in *Heartbreak House*, put his finger on the weakness of too much actors' lib, scotching the idea that directors' theatre was necessarily repressive, when he spoke to Peter Whitebrook of *The Scotsman*:

Look, directors and designers only enhance an actor's work. I distrust actors who say that they could work without them, as they usually have as much idea of position and what something will look like as a giraffe has of skating. I also distrust actors who say they must delve into themselves over a long period to find a character. The way it works here is that I offered the idea of Randall being a kleptomaniac and Philip gave me the scenario to play it. So of course there's collaboration, there has to be, the work-rate is too intense to be otherwise.

As it happens, this was a production that Michael Ratcliffe, for one, felt let down by in the acting department: 'The centre does not hold, never lives up to Randall loose among the silver, the Tommies on the lawn, Ellie watching, and the ominous red tree.'

Even actors who have soared gloriously at the Citizens often grow apart from its methods. This, I think, is inevitable, and my heart shrivels each time I see one of the former, glittering stage-orators in the Gorbals plodding through mundane television scripts as a barmaid or policeman. On the brink of her career, Charon Bourke states that she would be perfectly happy to pay the bills from her TV acting and to work in Glasgow the rest of the time. But she knows that career pressures might compel her to join the National or the RSC, should the chance come along. It is a terrible indictment of how the metropolitan London-based system works against the significance of the regional and British theatre as a whole.

But other Citizens actors find that, when they leave, they have to acknowledge what they evaluate with hindsight as shortcomings in the system. This is a natural process of extirpation and renunciation. Sian Thomas, for instance, did not so much leave as simply decide not to go back, having begun to resent the lack of discussion about acting. She also finds herself questioning the governing aesthetic:

> The theatre at large, ultimately, is about writers and actors. The rest is extra. I do think directors are important; but they are only important for the energy they impart to actors. In some ways, Philip is trying to say "No, the bit that really matters is the design, the middle bit of the sandwich", and he sometimes tries to discredit some of the plays he does by being very witty and very cynical. He wants, in a curious way, to deprive the actor of the power that naturally belongs to him.

Thomas wants to work with strong directors, 'big men and women who can see all points of view', who have both an aesthetic vision and an interest in the psychology of acting. She advocates a marriage between Philip Prowse and Mike Alfreds, but concedes that such an arrangement, attractive in theory, would not last for one second.

David Hayman had two great jolts to his creative system: when directing, as he did on three occasions at the Citizens, he discovered that his own way of working was different from that of his peers; and his father, a steelworker, was suddenly made redundant in the middle of the 1970s, which opened his eyes to a more directly political sense of responsibility as an artist. He also feels strongly that the quality of the acting at the end of the 1970s was markedly inferior to the quality of the vision: 'A lot of people were swamped by it [the vision], and I did feel that the next development of the company should be the emotional and technical one.'

Paola Dionisotti notes that what the Citizens were doing in the early 1970s was in direct opposition to how people were being taught to act in drama schools ('It had all become rather private, with wonderful emotional things happening behind a sofa that no one could see; we were told quite clearly. at Drama Centre that acting was nothing to do with showing-off') but that, having been taught how to play big roles with confidence, how to enjoy 'giving it' to an audience, she rejected the idea that actors should work in isolation from each other and not in collaboration with the director.

Ian McDiarmid remembers how, on leaving the Citizens, one joined companies where 'sensitive under-playing' was highly valued and where the worst thing you could do, worse even than killing your grandmother, was 'to go over the top'. In the 1970s, 'egotism' and 'self-indulgence' were insults everywhere in the British theatre except in Glasgow, says Jonathan Kent, where such vices carried with them, rather, the highest accolades. But both McDiarmid and Kent, who now run the Almeida Theatre in London as actors and directors, reckon that the emotional emphasis, the substitution of feeling for language, is a denial of the fact that language *is* feeling, the two go together. Kent astutely points out that the Citizens' view of theatre as an emotional extension, not a forum for social change, from which stems their ideology of acting, was, in the early 1970s, a deliberate flouting of the accepted wisdom both at the RSC (Leavisite intel-lectualism allied to a Marlowe Society verse-speaking tradition) and the Royal Court and fringe (social realism and political conscience).

In this way, the Citizens has always been an aesthetically dissident theatre, one refreshingly deviant from the entire mainstream, and not just the commercial sector; many actors recount how they turn up to auditions at places like the Royal Court and are shown the door the minute they mention their Glasgow credentials. The cult of personality is one to which the more puritanical wing of the British theatre has remained determinedly immune over the past twenty-five years. But Havergal and Prowse wanted to fill their stage with attractive, eye-catching, preferably sexy young people. In the first place, actors were hired for what McDiarmid calls their sense of self, their charisma and animal energy.

Fidelis Morgan relates the impact of a Citizens production to what Sybil Thorndike always talked about as 'the animal smell':

> You sit there and you do always have that feeling that they might spit on you at any time; and you know, too, that various members of the company, who are familiar to the audience, are the subject of interested speculation on their part as to what they might get up to next. It's a great feeling on both sides, that rapport, and it's all to do with theatre being theatre and not a screen, not something we've all gone away with and got perfect. It's real live people in front of your eyes, and anything might happen.

While asserting that most of the actors in Glasgow are

not actorish or flippant, Morgan confirms that the directors know within two minutes of meeting an actor whether or not they will get on with him or her : 'As a result, you end up getting a body of actors who are not exactly similar — they all have their tics, obviously — but they all tend to be eccentric in a rather straightforward way. You always find people there who've got personality.'

A strong quartet: Citizens on parole

In attempting to dig deeper into the calibre and diversity of the actors' personality, and how that quality relates to the nature of the Citizens' work, I offer brief biographical sketches of a carefully chosen, but not un-typical, quartet: Laurance Rudic, a Glaswegian and a permanent fixture, almost, over the past twenty years; Sian Thomas, a regular between 1977 and 1981; Fidelis Morgan, who first acted with the Citizens in 1978, and has also worked for a season there as an assistant director; and David Hayman, the local boy and first Hamlet, now a notable film actor and director, whose career over the past ten years offers the severest contrast possible with his previous ten in the Gorbals.

Laurance Rudic (b.1952) is only really known for his connection with the Citizens, and his career there is an effective rebuttal of the *canard* that actors who never work anywhere else are second-rate actors. A rather strange and private man, Rudic studied drama in Glasgow and claims to have been dying the theatrical death before he fell in love with Lindsay Kemp. Kemp was then based in Edinburgh, and Rudic spent all his spare time as a student helping out on his shows and appearing in such productions as Kemp's *Woyzeck* and *Flowers*, a remarkable homoerotic extravaganza based on Genet's novel *Our Lady of the Flowers*. The great thing about Kemp for Rudic was that he performed as he lived, without fear and miles out of the closet. He remembers how one night Kemp went absolutely crazy during a show; he had fallen in love with a boy in *Flowers* and, tanked up on gin and hash, broke off in mid-performance to declare in floods of tears that all his actors were leaving him, nobody cared for him any more, the world was against him, and so on. It remains for Rudic the most extra-ordinary night of his life. But the inspiration extended also to Kemp's use of music, dance, design and make-up. It was like nothing at all he was being taught at drama school.

The paradox here is that Rudic is not all that much of a sensualist himself. He lives quietly and abstemiously and travels alone a good deal in India. He likes living in different cultures and trying to understand them. These experiences broaden his philosophical outlook and have also, he feels, directly enhanced his work. He claims now to be 'more relaxed about who I am and what is my position in the world' and no longer has the problems he used to have when confronting an audience. The picture he forms of himself as an actor, in what he does on the stage, now comes into clearer focus.

When the Havergal company started up in 1970, Rudic knew he had to join the minute he saw the work. His first role was in *The Balcony*. He started immediately going through his 'first serious phase', because he realised at this point that he wanted to follow a more structured theatre route while incorporating all that he had learned with Kemp. He wanted to know more about the art of acting. He disagrees vehemently with those who believe the art of acting is not on the Citizens' agenda. 'In expecting me to create, the directors make me feel, as an actor, like an artist in my own right. This special context of the work, its world of imagination and risk-taking, simply does not exist anywhere else in the British theatre.'

Of average height and slim build, with dark hair and a sallow complexion, Rudic has reinforced the elegant, modernistic ambience of countless Citizens productions. But from small and decorative minor roles he has progressed over the years to play such demanding leads as the psychologically damaged son in *Altona*, the doctor in *Judith* and the decrepit old Manette in *A Tale of Two Cities*. As a Glaswegian, he finds that his voice tends to fall back down his throat, and that his tongue is lazy, so he works hard on bringing the sound up and forward in order to be able to play in the quieter style that he often wishes to adopt nowadays. He does not allow himself to get fat. He smokes a lot, but never misses his daily vocal exercises.

Rudic has no career plan, he has no life plan. He exists in a permanent state of pennilessness and bums around, sleeping on friends' floors when unable to afford anything better. He is a well-practised, and sought-after, house-sitter. He dislikes working in London but is not tied to the Citizens; committed, yes. But he counts the insecurity of that relationship with the directorate as important – even the most loyal and regular Citizens actors never know, when they finish on a production, if they will ever work there again. He alleges that if an actor was to treat the company as a safe haven, he would immediately be lost.

Sian Thomas (b.1955) is a stylish, attacking comedienne who has in recent years played Katherine in *The Taming of the Shrew* for the RSC and Célimène in *The Misanthrope* at the National. Both her parents were in the theatre (as is her younger sister, Sara Mair-Thomas, who played Bianca to her RSC Kate), and both studied at the Old Vic school with Michel Saint-Denis. Her father, Powys Thomas, who played Oberon in a famous George Devine production of *A Midsummer Night's Dream* in which all the characters were dressed as birds, went to Canada to work with Tyrone Guthrie and stayed on to found the National Theatre School of that country. Sian Thomas, aged seven, played Princess Margaret in a French Canadian production of *Richard III*, thought she was going to die of excitement, and so became an actress. After training back in England, at the Central School of Speech and Drama, she ended up playing big parts in bad rep productions until a life-line was thrown by the Citizens audition to which I have already referred.

She found the atmosphere at the Citizens both intoxicating and frightening and says it's the mood of sexuality that hovers in the air that makes you feel, as an actor, that you are in Europe, not in England or even Scotland. But she found, too, that, as in all creative institutions, there was a damaging, destructive side to the creativity. Which is why, she feels, it is important to know when to move away. Prowse she counts an absolute genius, but also a man apparently frightened of real contact with people. 'He is, of course, amazingly industrious. But working with an actor and going forward to discover something new and interesting, something you have not planned, is the sort of work he does not want to do. He wants control. But you cannot, as a director or a designer, control an actor's heart.'

The technical polish and steely characterisation Thomas brought to all her Glasgow performances again made a nonsense of the 'bad acting' charge. Outstanding in high comedy, she could also tug the heart-strings, as she did as Grusha in *The Caucasian Chalk Circle*, battling for her son's life through thick and thin; the son in this production was not played by a swaddled doll and, in the later stages, a child actor, but by the fully-grown Mark Rylance, whimpering and blubbing throughout as the embryonic, confused Hamlet he was later to become at the RSC. Thomas, for all her strictures, declares that the influence upon her of her time at the Citizens, as both actress and woman, is imperishable, unforgettable. The head of her drama school came to see her in the outrageous Goldoni production, *The Good Humoured Ladies*, and was horrified. 'At Central, they had always maintained that we should have a theatre of seduction, not of rape. Well, to them, the Glasgow Citizens was a theatre of rape, and they hated it.'

Fidelis Morgan (b.1952) comes from a large family of Irish Catholics ('not devout, more like the Borgias, really') and was born in a caravan on Salisbury Plain. Her

Liverpudlian father, a dentist, had friends in the 1960s who owned most of Carnaby Street, so he found himself caring for pop stars' teeth. With her mother and two younger sisters, she hung around on the periphery of such glamorous occasions as the opening of Mr Chow's Chinese restaurant in South Kensington. The family lived in a huge house on the Isle of Wight, with caves in the garden which came in handy for a series of what she remembers as rather orgiastic parties. Fidelis Morgan regards herself as the sensible one; the middle sister models lingerie for the Janet Reger catalogues, while the younger one, now working on computer slide designs, was for a time a private detective until she managed to get herself arrested for impersonating a social security officer.

After studying with the Restoration Theatre expert Jocelyn Powell in the drama department of Birmingham University, Morgan auditioned for RADA where 'some stupid man' made her march round a room shouting out numbers at the top of her voice. She told him she could not shout any louder − proud though she is of her foghorn sound effects − and he said 'Listen, my girl, if you want to get on in the theatre you've got to learn to be thick and to do as you're told.' So she picked up her handbag and left, muttering something along the lines of no wonder the theatre's in the state it is if that was how he went around carrying on in front of the poor benighted creatures who came under his wing She gained an Equity card playing a Kit-Kat girl in *Cabaret* at Perth Rep, and it took only a few days to work out that she was not very happy doing that, nor was she feeling very creative. Her fellow chorus girls were bitching away about the Glasgow Citizens, which made her suspect they were probably worth going to see. So she drove down to see *Happy End*: 'It was an extraordinary experience to walk in there for the first time. The theatre was red and green and black, and the set was red, green and black checks. The cast was fabulous and it struck me as being everything I wanted theatre to be.'

That was in 1973, and soon afterwards she went round the world with the RSC as understudy to Glenda Jackson in Trevor Nunn's production of *Hedda Gabler*. When she finally joined the Citizens, she went in as Mrs Peachum and played a series of burdened peasants, graduating to salon divas, tart dowagers and even Kath, the Beryl Reid role, in *Entertaining Mr Sloane* ('A horrible play by a horrible little man who obviously loathed women').

Fidelis Morgan is also a playwright and writer whose edited compilation of the Restoration women dramatists, *The Female Wits*, is one of the most revelatory volumes in recent feminist theatrical literature. She has also published a biography of Delarivier Manley, one of those 'lost' Restoration playwrights, as well as a fascinating edition, both scrupulous and imaginatively embroidered, of the narrative of Charlotte Charke, the actress daughter of Colley Cibber. Her latest project is nothing less than a history of the English actress.

What Morgan likes about the Citizens is what drew her to the Restoration period and the classical idea of theatre before the invention of film and television. There were only two theatres in Restoration London, and the audience went again and again, developing a personal relationship, 'friendship' even, with the actors.

It used to be like that at the Old Vic in the 1960s; as a schoolgirl, I used to go and see everything sitting on a bench seat for two bob and I used to think, I wonder what Ronald Pickup's going to be doing in this one. I don't give two hoots about what he's up to now, but at that time I cared about him enormously, as I cared enormously about Derek Jacobi, or Sheila Reid, or Geraldine McEwan. The best things I've ever seen have always had Maggie Smith in them; she has a great personality, and she also does the absolute truth of a play.

When I went to see **David Hayman** (b.1950) in Soho, he was editing a ninety-minute film, funded by the British Film Institute and Channel Four, about a notorious Glaswegian hardman and friend of Jimmy Boyle who had gone AWOL from the Army and had shot dead a barman in Rupert Street, London, for the sake of a few pounds. The film, *Silent Scream*, is about the last twenty-four hours of this character's life, seventeen years of which had been spent in prison, ending in the Barlinnie special unit where he died after taking a drug overdose.

Flashing back through his past life, the prisoner re-visits the bleak housing estate where he lived as a boy, re-lives escapades around the Necropolis, sees once more the sectarian Orange Marches through the Glasgow streets, and experiences his first day of parole, the painful process of hospitalisation and his recurrent brushes with authority figures. If, as he says, 'madness is a matter of contemporary morals', is it ethically correct for him, a certified drug addict, to be confined in prison for treatment? Hayman says he is not setting out to plead the cause of social conditioning in an environment of which he, as a native of Bridgeton, has first-hand knowledge, but to discuss the brutalities of the Scottish prison system.

Hayman's father's family hails from the island of Arran on the west coast of Scotland, his mother from Glasgow via Australia where her antecedents had been sent as convicts. The boy David strutted his stuff to glorious effect for ten years at the Citizens, but his life changed when his father lost his job and when he was offered a script to direct at the Traverse Theatre in Edinburgh. That script was *The Slab Boys* by John Byrne, and the huge irony is that Byrne had first submitted it to Havergal, who had sent it across to the Grassmarket experimental emporium with a strong recommendation that they should seriously consider producing it as it wasn't the sort of thing they did at the Citizens.

(The play, about teenage apprentices in a Paisley paint-mixing factory, was a runaway hit. Byrne later completed a vaguely autobiographical trilogy, all three plays were seen at the Royal Court in London, and Byrne followed up with a scorchingly funny TV series *Tutti Frutti*, starring Robbie Coltrane. First hint of Byrne's wildly funny writing talent — he was already known as a painter and occasional set designer — had come with *Writer's Cramp* on the Edinburgh Festival fringe of 1977; the cast of three — Bill Paterson, Alex Norton and John Bett — had all started out in the TAG branch of the Citizens before moving on to join John McGrath's 7:84 company in the early 1970s.)

Just before directing *The Slab Boys*, Hayman, who had worked as a child actor on television, played his first grown-up role on camera, that of Jimmy Boyle in *A Sense of Freedom* (an earlier stage play by Tom McGrath about Boyle, *The Hardman*, had been a notable success for Peter Kelly) and when it was transmitted on national television, the local star was seen in a controversial and much-discussed role by an audience of twenty million. As he admits, the nature of his market value, his price, changed overnight. And, as an actor, Hayman knew that he hungered, after ten years at the Citizens, to explore film and naturalism. He fell for a time into a television stereotype derived from the Jimmy Boyle performance, playing hit-men and thugs in very good TV series like *The Sweeney* and *Minder*. But he quickly tired of this and started directing plays at the Bush Theatre and Royal Court in London.

He looks back on the Citizens era with a strange mixture of affection and objectivity. He claims that the period gave him both his strengths and his weaknesses. He still looks very fit, the famished wolf appearance of his lean and hungry days in the Gorbals, glitter and eyeshadow notwithstanding, recycled in his casually fashionable attire of black leather jacket and jeans, rubber-soled shoes and white socks. The hair is as short as when he played Nijinsky in *Chinchilla* ten years ago. But the exoticism of that time has been expunged from his life, overtaken by tight filming schedules and a professional routine of energy-sapping flitting between Glasgow and London. His wife has been a social worker in Edinburgh, Glasgow and London, and they have two small sons. He has talked on television with the Bishop of Edinburgh about his sense of the religious in life, although he pays no dues to any denomination.

Hayman is not remotely precious about his work, but he has changed tack completely. In one or two Press interviews he has been misconstrued as rejecting his past life. But he understands more than anyone the impact of the Citizens on the Scottish theatre community. He comments drily on the rapturous reception accorded in some quarters to Gerry Mulgrew's touring Communicado company, or the current TAG work and its successive bright young directors Ian Brown and Alan Lyddiard, or Ian Wooldridge's regime at the Edinburgh Lyceum: 'It's all come from the Citizens, only they don't pull it off as well as Philip, Giles and David.' As artistic director of 7:84 he claims to produce subtler plays than did John McGrath and intends to tackle the subject of the Scots working-class hero who sells out. He obviously does not include himself in this category, citing the case of Jimmy Reid, the former Communist leader of the Clydeside ship-builders' trades union who became a media star and now writes a highly paid column in a tabloid newspaper. 'That is a paradigm of the Scots condition. We always fall at the last hurdle, and I want to do something about that. McGrath wouldn't touch the subject. He was always putting political dogma and statements on the stage, rather than investigating the personal political angle.'

Alone of all the actors who have worked with the

Havergal directorate, Hayman could almost claim associate director status. He admits he sometimes cashed in on this, pushing his luck and the patience of his acting colleagues, as in *Happy End* when, playing a one-legged beggar, he tried to retrieve a cork from a bottle and extended the business so it went on for ever: 'I always grabbed moments like that because for me the essence of theatre is taking the audience along a knife-edge, building that sense of reality in danger that you simply cannot do on film or TV.' He remembers another beggarly moment of creative input when he was discussing with Prowse the latter's production of *The Changeling* 'one stoned evening' and how they might represent twenty beggars on the stage. Hayman volunteered to solve the problem by slithering around the action all night muttering 'Flores para los muertos?' That motif, a highly effective one pinched from Tennessee Williams, set the pace and tone of the entire show.

Everything the Citizens stood for he now sees in some ways as a denial of his city and environment; he is less adept at making the resonant, wider political connections than are visitors and chroniclers from outside. But having left school without a single O-level to his credit, and having started work in the steel industry, he found a passport to foreign cultural parts on his own doorstep. He sat, he says, at the feet of three masters, three life-embellishers, who had access to world treasures, and who shared their enthusiasm and knowledge with him and his colleagues in their formative years. In such a context, the acting itself was secondary to the visions conjured, the artistic journeys proposed, the chasms leapt.

We return to the fundamental point about the Citizens. It is not just a question of acting, of theatre, of plays, of scenery. What goes on there is an expression of integrated purpose, itself part of an insistence on creating some form of intelligent, escapist entertainment that will embrace its audience and transform its community. The technical details of performance, therefore, are of less significance than the spirit which infuses them, a spirit that is in the first and last place irradiated by the actors on the stage. And of that spirit you are never in doubt when sitting in the plush brightness of the Gorbals auditorium. If that sounds like an excuse for what might be counted in strictest critical terms unpolished or underachieved expression, then that is what it must be.

One of the most remarkable things about the Citizens, as we have already noted, is its unequalled track record as a nursery for the very best young British actors. And every one of those actors who has experienced what Angela Chadfield calls the 'loose vivacity of MacDonald, the visual brilliance of Prowse and the old-style English generosity of Havergal' knows deep down that he or she will experience nothing comparable, and nothing so valuable, in the coming years of unpredictable hurly-burly, mixed-economy compromise, and over-priced mediocrity that pass for the great bulk of the British entertainment and theatre industries. They have been marked for life. They have been enrolled as true Citizens.

10

CONCLUSION

On 2 March, 1990, the Queen came to Glasgow to witness the official acceptance of the Cultural City baton, handed on by Jacques Chirac, the Mayor of Paris. After lunch with the Lord Provost, Her Majesty placed herself for one hour at the disposal of Strathclyde Regional Council. How did Strathclyde entertain her? By taking her to the Citizens. She did not see a Citizens production, but she met the staff and witnessed a performance by schoolchildren, some of them disabled and many representing the ethnic variety of the community.

There could be no more appropriate symbol of the theatre's success under Havergal than this royal visit. Strathclyde has also underwritten a third Summer Season at the Citizens, adding £100,000 for the third year running to the core grant of £80,000. Glasgow District Council, which five years ago was giving the theatre only £75,000, has confirmed a grant for 1990–91 of £300,000 which represents a 9 per cent increase on last year's figure. With this level of support from the local authorities, the Citizens would like more of an increase from the Scottish Arts Council, but the SAC has remained averse to seeing the Citizens as any more deserving than its other major drama clients. The SAC grant for 1990−91 will be £438,000, plus £20,000 development money.

1990 has been slightly marred for the Citizens by the Richard Harris affair. Originally announced as joining the company to play the lead in *Enrico Four* in February, Harris withdrew from the production because he disliked the new translation by Robert David MacDonald. Despite this set-back, the play opened on the allotted date, with Greg Hicks giving a superlative display as the mad king.

The episode demonstrates the folly of suddenly ditching a policy of twenty-one years of having nothing, or not very much, to do with London − that fundamental creed advocated in the Glasgow Rep's 1909 manifesto, and approved, in theory at least, by James Bridie. Richard Harris, long absent from the stage while pursuing his film career, was launching a surprise assault on the West End of London in Pirandello's *Henry IV*. At the planning stage, he went to see Philip Prowse's revival of *The Vortex* at the Garrick Theatre. His reaction was ecstatic − according to several witnesses he went bananas with enthusiasm − and he demanded that Duncan Weldon, who was to produce the Pirandello for Triumph Theatre Productions, should hire Prowse as his director. Thelma Holt, the producer and former director of the Round House, where *Don Juan* had played, and a Citizens board-member, acted as marriage-broker between Triumph and Glasgow. But a petition for divorce was filed even before consummation.

Pirandello's *Henry IV* was always a play the Citizens might have done. Harris agreed to open in Glasgow, and Weldon promised the Citizens an extra £27,500 towards the cost of extra actors and a set solid enough to withstand the rigours of touring after Glasgow, and of coming into the West End. Harris knew and liked one of the translations already available in English. The Citizens, as we have seen, always do their own new translations and give them to the cast only on the first day of rehearsals. On this occasion, a concession was made to Harris, and Robert David MacDonald despatched his new text to the film star at the end of October, though Harris, filming and travelling, did not actually receive it until Christmas.

Just before he was due to arrive in Glasgow, Harris pulled out, unhappy with the proposed text. The Citizens' connection with Triumph was severed, and Harris and Weldon hurriedly set up a new production of the same play, with an old translation, which opened on the road in Cardiff at the end of March, arriving in the West End in May. Weldon paid the Citizens £12,500, almost as a goodwill gesture, for a set he was unable to use.

This left the Citizens down by £15,000, a disastrous loss by their financial standards of book-keeping. The end of the financial year was looming and there was no way of taking the sort of inventively cheeseparing action on the programme which had characterised the company's response to the two previous unscheduled disasters — the costs of *Rosenkavalier* in 1983, and the loss of pantomime revenue because of the teachers' strike in 1985. But by freezing all expenditure on running costs and repairs, and by cutting back wherever possible (£1,000, for instance, was snipped from the budget of *The Four Horsemen of the Apocalypse* in March), the books for the year would finally show a loss of only a few thousand pounds.

Giles Havergal was severely shaken by the episode, and is unlikely to be trapped in any more alliances with screen stars and London managements. Nonetheless, the Prowse/Glenda Jackson *Mother Courage* transferred to the Mermaid in London in July 1990, "bought out" by the producer Bill Kenwright, and with no mention of the Citizens in the programme or publicity. Only a small royalty on the translation returned to the coffers in Glasgow. The Citizens company itself had still not officially come to London since its one and only visit in 1980.

Continuity and renewal are the name of the game in all theatre, but as we approach the second millennium, the general signs for future survival are not encouraging. The story of the Citizens is unique, and not just because of the quality of the work. The company is a distant beacon in the darkening surrounds of the hard-hit and ailing subsidised companies south of the border. The overall position, with a partial slant, was described by Terry Hands in an interview he gave to Irving Wardle in the *Independent on Sunday* just after he had announced the projected closure of the RSC's London base in the Barbican for four months at the end of 1990:

> When I was young there was the Old Vic, and Stratford and the reps and we all lived perfectly well together. Not in rivalry, but in the sense that all these riches are there to be owned by everybody ... If we wish to preserve, with all its faults, a national view of the arts,

not any particular company, the only thing left representing it, and training actors, directors, and technicians, is the RSC. The rest is gone.

But the rest is not entirely gone for as long as the Citizens flourish, nor is the traffic of RSC talent remotely one-way: we have seen how very many good young actors, directors and designers have been hired and encouraged at the Citizens. But Hands's main point, that the theatrical culture of Britain is under threat owing to economic hardship and loss of morale in the repertory movement, is just. The salvation may not necessarily lie in the shoring up of the RSC as currently constituted, nor would that company's revitalisation do very much for the Scottish theatre anyway.

The example of the Citizens to the rest of Britain is clear. It has thrived by virtue of its unqualified commitment to a community, its belief in its own work, and its exceptional standards of managerial competence. Only with that combination of factors, and a comparable artistic determination, will the theatre of our four nations — as opposed to its narrow metropolitan representation, increasingly subject to distorting commercial pressures — survive and prosper.

The Glasgow Citizens has set the pace and shown the way. But the blueprint may not be applicable elsewhere. For the Citizens' identity is, finally, one of absolute, unbridled individuality made possible by the fulfilment of profound social and political obligations.

PRODUCTION LIST 1969 – 1990

NAME OF PLAY	DATE	PLAYWRIGHT	DIRECTOR	DESIGNER
The Milk Train Doesn't Stop Here Any More	Sep/Oct 1969	Tennessee Williams	Giles Havergal	Philip Prowse
Sam Foster Comes Home	Oct/Nov 1969	Don Taylor	Stephen Hollis	Bob Ringwood
Les Liaisons Dangereuses	Nov 1969	Laclos	Giles Havergal	Philip Prowse
A Delicate Balance	Dec 1969	Edward Albee	Michael Rudman	Bob Ringwood
Nicholas Nickleby	Dec 1969/Jan 1970	Caryl Brahms & Ned Sherrin	Giles Havergal	Philip Prowse
The Shadow of a Gunman	Jan/Feb 1970	Sean O'Casey	Robert Walker	Graham Whyte
Heartbreak House	Feb 1970	Bernard Shaw	Vincent Guy	Bob Ringwood
Ebb Tide	Mar 1970	Robert David MacDonald	Vincent Guy	Graham Whyte
Look Back in Anger	Mar/Apr 1970	John Osborne	Giles Havergal	Bob Ringwood
Colombe	Apr/May 1970	Jean Anouilh	Vincent Guy	Graham Whyte
The Importance of Being Earnest	May 1970	Oscar Wilde	Giles Havergal	Philip Prowse
Hamlet	Sep 1970	William Shakespeare	Giles Havergal	Philip Prowse
Rosencrantz & Guildenstern are Dead	Oct 1970	Tom Stoppard	Giles Havergal	Bob Ringwood
Mother Courage	Oct/Nov 1970	Bertolt Brecht	Robert Walker	Philip Prowse
Saint Joan	Nov 1970	Bernard Shaw	Giles Havergal	Bob Ringwood
A Taste of Honey	Dec 1970	Shelagh Delaney	Keith Hack	Digby Howard
Aladdin	Jan 1971	Terry Jones and Michael Palin	Giles Havergal	Bob Ringwood
The Hostage	Jan/Feb 1971	Brendan Behan	Robert Walker	Philip Prowse
Waiting for Godot	Feb/Mar 1971	Samuel Beckett	Keith Hack	Digby Howard

Title	Date	Author	Director	Designer
A Streetcar Named Desire	Mar 1971	Tennessee Williams	Giles Havergal	Philip Prowse
She Stoops to Conquer	Apr 1971	Oliver Goldsmith	Stephen Hollis	Terry Griffiths
The Balcony (Le Balcon)	Apr/May 1971	Jean Genet	Giles Havergal	Philip Prowse
Twelfth Night	May/June 1971	William Shakespeare	Giles Havergal	Philip Prowse
The White Devil	Aug/Sep 1971	John Webster	Giles Havergal	Philip Prowse
The Life of Galileo (Das Leben des Galileo Galilei)	Sep/Oct 1971	Bertolt Brecht	Keith Hack	Maria Bjornson/ Sue Blane
Three Sisters	Oct 1971	Anton Chekhov	Giles Havergal	Maria Bjornson
Loot	Nov 1971	Joe Orton	Steven Dartnell	Sue Blane
Danton's Death (Dantons Tod)	Nov/Dec 1971	Georg Büchner	Philip Prowse	Philip Prowse
Cinderella	Dec 1971/Jan 1972	Sid Colin	Giles Havergal	Maria Bjornson/ Sue Blane
The Relapse	Jan/Feb 1972	John Vanbrugh	Philip Prowse	Philip Prowse
The Crucible	Feb/Mar 1972	Arthur Miller	Steven Dartnell	Maria Bjornson
Saved	Mar/Apr 1972	Edward Bond	Steven Dartnell	Philip Prowse
In the Jungle of the Cities (Im Dickicht der Städte)	Apr/May 1972	Bertolt Brecht	Keith Hack	Maria Bjornson
Antony and Cleopatra	May 1972	William Shakespeare	Giles Havergal	Philip Prowse
Tamburlaine	Jan/Feb 1973	Christopher Marlowe	Keith Hack	Philip Prowse
The Threepenny Opera (Die Dreigroschenoper)	Oct/Nov 1972	Bertolt Brecht	Richard Stroud	Maria Bjornson
Venice Preserv'd	Oct/Nov 1972	Thomas Otway	Robert David MacDonald	Philip Prowse
Tartuffe	Nov/Dec 72, Feb/Mar 73	Jean-Baptiste Molière	Giles Havergal	Philip Prowse

NAME OF PLAY	DATE	PLAYWRIGHT	DIRECTOR	DESIGNER
Puss in Boots	Dec 72/Jan 73	Myles Rudge	Giles Havergal	Maria Bjornson/Sue Blane
The Government Inspector (Revizor)	Feb/Mar 1973	Nikolai Gogol	Robert David MacDonald	Sue Blane
Troilus and Cressida	Mar/Apr 1973	William Shakespeare	Philip Prowse	Philip Prowse
Happy End	Nov 1973	Thomas Beckett Brecht/Weill	Robert David MacDonald	Philip Prowse
The Devils	Dec 1973	John Whiting	Giles Havergal	Philip Prowse
Dick Whittington	Dec 73/Jan 74	Myles Rudge	Giles Havergal	Sue Blane
Arden of Faversham	Jan 1974	Anonymous	Steven Dartnell	Geoffrey Rose
The Taming of the Shrew	Feb 1974	William Shakespeare	Giles Havergal	Philip Prowse
Macbeth	Mar 1974	William Shakespeare	Steven Dartnell	Geoffrey Rose
The Collection/A Slight Ache	Apr 1974	Harold Pinter	Steven Dartnell	Geoffrey Rose
Camille	Apr 1974	Robert David MacDonald	Robert David MacDonald	Philip Prowse
Early Morning	May 1974	Edward Bond	Philip Prowse	Philip Prowse
St. Joan of the Stockyards (Die Heilige Johanna der Schlachthöfe)	Sep 1974	Bertolt Brecht	Robert David MacDonald	Philip Prowse
Coriolanus	Oct 1974	William Shakespeare	Jonathan Chadwick	David Fisher
Indians	Oct/Nov 1974	Arthur Kopit	Malcolm McKay	David Fisher
Camino Real	Nov 1974	Tennessee Williams	Philip Prowse	Philip Prowse
Kennedy's Children	Nov 1974	Robert Patrick	John Chapman	David Fisher
Jack and the Beanstalk	Dec 74/Jan 75	Myles Rudge	Giles Havergal	Colin Winslow
The Government Inspector (Revizor)	Jan/Feb 1975	Nikolai Gogol	Robert David MacDonald	Philip Prowse

Title	Author	Date	Director	Designer
The Duchess of Malfi	John Webster	Feb 1975	Philip Prowse	Philip Prowse
Romeo & Juliet	William Shakespeare	Feb/Mar 1975	David Hayman	Philip Prowse
De Sade Show	Robert David MacDonald	Mar 1975	Robert David MacDonald	Philip Prowse
Hamlet	William Shakespeare	Sep/Oct 1975	Philip Prowse	Philip Prowse
Sailor Beware	Falkland Cary	Oct/Nov 1975	Giles Havergal	Philip Prowse
Thyestes	Lucius Seneca	Nov 1975	David Hayman	David Hayman
Aladdin	Myles Rudge	Dec 75/Jan 76	Giles Havergal	Colin Winslow
De Sade Show	Robert David MacDonald	Jan 1976	Robert David MacDonald	Philip Prowse
Mirandolina (La Locandiera)	Carlo Goldoni	Jan/Feb 1976	Robert David MacDonald	Philip Prowse
The Changeling	Thomas Middleton	Feb 1976	Philip Prowse	Philip Prowse
Woyzeck	Georg Büchner	Mar 1976	Robert David MacDonald	Philip Prowse
Maskerade (Maskarad)	Mikhail Lermontov	Sept/Oct 1976	Robert David MacDonald	Philip Prowse
The Seven Deadly Sins of the Lower Middle Class (Die Sieben Todsünden der Kleinbürger)	Bertolt Brecht/Kurt Weill	Sep/Oct 1976	Geoffrey Cauley	Philip Prowse
What the Butler Saw	Joe Orton	Oct/Nov 1976	Giles Havergal	Geoffrey Rose
Elizabeth I	Paul Foster	Nov 1976	David Hayman	David Hayman
Cinderella	Sid Colin	Dec 76/Jan 77	Giles Havergal	Colin Winslow
The Country Wife	William Wycherley	Jan/Feb 1977	Philip Prowse	Philip Prowse
The Importance of Being Earnest	Oscar Wilde	Feb/Mar 1977	Giles Havergal	Philip Prowse
Figaro (Le Mariage de Figaro)	Pierre Beaumarchais	Apr/May 1977	Robert David MacDonald	Philip Prowse
Chinchilla	Robert David MacDonald	May 1977	Philip Prowse	Philip Prowse
Semi-Monde	Noël Coward	Sep 1977	Philip Prowse	Philip Prowse

NAME OF PLAY	DATE	PLAYWRIGHT	DIRECTOR	DESIGNER
Vautrin	Oct 1977	Honore de Balzac	Robert David MacDonald	Philip Prowse
Loot	Nov 1977	Joe Orton	Giles Havergal	Geoffrey Rose
Mother Goose	Dec 77/Jan 78	Myles Rudge	Giles Havergal	Sue Blane
Summit Conference	Jan/Feb 1978	Robert David MacDonald	Philip Prowse	Philip Prowse
No Orchids for Miss Blandish	Feb/Mar 1978	James Hadley Chase	Robert David MacDonald	Geoffrey Rose
Painter's Palace of Pleasure	Mar/Apr 1978	John Ford & John Webster	Philip Prowse	Philip Prowse
The Threepenny Opera (Die Dreigroschenoper)	Sep/Oct 1978	Bertolt Brecht/Kurt Weill	Philip Prowse	Philip Prowse
The Spanish Tragedy	Oct/Nov 1978	Thomas Kyd	Robert David MacDonald	Geoffrey Rose
The Seagull	Nov 1978	Anton Chekhov	Philip Prowse	Philip Prowse
Dick Whittington	Dec 78/Jan 79	Myles Rudge	Giles Havergal	Sue Blane
Orpheus (Orphée)	Jan/Feb 1979	Jean Cocteau	Geoffrey Cauley	Geoffrey Cauley
Macbeth	Feb/Mar 1979	William Shakespeare	Giles Havergal	(no designer)
Country Life (La Villegiatura)	Mar/Apr 1979	Carlo Goldoni	Robert David MacDonald	Philip Prowse
Chinchilla	Sep 1979	Robert David MacDonald	Philip Prowse	Philip Prowse
The Good Humoured Ladies (Le Morbinose and Le Donne di Buon Umore)	Sep 1979	Carlo Goldoni	Robert David MacDonald	Sue Blane
Pygmalion	Oct/Nov 1979	George Bernard Shaw	Giles Havergal	Sue Blane
The Maid's Tragedy	Nov 1979	Francis Beaumont & John Fletcher	Philip Prowse	Philip Prowse
Puss in Boots	Dec 79/Jan 80	Myles Rudge	Giles Havergal	Sue Blane
Fears & Miseries of the Third Reich (Furcht und Elend des Dritten Reichs)	Jan/Feb 1980	Bertolt Brecht	Giles Havergal	Sue Blane

Title	Date	Playwright	Director	Designer
A Waste of Time (A la Recherche du Temps Perdu)	Feb/Mar 1980	Robert David MacDonald	Philip Prowse	Philip Prowse
The Battlefield (La Guerra)	Aug/Sep 1980	Carlo Goldoni	Robert David MacDonald	Philip Prowse
The Caucasian Chalk Circle (Der Kaukasische Kreidekreis)	Oct 1980	Bertolt Brecht	Giles Havergal	Geoffrey Rose
Don Juan	Nov 1980	Robert David MacDonald	Philip Prowse	Philip Prowse
Babes in the Wood	Dec 80/Jan 81	David Dearlove	Giles Havergal	Shirley Bucklow
Desperado Corner	Jan 1981	Shawn Lawton	Di Trevis	Geoffrey Rose
The Massacre at Paris	Jan/Feb 1981	Christopher Marlowe	Philip Prowse	Philip Prowse
Madame Louise	Mar 1981	Vernon Sylvaine	Giles Havergal	Geoffrey Rose
Desperado Corner	Apr 1981	Shawn Lawton	Robert David MacDonald	Geoffrey Rose
A Waste of Time (A la Recherche du Temps Perdu)	Sep 1981	Robert David MacDonald	Philip Prowse	Philip Prowse
Hamlet	Oct 1981	William Shakespeare	Robert David MacDonald	Philip Prowse
Marriage à la Mode	Nov 1981	John Dryden	Giles Havergal	Philip Prowse
Jack and the Beanstalk	Dec 81/Jan 82	Myles Rudge	Giles Havergal	Colin MacNeil
Puntila and Matti (Herr Puntila und Sein Knecht Matti)	Jan/Feb 1982	Bertolt Brecht	Giles Havergal	Terry Bartlett
The Balcony (Le Balcon)	Feb 1982	Jean Genet	Philip Prowse	Philip Prowse
The Blacks (Les Nègres)	Mar/Apr 1982	Jean Genet	Philip Prowse	Philip Prowse
The Screens (Les Paravents)	Mar/Apr 1982	Jean Genet	Philip Prowse	Philip Prowse
The Roman Actor	Sep/Oct 1982	Philip Massinger	Philip Prowse	Philip Prowse
Red Roses for Me	Oct 1982	Sean O'Casey	Giles Havergal	Geoffrey Rose

NAME OF PLAY	DATE	PLAYWRIGHT	DIRECTOR	DESIGNER
Torquato Tasso	Oct/Nov 1982	Johannes Wolfgang Goethe	Robert David MacDonald	Michael Levine
Philosophy in the Boudoir (La Philosophie dans le Boudoir)	Nov 1982	Marquis de Sade	Philip Prowse	Philip Prowse
The Mother (Die Mutter)	Nov/Dec 1982	Bertolt Brecht	Giles Havergal	Geoffrey Rose
The Impresario from Smyrna (L'Impresario delle Smirne)	Jan 1983	Carlo Goldoni	Robert David MacDonald	Michael Levine
The Merchant of Venice	Jan/Feb 1983	William Shakespeare	Philip Prowse	Philip Prowse
Arms and the Man	Feb 1983	George Bernard Shaw	Giles Havergal	Colin MacNeil
The Custom of the Country	Mar 1983	John Fletcher/Philip Massinger	Robert David MacDonald	Michael Levine
Sirocco	Mar 1983	Noël Coward	Philip Prowse	Philip Prowse
Webster	Mar/Apr 1983	Robert David MacDonald	Philip Prowse	Philip Prowse
The Last Days of Mankind (Die Letzten Tagen der Menschheit)	Sep 1983	Karl Kraus	Robert David MacDonald	Terry Bartlett
Rosenkavalier (Der Rosenkavalier)	Sep/Oct 1983	Hugo von Hofmannsthal	Philip Prowse	Philip Prowse
Juno and the Paycock	Oct/Nov 1983	Sean O'Casey	Giles Havergal	Kenny Miller
Oroonoko	Nov 1983	Thomas Southerne	Philip Prowse	Philip Prowse
The Snow Queen	Dec 83/Jan 84	Stuart Paterson	Ian Wooldridge	Colin MacNeil
Private Lives	Jan/Feb 1984	Noël Coward	Giles Havergal	Kenny Miller
The Machine Wreckers (Die Maschinenstürmer)	Feb 1984	Ernst Toller	Giles Havergal	Kenny Miller
Altona (Les Séquestrés d'Altona)	Mar 1984	Jean Paul Sartre	Robert David MacDonald	Kenny Miller

Title	Date	Author		
A Woman of No Importance	Aug/Sep 1984	Oscar Wilde	Philip Prowse	Philip Prowse
French Knickers (La Vie Parisienne)	Sept/Oct 1984	Offenbach	Philip Prowse	Philip Prowse
She Stoops to Conquer	Oct/Nov 1984	Oliver Goldsmith	Robert David MacDonald	Kenny Miller
Judith	Nov 1984	Rolf Hochhuth	Robert David MacDonald	Kenny Miller
The Lion, The Witch and The Wardrobe	Dec 84/Jan 85	C.S. Lewis/Andrew Alty	Giles Havergal	Kenny Miller
Mary Stuart (Maria Stuart)	Jan/Feb 1985	Friedrich von Schiller	Philip Prowse	Philip Prowse
Blithe Spirit	Feb/Mar 1985	Noël Coward	Giles Havergal	Kenny Miller
The Plough and the Stars	Mar 1985	Sean O'Casey	Giles Havergal	Kenny Miller
Heartbreak House	Aug/Sep 1985	George Bernard Shaw	Philip Prowse	Philip Prowse
Arsenic and Old Lace	Oct/Nov 1985	Joseph Kesselrig	Giles Havergal	Kenny Miller
Faust (Parts I and II) (Faust I und II Teil)	Nov 1985	Johannes Wolfgang Goethe	Robert David MacDonald	Kenny Miller
Hansel & Gretel	Dec 85/Jan 86	Myles Rudge	Giles Havergal	Kenny Miller
The Spanish Bawd (La Celestina)	Jan/Feb 1986	Fernando de Rojas	Philip Prowse	Philip Prowse
Friends and Lovers (Il Vero Amico)	Feb 1986	Carlo Goldoni	Robert David MacDonald	Kenny Miller
Entertaining Mr. Sloane	Feb/Mar 1986	Joe Orton	Giles Havergal	Kenny Miller
An Ideal Husband	Aug/Sep 1986	Oscar Wilde	Philip Prowse	Philip Prowse
The Representative (Der Stellvertreter)	Oct 1986	Rolf Hochhuth	Robert David MacDonald	Kenny Miller
Hidden Fires (Le Chandelier)	Nov 1986	Alfred de Musset	Robert David MacDonald	Stewart Laing
Red Riding Hood and the Wolf	Dec 86/Jan 87	Myles Rudge	Giles Havergal	Kenny Miller
Death of a Salesman	Jan/Feb 1987	Arthur Miller	Giles Havergal	Kenny Miller
Anna Karenina	Feb 1987	Robert David MacDonald after Leo Tolstoy	Philip Prowse	Philip Prowse
The School for Scandal	Sept/Oct 1987	Richard Brinsley Sheridan	Giles Havergal	Terry Bartlett

NAME OF PLAY	DATE	PLAYWRIGHT	DIRECTOR	DESIGNER
Joan of Arc (Die Jungfrau von Orleans)	Oct 1987	Friedrich von Schiller	Robert David MacDonald	Stewart Laing
No Man's Land	Nov 1987	Harold Pinter	Giles Havergal	Kathy Strachan
Aladdin and his Wonderful Lamp	Dec 87/Jan 88	Myles Rudge	Giles Havergal	Colin MacNeil
The Vortex	Jan/Feb 1988	Noël Coward	Philip Prowse	Philip Prowse
'Tis Pity She's a Whore	Feb/Mar 1988	John Ford	Philip Prowse	Philip Prowse
Frankenstein	Mar/Apr 1988	Mary Shelley	Jon Pope	Kathy Strachan
Lady Windermere's Fan	May/June 1988	Oscar Wilde	Philip Prowse	Philip Prowse
Dr. Angelus	June 1988	James Bridie	Giles Havergal	Stewart Laing
The Lady from the Sea	Sep 1988	Henrik Ibsen	Tom Cairns	Tom Cairns
Richard III	Sep/Oct 1988	William Shakespeare	Jon Pope	Kathy Strachan
Phedra (Phèdre)	Oct/Nov 1988	Jean Racine	Philip Prowse	Philip Prowse
Pinocchio	Nov/Dec 88/Jan 89	Myles Rudge	Giles Havergal	Stewart Laing
The Alchemist	Jan/Feb 1989	Ben Jonson	Robert David MacDonald	Stewart Laing
Douglas	Feb/Mar 1989	John Home	Robert David MacDonald	Stewart Laing
A Tale of Two Cities	May/Jun 1989	Charles Dickens	Philip Prowse	Philip Prowse
The Crucible	Aug/Sep 1989	Arthur Miller	Giles Havergal	Stewart Laing
Macbeth	Oct 1989	William Shakespeare	Jon Pope	Stewart Laing
Travels With My Aunt	Nov 1989	Graham Greene	Giles Havergal & Jon Pope	Stewart Laing
The Sorcerer's Apprentice	Nov/Dec 89/Jan 90	Myles Rudge	Giles Havergal	Stewart Laing
Enrico Four	Feb/Mar 1990	Luigi Pirandello	Philip Prowse	Philip Prowse

The Four Horsemen of the Apocalypse	Mar 1990	V. Blasco Ibanez	Jon Pope	Stewart Laing
Antony	Apr 1990	Alexandre Dumas	Robert David MacDonald	Terry Bartlett
Mother Courage	May/Jun 1990	Bertolt Brecht	Philip Prowse	Philip Prowse

SELECT BIBLIOGRAPHY

Ansorge, Peter. *Disrupting the Spectacle* (Pitman 1975)

Bannister, Winifred. *James Bridie and his Theatre* (Rockliff 1955)

Braun, Edward (ed.). *Meyerhold on Theatre* (Methuen 1969)

Chambers, Colin. *The Story of Unity Theatre* (Lawrence and Wishart 1989)

Ellmann, Richard. *Oscar Wilde* (Hamish Hamilton 1987)

Glasser, Ralph. *Growing Up in the Gorbals* (Chatto & Windus 1986)

Gomme, Andrew; Walker, David. *Architecture of Glasgow* (Lund Humphries 1987)

House, Jack. *The Heart of Glasgow* (Richard Drew 1965)

Hutchison, David. *The Modern Scottish Theatre* (Molendinar Press 1977)

Isaac, Winifred. *Alfred Wareing* (Green Bank Press 1948)

Kemp, Arnold (ed). *The Glasgow Herald Book of Glasgow* (Mainstream 1989)

Lindsay, Maurice. *Glasgow* (Hale 1972)

McGrath, John. *A Good Night Out* (Eyre Methuen 1981)

McGrath, John. *The Bone Won't Break* (Methuen 1990)

McLeish, Robert; McKenny, Linda (ed.). *The Gorbals Story* (7:84 Publications 1985)

McMillan, Joyce. *The Traverse Theatre Story* (Methuen 1988)

Marzaroli, Oscar, and McIlvanney, William. *Shades of Grey: Glasgow 1956–87* (Mainstream 1987)

Massie, Alan. *Glasgow* (Barrie & Jenkins 1989)

Mavor, Ronald. *Dr Mavor and Mr Bridie* (Canongate and the National Library of Scotland 1988)

Miller, Jonathan. *Subsequent Performances* (Faber 1986)

Nichols, Peter. *Feeling You're Behind* (Weidenfeld & Nicolson 1984)

Oliver, Cordelia. *It is a Curious Story* (Mainstream 1987)

Rudnitsky, Konstantin. *Russian and Soviet Theatre* (Thames and Hudson 1988)

Schmidt, Paul (ed.). *Meyerhold At Work* (Carcanet New Press 1981)

Sontag, Susan. *A Susan Sontag Reader* (Penguin 1982)

Ward, Robin. *Some City Glasgow* (Richard Drew 1982)

Willett, John. *The Theatre of Erwin Piscator* (Eyre Methuen 1978)

Williamson, Elizabeth; Riches, Anne; Higgs, Malcolm. *Glasgow* (Penguin 1990)

Wilmut, Roger. *Kindly Leave The Stage!* (Methuen 1985)

INDEX

MICHAEL COVENEY is the theatre critic of *The Observer*. He was born in Stepney, East London, in 1948 and educated at St Ignatius College, London, and Worcester College, Oxford. He worked initially as a piano player, a teacher, and as a script reader for the Royal Court Theatre. He became a regular contributor to the arts page of the *Financial Times* in 1972, and, in 1973, assistant editor of *Plays and Players*. He was editor of *Plays and Players* from 1975 to 1978.

He was on the staff of the *Financial Times* from 1981 to 1989 as theatre critic and deputy arts editor, moving to *The Observer* in January 1990. He is the London correspondent and editorial adviser on *Theatre in Europe*, Giorgio Strehler's magazine published in Paris and Milan. He broadcasts regularly and has contributed to many publications, including the *New York Times*, a series of theatre annuals, and a celebration of John Gielgud.